P9-BTO-676

Issues of Theological Conflict

Evangelicals and Liberals

Issues of Theological Conflict

Evangelicals and Liberals

by

RICHARD J. COLEMAN

WILLIAM B. EERDMANS PUBLISHING COMPANY
Grand Rapids, Michigan

Copyright © 1972 by William B. Eerdmans Publishing Company

Revised edition copyright © 1980 by Wm. B. Eerdmans Publishing Co.
225 Jefferson Ave. S.E., Grand Rapids, Mich. 49503
All rights reserved
Printed in the United States of America

Library of Congress Cataloging in Publication Data

Coleman, Richard J.
Issues of theological conflict.

Previous ed. (1972) published under title: Issues of theological warfare.
Bibliography: p. 275.
1. Liberalism (Religion)—United States. 2. Evangelicalism—United States. I. Title.

BR1615.C63 1980 230 79-19494
ISBN 0-8028-3185-0

To my Father
and the memory of my Mother

CONTENTS

PREFACE

The time has come, in fact it is long past, to take completely seriously the growing and deepening division between liberal and evangelical Protestants. All across the nation there is a mounting dissatisfaction among laymen with the way liberal professional leaders are moving the church, formation of numerous associations for mutual support and political power, convention after convention racked by liberal-conservative controversies, emergence of independent newspapers and journals which thrive on protest, and increased polarization of theological positions. Not only is the ecumenical movement threatened; the very existence of major denominations is being questioned. On the one hand there is the gloomy prospect that as the division between Protestants and Roman Catholics fades in the 1970s, a new division between liberals and evangelicals will take its place. At the same time there are hopeful signs that in some ways evangelicals and liberals are better prepared to discuss their theological differences.

What has happened so far is an increasing tempo of confrontation along sociopolitical lines. What is needed in equal intensity is a confrontation over the basic theological issues which divide evangelicals and liberals. The main purpose of this book is to define the issues as both evangelicals and liberals understand them, and to stimulate and encourage dialogue that faces the issues squarely. Certainly there have been attempts to do this, but unfortunately most have been either so inadequate or so clouded by prejudice as to render them useless. The present work is unique, I believe, in placing the arguments and positions of both evangelicals and liberals side by side rather than under separate covers. I have attempted to state as clearly and objectively as possible what each group holds to be true. The book reflects my deep conviction that the evangelical and the liberal have something positive to offer to each other.

In addition to understanding the issues and promoting dialogue, a second reason for the book is to help ministers and laymen identify the sources of tension between them. Rare indeed is the church today that has not been confronted with some crisis as a result of the theological division between liberal and conservative Christians. Greater familiarity with the issues will surely bring to both parties a deeper respect and sensitivity for differing viewpoints and backgrounds.

A third important reason for writing this kind of book is to attempt to shed new light on some very significant theological questions. Academic debate has always gone on between men with similar points of view. Something is to be gained, however, when the evangelical is made to answer to the criticisms of the liberal and the liberal to the judgments of the evangelical. Many theological issues which have long been passed over come suddenly to the surface when two quite different perspectives meet.

The book is intended primarily for the theologically trained. It is my belief that if dialogue is to happen, it must be initiated by ministers, seminary faculty and students, and denominational leaders who have a clear understanding of the issues involved. The first chapter sets the stage and introduces the participants. The following two chapters, entitled "The Heart of the Matter," define the two basic issues. The fourth and fifth chapters may be seen as practical extensions of the first two. The sixth chapter brings into focus all that has been discussed in the pressing question of "The Church and Social Involvement." The conclusion of each chapter is in no way intended to offer a final solution. Instead, taking a lesson from Vatican II, I have tried to use language that opens the door to further study and discussion. Extensive footnotes and other resource material are provided to facilitate additional study.

I do not doubt that there will be some disagreement with my use of the terms "evangelical" and "liberal." We more often speak of a conservative-liberal split; but the designation "conservative" carries many negative connotations which fail to do justice to the peculiar essence of American evangelicalism. There is a very real danger, however, that we will get hung up on terms and use that as an excuse not to debate the issues which divide us. Labels are never completely satisfactory, but some kind of general categories is required to identify the broad positions which are obviously splitting the major denominations. Clearly it is time to begin the dialogue which the Christian church so desperately needs, not by rash oversimplification, but by careful analysis and mutual respect for one another's heritage. We have waited too long for these two vital and historic traditions to nourish and balance each other. Some may feel this kind of book only increases tensions. I say it is far better to face up to the situation—even if it means a theological warfare that is painfully honest.

My thanks and acknowledgments extend to many persons. I owe a deep debt of gratitude to Dr. Arthur Mandy, who helped me discover the prejudices within myself, and to Professor J. Christian Beker, who teaches his students to ask the hard questions of Scripture. Deep appreciation goes to the reference department of the Pittsfield Public Library, and especially to Mrs. Daniel Zack, for their diligence in obtaining books. It would be nearly impossible to mention all the ways my wife, Ruth, assisted in the writing of this book. Finally, my sincere thanks to the several readers, friends, and teachers, both liberals and evangelicals, who gave encouragement and suggestions along the way.

PREFACE TO THE REVISED EDITION

It is no longer necessary to belabor or document the axial split within Protestantism between evangelicals and liberals. In the first edition of this book I played the role of prognosticator and spoke of a "pending schism" and a "mounting dissatisfaction among laymen." Time has proven this prediction to be more than correct, as the new fact of religious life in America is the emergence of an established evangelicalism. We easily recognize that evangelicals come in various colors, and their sudden growth and diversification has led to another fact of life, namely, internal contentions over such central questions as biblical inerrancy, social action, and ecumenism. Since the first edition many sociological changes have occurred, but the principal theological issues have remained constant. This is not to say, however, that there has been no progress or that arguments have not been refined. My first task in this new edition has, therefore, been to detail where advances have taken place.

I have resisted the temptation to focus upon the controversy among evangelicals themselves, even though this is the more lively and dramatic debate, for this could be a grave mistake. I am convinced more than ever that liberals need to hear the challenge of evangelicalism, just as evangelicals need to clearly hear the challenge of liberalism, and that they both need to be questioned by each other without arguments being filtered through their own mouthpieces. The idea of dialogue between evangelicals and liberals in 1972 may have been an "idea before its time," but I am encouraged by movements that have made this a more realistic possibility. Both groups have experienced gradual shifts, some conscious and some unconscious, so that with justification we can now speak of liberal evangelicals and evangelical liberals. The next decade will be most interesting and vitally important for American Protestantism as new forces converge and interact, and one hopes that this new edition will again offer directions for the future.

The other crucial "happening" that has affected both evangelicals and liberals is the further identification of Christianity with the cultural values of society. For over half a century conservatives were a voice crying in the wilderness against the liberal captivity in the hands of secularism. The familiar refrain was that liberal theology had become a pale specter of the Christian faith incapable of bearing a distinctive witness. While some liberals are beginning to discover for themselves how firmly wedded to secular society they have become, conservatives, who are beginning to enjoy majority status, are at the point of finding themselves in a similar situation. If the observation that the middle ground in American Protestantism has been eroded away—if it ever did exist—then it remains to be seen if a new biblical expression coming from the fringes of liberalism and evangelicalism can forge a new middle course. The prospect is certainly worth watching.

This new edition of *Issues of Theological Conflict: Evangelicals and Liberals* is a thorough revision. Replacing the introduction is a new chapter that defines the historical context and our theological roots, examines "how we divide" and whether evangelicals and liberals need each other. The material throughout has been updated and the footnotes enlarged to give the reader access to the most recent scholarship. Special attention has been given to the questions of biblical authority (inerrancy) and cultural subversion, since they are the determining issues of the immediate future.

I am indebted to Priscilla Phenix for her editorial eye and for compiling the bibliography. I thankfully acknowledge the words of encouragement I received when the first edition of this book appeared. Many have felt that the gulf between evangelicals and liberals is too great to be bridged; but others, for whom I rejoice, believe that truth is never the possession of one party or one denomination. Let us hope and pray that the Spirit will again reconcile Christians to each other and will number our days as a divisive force among other divisive forces in the world today.

I. THE FORGING OF A NEW MIDDLE

THE CENTER THAT NEVER WAS, BUT COULD BE

In many ways it has been seven short years filled with many changes since the first edition of this book appeared. During these years the theological issues dividing evangelicals and liberals have not substantially shifted, but the climate in which those issues are to be discussed has been dramatically recast. I felt compelled to reflect the new mood of the times by introducing the theme of "Forging a New Middle." Our task in the first chapter is to spell out what has happened in seven years. But even more importantly, we must ponder the shape of things to come, because no one wants to repeat the mistakes of the past.

In 1974 Diogenes Allen, Associate Professor of Philosophy at Princeton Theological Seminary, commented that the "most significant event [in the past several years] had been the collapse of the middle ground between liberalism and fundamentalism."[1] The middle ground he had in mind was neoorthodoxy, and the failure was the vacuum left by the death of Barth, Brunner, Tillich, Bultmann, the Niebuhrs, and a host of lesser known theologians whose roots stretch back into the nineteenth century. We understand what Diogenes Allen means when he refers to neoorthodoxy's forging something of a middle ground between a European liberalism and an American conservativism, but we question whether neoorthodoxy accomplished anything more than building superstructures across deep chasms. We will touch upon this question again when we explore the "historical setting" that

[1]Diogenes Allen, *Theology Today*, vol. XXX, no. 4 (January, 1974), p. 333.

shaped our present situation; but suffice it to say that undoubtedly a new vacuum has been created by the contemporary disillusionment with the artificial synthesis of dialectical theology.

There is no other country in the world where religion holds a place comparable to its position in America. Everyone seems to agree that the last two decades have witnessed a radical reorientation in the religious lifestyles of Americans. Even the most casual look at the historical roots of the various Christian institutions is enough to convince the layman that most generalizations do not apply to our peculiar situation. Springing from a broadstream pietistic heritage came such different movements as fundamentalism and the Social Gospel. Both of these movements enjoyed a certain privileged status in American history, but both were short-lived, and for almost exactly opposite reasons. Fundamentalists could only stiffen their backsides in a defensive posture against a progressive modernism, while the jellyfish nature of a new form of twentieth-century liberalism proved no match for the engulfing tide of secularism. The devastating effects of World War II were such that the American people were hungry for any kind of faith that would offer them meaning for their lives—but a meaning that was neither overly pessimistic nor overly optimistic. From the ashes of an inflexible fundamentalism was built an evangelical conservativism, sometimes known as neoevangelicalism, that kept one foot in the past but the other foot pointed toward the future. The liberal experiment in the 1950s and '60s was just that—a hodgepodge of experiments ranging from biblical theology to a new hermeneutic. Sociologists and theologians are telling us that a new evangelical consensus is about to be crowned whereby Americans no longer need to feel ill at ease with phrases like "born again" or "praise the Lord." But it is a strange kind of consensus, because liberal Protestantism as represented in mainline denominations is by no means dead. There are stirrings afoot, however, in both liberal and evangelical camps, because neither has been able to weld together a comprehensive theology that synthesizes the issues that have persistently divided Christians in America.

Anyone who looks at the present historical setting with open eyes is reluctant to make hard and fast judgments. Religious and institutional loyalties are shifting so rapidly that it is difficult to determine what is mainline anymore. It is not absurd, for example, to speak of evangelical liberals or liberal evangelicals. Richard Quebedeaux has pictured the ferment that is heating up in that amorphous stream known as neoevangelicalism or simply evangelical Protestantism.[2] We will have more to say about the issues that seem to be troubling the conservative movement, but in general it can be pointed out that these issues, such as biblical inerrancy and the relationship between mission as evangelism and as social justice, are far from superficial. The very fact that there is no consensus among evangelicals on such issues ought to alert us that they were never adequately resolved.

But a similar picture can be painted of that equally ill-defined complex of traditions known as liberalism. Since 1960 the theological pendulum has been swinging erratically. Radical liberalism, such as the secular-city debate and the new theologies (surveyed by Martin Marty and Dean Peerman), did nothing to stabilize or solidify what was worth saving from their not so distant past. The most promising new venture was biblical theology (which also generated a series entitled "Studies in Biblical Theology"), because it proposed to correct the deficiencies of an overly negative historical criticism. Those involved in constructing an overarching biblical theology now realize that it failed to come to grips with the inspiration of Scripture.[3] Simultaneously the ecumenical thrust promised to unite Christians under one banner, if not under one roof. The essential demise of the Consultation on Church Union (COCU) can be attributed in part to the same failures that undid the biblical theology movement, but it can also be traced to the vibrant but silent evangelical minority that gradually concluded that they had some items to add to the agenda. In addition, the fire suddenly died out of the socio-political involvement of liberals in the 1960s. Church leaders who had been plugged into social action groups are now serving on revitalized committees for evangelism and stewardship. Again it can safely be surmised that "holistic" mission was an

[2]Richard Quebedeaux, *The Young Evangelicals* (New York: Harper & Row, 1974) and *The Worldly Evangelicals* (New York: Harper & Row, 1978).

[3]Brevard S. Childs, *Biblical Theology in Crisis* (Philadelphia: Westminster, 1974), p. 103 and *passim*.

idiom used only by conciliar executives with no reference to what was happening in the local church.

When William G. McLoughlin asked the rhetorical question, "Is there a Third Force in Christendom?" he had in mind the conservative fringe groups that were coming into prominence.[4] After studying the situation, McLoughlin had concluded no, but he did forecast that if a third force were to come between Catholicism and mainline Protestantism it would be "the pietistic spirit of American culture itself." Robert N. Bellah (in that same 1967 issue of *Daedalus*) named that special blending of religious commitment and American ideas "civil religion." McLoughlin was, of course, wrong in his prediction, since to be American no longer means to be Protestant, Jew, or Roman Catholic (*à la* Will Herberg), but rather to be a *conservative* or *liberal* Protestant, Jew, or Roman Catholic. On religious issues, Americans do divide differently than they did in the '50s, and it is precisely because of new overriding issues that we must pay more attention to the culpability of civil religion. We are indebted to Bellah for bringing clearly to the foreground what was once distant and misty, namely, that there is in America a civil religion with its own rituals, morals, missionary tasks, and sacred documents.

The editor of *Sojourners* (formerly the *Post-American*), Jim Wallis, spells out the consequence of this newly revealed but very old facet of American life:

> The most important distinctions in theology are no longer between high church and low church, evangelicals and ecumenicals, Protestants and Catholics, Calvinists and Armenians, or whatever else. What matters most today is whether one is a supporter of establishment Christianity or a practitioner of biblical faith.[5]

Establishment Christianity here could be either the evangelical or the liberal status quo. Approaching the question from a different angle, James Smart warns of the "cultural subversion of

[4]*Daedalus,* vol. XCVI, no. 1 (Winter, 1967), pp. 43–68.

[5]Jim Wallis, *Agenda for Biblical People* (New York: Harper & Row, 1976), p. 1.

the Biblical faith."[6] If these two authors are correct, as I believe they are, then anti-establishment evangelicals and liberals, regardless of their particular stripes, are facing a common foe. This is the primary reason they will join forces to forge a new middle course.

I write of the forging of a new middle, but I do not expect to see in the near future a cohesive, unified force sweeping America. What I do expect to see is the development and deepening of the stirrings now at work. It would be an oversimplification to call attention to the solidification and broadening within the evangelical left, or what Quebedeaux calls the "young evangelicals," just as it would be superficial to refer to a conservative swing within liberalism. Cyclical swings are the natural course of events. My expectations have a much firmer foundation. For about ten years the theological community has been at work defining and clarifying the issues I raise in this book, and in another sense the church has been wrestling with them all of its life. At this particular point in our history neither church union nor denominational splits are the pressing business. Rather, we are passing through a period of searching. Both liberals and conservatives are reexamining their past, especially the past twenty to thirty years, and for good reasons. We can now judge the effects of modernism and secularism, and we don't like the results. Evangelicals from their perspective have matured to the point where they are no longer on the defensive and can not only recognize but admit their reactionary extremes. Liberal theology has been in such a flux that it sincerely longs for an approach that is consistent, practical, and faithful to the biblical witness.

The remainder of this book will allow me to be more specific about names, books, and movements. Let me simply identify four determining factors in the forging of a new middle.

(1) Neoorthodoxy Reconsidered—The creative influence of neoorthodoxy is not as passé as we think. An immature fundamentalism and reactionary conservativism found little use for Karl Barth and those like him. They were too preoccupied with apologetic diatribes, defending the inerrancy of Scripture, creat-

[6]James Smart, *The Cultural Subversion of the Biblical Faith* (Philadelphia: Westminster, 1977).

ing a new revivalism centered around Billy Graham, and unifying their own strengths. Neoorthodoxy has been severely criticized in the past by conservatives who discerned remnants and disguised forms of nineteenth-century liberalism, and who faulted the dialectical theologians for not being radical (conservative) enough in their correction of liberalism's theological starting point. The climate is changing, however, and the evangelical critics are acknowledging a little more and finding real potency and balance in the neoorthodox approach to critical issues. One reads the erudite and respected G. C. Berkouwer's *A Half Century of Theology* and is greatly surprised to see how open and receptive he is to Karl Barth.[7]

We might wish the liberal community had come as far in their appreciation of these modern-day German reformers. The liberals of the 1940s and '50s in both Europe and North America were conscious of the neoorthodox contribution, but then they lost interest. They perceived correctly in many instances that neoorthodoxy had constructed a superstructure that spanned too many gulfs. Specifically, liberals found its superficial treatment of the historical-critical method, its separation of faith from culture and the social sciences, its emphasis on man's inadequacy rather than his possibilities in a new era of technology and urbanization, and its biblical positivism and super-realism unsatisfactory.[8] Barth's otherworldly transcendence seemed a cop-out insofar as Americans appraised the latter half of the twentieth century. But little by little, as the warm embrace of secularism was reconsidered,

[7]G. C. Berkouwer, *A Half Century of Theology* (Grand Rapids: Eerdmans, 1977). Donald G. Bloesch is another example of an evangelical who is cautiously moving closer to Karl Barth. See Bloesch, *Jesus Is Victor!: Karl Barth's Description of Salvation* (Nashville: Abingdon, 1976). Concerning the trend toward neoorthodoxy at Fuller Seminary, see Gerald T. Sheppard, "Biblical Hermeneutics: The Academic Language of Evangelical Identity," *Union Quarterly Review* (Winter, 1977), pp. 81–94.

[8]By super-realism I mean the reliance upon categories such as *Urgeschichte* ("pre-history"), "trans-historical," and "mighty acts"; by biblical positivism I mean the almost naive acceptance of a biblical authority based upon mythological language, a biblical superstructure, and the transcendent word which creates its own receptivity; and by the separation of faith and culture I mean the resulting dualism between divine and secular, transcendence and immanence, theistic belief and the everyday

the search for a theology that creates its own agenda intensified. The unexpected broad support the January 1975 Hartford Appeal received is one indication of a growing sentiment that "today an apparent loss of a sense of the transcendent is undermining the Church's ability to address with clarity and courage the urgent tasks to which God calls it in the world."[9]

(2) Theology's Starting Point—Christian theology has always had an intense interest in the question: "What is the proper starting point from which to begin to talk about God?" The classic distinction has been between an anthropological and a non-anthropological starting point,[10] the liberal consistently choosing the former and the conservative the latter. Neoorthodoxy, of course, reacted against the nineteenth century's tendency to locate our understanding of God in the theoretical structures of consciousness (Lessing) or feeling (Schleiermacher). Since 1950, liberals have tended to return to human experience as a legitimate starting point in order to integrate Christian theistic belief with the everyday experience of contemporary man.[11]

---

experience of contemporary man. Yet concerning the latter it must not be forgotten that the separation of faith and culture was the reaction of neoorthodoxy to the synthesis of the two by nineteenth-century liberal theology, and that Barth, from his tower of transcendence, first resisted the identification of Christianity with Nazism.

[9]See *Against the World for the World: The Hartford Appeal and the Future of American Religion*, ed. Peter Berger and Richard Neuhaus (New York: Seabury, 1976), p. 1. The eleventh theme or modern heresy lifted up by the Hartford Appeal is especially relevant: "An emphasis on God's transcendence is at least a hindrance to, and perhaps incompatible with, Christian social concern and action."

[10]Other ways to describe this contrast in starting points include natural revelation vs. special revelation (direct vs. indirect, see chapter III), Apollonian and Dionysian styles (p. 79, Chapter II), Cartesian vs. non-Cartesian, and the uniquely Roman Catholic distinction between truth understood dogmatically and unchanging truth or truth as existentially related to the self and thus in a state of continual development (see especially the writings of Leslie Dewart for the latter).

[11]Langdon Gilkey makes a case that the present situation in theology does not represent a return to classical liberalism. The present challenge as he saw it in 1969 was to return to the basic principle of liberalism—to locate God in the course of history and ordinary experience—but to avoid the tragic error of dissolving God's transcendence into divine immanence and thereby opening the way for an

Countless books have examined our cultural condition for signals of transcendence, elucidated psychological and philosophical categories that make the gospel intelligible and applicable to people, and examined the existential situation of the addressee. Yet, if I read the signs of the time correctly, there is a growing disenchantment with an approach that focuses on the proper appropriation of the kerygma rather than its content. There is an uneasy feeling that Cartesianism[12] has acted as a sieve through which the biblical content is filtered. One wonders from a hermeneutical perspective whether the stress on asking the question and examining the preconditions (*à la* Bultmann) did not emasculate the answer and prevent the text from challenging our premises. The Hartford Appeal was fully aware of this "debilitating theme" in contemporary liberalism: "Modern thought is superior to all past forms of understanding reality, and therefore normative for Christian faith and life" (Theme 1); and "Jesus can only be understood in terms of contemporary models of humanity" (Theme 4).

Liberalism is not alone in coming to terms with its theological heritage. The new evangelicalism arose in the late 1940s as a reaction to a severe fundamentalism that refused to take modern society seriously. The conservatives who initiated neoevangelicalism wanted to retain the principles of orthodoxy but be freer in how they would interpret them to a new era. The open divorce among evangelicals resulted from one group's ability to recognize that urbanization and technology were the new facts of life and the other group's unwillingness to adapt to these facts. The issue of how far one goes in reinterpreting Christian doctrine continues as a new generation of evangelicals begins to make its views known.

It is noteworthy that Carl F. H. Henry, the dean of neo-

---

unquestioned continuity between the Christian faith and a progressing secular order. Gilkey, along with Peter Berger (*Rumor of Angels*), proceeded to delineate areas of ordinary secular experience where dimensions of the ultimate were present. See Gilkey, *Naming the Whirlwind: The Renewal of God-Language* (Indianapolis: Bobbs-Merrill, 1969).

[12]Helmut Thielicke's terminology in *The Evangelical Faith*, vol. I: *The Relation of Theology to Modern Thought-Forms* (Grand Rapids: Eerdmans, 1974).

evangelism, has devoted the first of his projected four volumes of systematic theology to a prolegomenon evaluating the philosophical, cultural, scientific, and theological presuppositions of the times.[13] Henry is by no means alone in his willingness to enter into dialogue with radical and liberal theologians, but he begins with a prolegomenon at a time when many liberal thinkers are eager to move beyond cultural analysis. Henry does not depart from naming special revelation as the source of all particular Christian truths, but one feels that he reflects an even greater openness to take seriously what other disciplines say about the human condition. The unspoken assumption is that even an axiomatic methodology cannot claim infallibility and therefore must consider truth as it is found in the human condition.

On a different front, a relational theology developed in the 1960s as another reaction to a reproductive method that merely repeated the fundamental doctrines. Prominent relational theologians are Keith Miller, an Episcopal layman and author of many practical books on building and maintaining relationships; Lyman Coleman, author of the popular *Serendipity* books for young people and their leaders; Lloyd Ogilvie, senior minister of the First Presbyterian Church of Hollywood, California, and frequent guest speaker and lecturer; and Bruce Larson, an ordained United Presbyterian minister and the movement's principal theoretician. What unites all these men is the conviction that contemporary evangelical theology has neglected the relational side of the gospel. Together with the radical social activist wing of the new evangelicalism, relational theologians have a distinct dis-

[13]Carl F. H. Henry, *God, Revelation and Authority,* vol. I: *God Who Speaks and Shows, Preliminary Considerations* (Waco: Word, 1976). Henry, addressing fellow evangelicals in a different context, makes the observation: "Those who contend that the theology of revelation is the most persuasive context for forging world-life concerns must explain the dearth of serious philosophical exposition of rational theism in our evangelical college circles." *Evangelicals in Search of Identity* (Waco: Word, 1976), p. 95. The liberal, of course, would respond by saying, "just so, you cannot expect theology to speak to secular man when it eschews philosophical or empirical analysis and confines itself to *a priori* propositions." We must critically ask: is Henry guilty of writing a theology of revelation that only gives lip service to philosophical and empirical analysis?

taste for doctrines and creeds having no practical application. The mark of orthodoxy for them is not right conceptual thinking but "the quality and scope of relationships" (Larson).

I can imagine several areas of cross-fertilization as liberals rediscover the value of a theological system firmly attached to the transcendent, and as evangelicals learn to appreciate a theology that speaks to our experience of reality. Ultimately the starting point may be no more important than the end point as long as the hermeneutical circle is completed. Evangelicals and liberals have their own distinctive heritage to draw upon, but persistent weaknesses could best be overcome by turning to the creative writers of a different tradition.

(3) Biblical Authority—The related issues of biblical inspiration and critical historicalism have been the "thorn in the flesh" of liberal-evangelical relationships. By consensus it is still the pivotal question to be addressed before any substantial progress can be made. Professor Clark Pinnock, who has written widely on this topic, identifies three positions within the evangelical coalition.[14] First are the militant advocates of an unqualified biblical inerrancy who continue in the footsetps of Warfield-Hodge and the fundamentalists. For them inerrancy is an essential Christian doctrine which, if denied, is tantamount to rejecting the Christian faith. Harold Lindsell's book *Battle for the Bible* (1976) is the latest articulating this strict position, and he probably speaks for most evangelicals. The second group holds a modified position on inerrancy. This group is content to affirm that the Bible is inerrant in all that it intends to teach. They wish to hold on to the term "inerrant" but they also wish to broaden its meaning to accommodate certain qualifications, such as variants in the synoptic gospels, parallel accounts that do not agree, and minor historical inaccuracies. These evangelicals are often scholars who have been exposed to the historical-critical method, and have most recently proclaimed their beliefs in a section of the Lausanne Covenant dealing with Scripture (The International Congress on World Evangelization). Although the dividing lines are less than precise, influential voices include R. K. Harrison (*Introduction to the Old Testament*), James Orr (*Revelation and Inspiration*), Clark

[14]*Theology Today*, vol. XXXV, no. 1 (April, 1978), pp. 65–69.

Pinnock (*Biblical Revelation*), Bernard Ramm (*Special Revelation and the Word of God*), Jack Rogers (*Scripture in the Westminster Confession*), and James I. Packer (*"Fundamentalism" and the Word of God*).

Third, and in a distinct minority, are evangelicals who believe the term "inerrancy" is not appropriate to describe the scriptural witness. They are strong defenders of the authority of the Bible, but are convinced that the Bible claims to be an infallible guide only on matters of faith and practice. Among the most capable scholars evangelicalism has produced, this group has most actively formulated an alternative concept of biblical authority. They include F. F. Bruce (University of Manchester, England), George E. Ladd (Fuller Seminary), G. C. Berkouwer (Professor Emeritus, Free University of Amsterdam), Daniel P. Fuller (Fuller Seminary), and Bruce Metzger (Princeton Theological Seminary).[15] In sharp contrast to the first position, these architects of a new understanding of infallibility and inspiration are convinced that the sufficiency of Scripture is not destroyed by recognizing the Bible as culturally and historically conditioned.

Liberals are tempted to regard the inerrancy debate as a parochial dissension they can safely ignore. Those more informed, however, know that a "crisis of the Scriptural principle" (Pannenberg) is at hand. A movement intensifying among liberals has proposed to reexamine the critical-historical method as it was adopted from the nineteenth century. The first reaction, slow in coming, was to reverse many of the radical critical results of a biblical scholarship bent on revealing the human seams in Scripture. As a whole, biblical commentaries today are much more cautious and conservative in their conclusions regarding authorship, dating, textual emendation, and later redactions. What was

[15]It is also necessary to mention, with some caution, H. M. Kuitert, *Do You Understand What You Read?* (1970), Harry R. Boer, *Above the Battle? The Bible and Its Critics* (1975), H. N. Ridderbos, *The Authority of the New Testament* (1963), Paul K. Jewett, *Man as Male and Female* (1975), and Stephen T. Davis, *The Debate about the Bible* (1977). One begins to wonder if Clark Pinnock is moving ever closer to this third option. See *Journal of the American Scientific Affiliation* (June, 1979) for his most recent considerations.

once a preoccupation with splitting the text into as many pieces as possible is now being replaced by a structural analysis that looks at Scripture in terms of the largest blocks possible.[16] Bishop John A. T. Robinson, a respected New Testament scholar who popularized an iconoclastic approach to theology in *Honest to God*, clearly illustrates the shift that has occurred. Robinson, in his newest study *Redating the New Testament* (1976), argues that all the New Testament books were written before A.D. 70, that Paul wrote *all* the letters attributed to him, and that the apostle John was indeed the author of the Fourth Gospel. Thus it is no longer daring to question the more sacrosanct conclusions of historical criticism.

An even more important development in the last decade has been a desire to recast the critical-historical method into a new mold. European scholars such as Pannenberg and Rolf Rendtorff[17] are constructing a theological approach that takes history seriously as the locus of divine revelation. This school of thought will not allow the academic world to pass over the acts of God in Israel's history or the historical Jesus as if they did not really matter. Peter Stuhlmacher, a student of Ernst Käsemann and his successor in the chair of New Testament at Tübingen, has taken a long, hard look at the narrow, closed-minded, autonomous mentality of critical-historicalism.[18] Stuhlmacher does not stand alone, for a group of young German scholars also feel that

[16]On structuralism as a new method of biblical interpretation, see Robert M. Polzin, *Biblical Structuralism: Method and Subjectivity in the Study of Ancient Texts* (Philadelphia: Fortress, 1977), and the entire issue of the journal *Interpretation*, vol. XXVIII (1974). Under the editorship of Dan O. Via, Jr. (New Testament) and Gene M. Tucker (Old Testament), Fortress Press is publishing a series of "Guides to Biblical Scholarship" which covers a wide spectrum of issues and recent developments. Also recommended are the two companion volumes by Gerhard F. Hasel, *New Testament Theology/Old Testament Theology: Basic Issues in the Current Debate* (Grand Rapids: Eerdmans, 1975; 1978), because they are comprehensive but not too technical.

[17]Wolfhart Pannenberg, ed., *Revelation as History* (New York: Macmillan, 1968); Pannenberg, *Basic Questions in Theology* (Philadelphia: Fortress, 1970), vol. I.

[18]Peter Stuhlmacher, *Historical Criticism and Theological Interpretation of Scripture*, trans. Roy A. Harrisville (Philadelphia: Fortress, 1977).

biblical interpretation will continue to be ineffectual if it is not freed from the rationalism and positivism of the Enlightenment.[19]

In the United States the critical-historical method has been most severely scrutinized by Brevard S. Childs (*Biblical Theology in Crisis*, 1974), Walter Wink (*The Bible in Human Transformation*, 1973), and James Smart (*The Strange Silence of the Bible in the Church*, 1970). The loudest criticism is the failure of the critical-historical method to interpret Scripture so as to "enable personal and social transformation" (Wink). The bankruptcy of the method is due mainly to placing more confidence in history and the possibility of objective results than in the biblical text itself. All three call for a more "holistic" approach whereby the student or interpreter enters into a genuine dialogue with the text—a dialogue in which the person is not afraid to be questioned as well as answered.

The present situation cannot be understood without first realizing that evangelicals and liberals have come from a period when they were diametrically opposed. The Graf-Wellhausen hypothesis was motivated by a desire to destroy the conservative view of the Bible as directly inspired without human participation. Historical criticism became a weapon to attack a whole ideology. On the other hand, conservatives set out to build an impregnable defense around Scripture by way of a doctrine of verbal inspiration and inerrancy.[20] While liberals were trying to reveal the human quality of biblical inscripturization, conservatives were trying to prove its divine origin. Both sides are coming to the realization that their mutual defenses became more important than letting Scripture speak its own revolutionary word. For evangelicals this means confessing that "the evangelical fixation on errorlessness has prevented us from getting ahead in biblical

[19]A comprehensive but compact review of the ongoing debate concerning the critical-historical method is Edgar Krentz's *The Historical Critical Method* (Philadelphia: Fortress, 1965), esp. pp. 73ff.

[20]A careful reading of Hodge and Warfield shows that there was no way possible to prove the Bible contained one error after you had accepted their conditions. See Richard J. Coleman, "Biblical Inerrancy: Are we going anywhere?" *Theology Today*, vol. XXXI, no. 4 (January, 1975), pp. 295–303.

interpretation, and explains why we must turn to nonevangelicals to get help working out the details."[21] This fixation on inerrancy has meant at times a greater concern to prove the Chronicler was accurate than to be faithful to what the Scripture said. As a result, a kind of biblicism became a theology about the Bible, a theology that unfortunately became more important—if not foundational—for conservatism than the message of Scripture.[22]

In the hands of liberalism, biblical criticism became not only a tool but also a weapon to demonstrate the human side of Scripture. The liberal obsession to translate the biblical faith into understandable categories was one thing, but it was something quite different when theological and philosophical categories became the ruling principles for its interpretation. Consequently biblical theology was based upon the presupposition of a rationalistic biblical criticism, a methodology that was so fiercely defended that the biblical writings themselves seemed almost secondary to what the commentator wrote. Bereft of a theology of biblical inspiration and authority and having failed to place the critical method itself under the authority of Scripture, liberal theology inevitably succumbed to the cultural norms of its day.

(4) The Mission of the Church—In evangelical circles a quiet revolution has occurred concerning the definition, scope, and thrust of the mission of the church. The revolution has been pervasive, and its birth can be traced back to the emergence of neoevangelicalism. When Carl F. H. Henry wrote his earthshaking book, *The Uneasy Conscience of Modern Fundamentalism* (1947), he certainly had in mind the evangelicals' uneasy conscience about the overly narrow definition of mission as practiced by fundamentalism. In 1966 there were two visible examples of the reawakening of the social and missionary concern of evangelicals: the Con-

[21]Clark Pinnock, "Three Views of the Bible in Contemporary Theology," in *Biblical Authority*, ed. Jack Rogers (Waco: Word, 1977), p. 68.

[22]The excellent article by Paul L. Holmer of Yale Divinity School draws out the full consequences of biblicism. See Holmer, "Contemporary Evangelical Faith: An Assessment and Critique," in *The Evangelicals*, ed. David Wells and John Woodbridge (Nashville: Abingdon, 1975), pp. 68–95.

gress on the Church's Worldwide Mission at Wheaton College, which attracted 938 delegates from 71 countries, and the First World Congress on Evangelism in Berlin with an even broader representation.[23] Commenting on the follow-up Congress on Evangelism in Minneapolis, Billy Graham demonstrated just how far the revolution had taken evangelicals.

> I think evangelical Christianity is now "where the action is." We have seen a breakthrough in Minneapolis, I think. For the first time the world realizes that evangelicals have always had a social conscience—maybe not always as strong as they should have had. . . . But there has been a social concern. And missionary zeal.
>
> All of this came out in Minneapolis, and I think people in some of the liberally oriented groups were quite surprised.[24]

The momentum did not stop at Minneapolis. The First World Congress on Evangelism in Berlin also went a long way in demonstrating the interdenominational unity of evangelicals and their commitment to an international style of church mission. The next logical step was the development of an ecumenical theology of evangelism, which was the main topic of business at the International Congress on World Evangelization at Lausanne in 1974. Assessing the strengths and weaknesses of both the Berlin and Lausanne congresses, Arthur P. Johnston, himself an active participant, wrote that it would be ill-advised to speak of these events as "mature expressions of evangelicalism," but they did demonstrate to the world that evangelicalism had withdrawn from its defensive stance, characteristic since the Scopes Trial of 1925, and could now be seen as a "significant international body capable of even greater evangelistic exploits in an age of technol-

[23]See Harold Lindsell, ed., *The Church's Worldwide Mission* (Waco: Word, 1966) for position papers and the adopted declaration of the Wheaton Congress. An inside view of the World Congress in Berlin is given by Carl F. H. Henry, *Evangelicals at the Brink of Crisis* (Waco: Word, 1967).

[24]*Christianity Today* (Nov. 7, 1969), p. 34.

ogy."[25] There are few who would find fault with Dr. Johnston's evaluation.

The liberal conciliar movement, as early as 1961 at the Third Assembly of the World Council of Churches at New Delhi, wanted to correct the one-sidedness of its definition of mission. The Council's theme, "Jesus Christ, the Light of the World!" testified that the "work of evangelism is necessary in this and in every age in order that the blind eyes may be opened to the splendor of light." Increasingly so, various ecumenical and denominational bodies have openly and quietly courted evangelical leaders for their input. Evangelicals, for example, were invited to and were represented at the Fifth Assembly of the World Council of Churches, Nairobi, 1975. Although few were voting delegates, they were influential in drafting the report "Confessing Christ Today," which was unanimously adopted by the Assembly.[26] Several of the better known evangelical leaders, such as John H. Yoder, David Hubbard, Jim Wallis, Ronald J. Sider, and W. Stanley Mooneyham who represented World Vision International, were invited because of their influential writings or organizations.

One of the important factors in moving both liberals and evangelicals to accept a more inclusive interpretation of the mission of the church is their willingness to look critically at their recent past. Listen, for instance, to the confession made by one thousand missionaries and church leaders who signed the Wheaton Declaration of 1966:

> We have sinned grievously.... We are guilty of an unscriptural isolation from the world that too often keeps us from honestly facing and coping with its concerns. We have often failed to apply Scriptural principles to such problems as racism, war, population explosion, poverty, family disintegration, social revolution and communism.[27]

[25]Arthur P. Johnston, *The Battle for World Evangelism* (Wheaton: Tyndale House, 1978), p. 216.

[26]The full text with introduction is found in *Breaking Barriers: Nairobi 1975*, ed. David M. Paton (Grand Rapids: Eerdmans, 1975), pp. 41–57.

[27]Lindsell, *Church's Worldwide Mission*, pp. 219–220.

The same tone of repentance is carried over in the 1977 Lausanne Covenant.

> Here too we express penitence both for our neglect and for having sometimes regarded evangelism and social concern as mutually exclusive. . . . When people receive Christ they are born again into his kingdom and must seek not only to exhibit but also to spread its righteousness in the midst of an unrighteous world. The salvation we claim should be transforming us in the totality of our personal and social responsibilities.[28]

As evangelicals speak of their lack of social conscience and orthodoxy's overly narrow understanding of redemption, liberals are learning to admit their neglect of the personal way the gospel calls people to repent and be saved. In 1974, one positive reaction to the confessional and forthright nature of the Chicago Declaration[29] was from the Division of Church and Society of the National Council of Churches. "Moved by the Holy Spirit," the committee declared:

> We have been too often inclined to criticize or ignore those who have tended to emphasize the personal rather than the structural. . . . We acknowledge that we have not sufficiently shown . . . the determination to be rooted in Christ's Gospel. . . . We affirm that God abounds in mercy and that he forgives all who repent and turn from their sins. So we seek a Christian discipleship that is no longer shy or diffident about proclaiming the complete Gospel of Christ, with both its personal and social implications [see Appendix for text].

[28]The full text is found in Johnston, *Battle for World Evangelism,* pp. 369ff.

[29]Meeting at a Thanksgiving workshop on "Evangelicals and Social Action" in Chicago of 1973, a small but diverse group of the "evangelical left" leaders drafted this 473-word Declaration (see Appendix and Ronald J. Sider, ed., *The Chicago Declaration* [Carol Stream, Ill.: Creation House, 1974]). Even though a follow-up workshop failed to accomplish much, the spillover from the Chicago Declaration has been considerable, including the newly organized Evangelicals for Social Action which itself is conducting prototype workshops.

Growing out of this mutual desire to address the remissions of a deficient past is a common attempt to appropriate a definition of mission that balances the personal and social. The Fourth Assembly of the World Council of Churches strove to dissolve the apparent opposition between a gospel of personal conversion and a gospel of social justice. At their two most recent international gatherings evangelicals and liberals have not fully explicated what a "holistic" mission of the church means. It cannot be said that either the Fifth General Assembly of the WCC (Nairobi) or Lausanne 1974 put together a positive statement that would satisfy both of them. Even though the formulas are framed mostly in series of negatives concerning this issue, we do see a healthy interaction between what were once two opposing, divided camps.

Among evangelicals one still detects a pointed tension between those who would define mission in terms of a partnership between social action and personal conversion and those who will settle for nothing less than a definition that gives the priority to evangelism and sees social action as another means of confronting men with the gospel of Jesus Christ.[30] On the other hand, there is a small but potent group of radical evangelicals who attack every form of cultural subversion, namely, materialism, racism, sexism, militarism, and economic injustice. Although not as visible, a similar tension lies within liberalism between those who are urging churches to get deeply involved in church growth and personal evangelism tactics and those who are very cautious of anything that does not include an outcry against institutional and structural injustice. Consequently, there exists a great need for a theology of mission that can serve to build at the local level mission committees that bear witness to the inner and outer dimensions of sin and salvation.

[30]In addition to being debated in numerous committees of the last two international world congresses, the issue has been argued by Arthur P. Johnston, representing the former, and John R. W. Stott, representing the latter. See Johnston, *Battle for World Evangelism*, and *World Evangelism and the Word of God* (Minneapolis: Bethany Fellowship, 1974); Stott, *Christian Mission in the Modern World* (Downers Grove, Ill.: Inter-Varsity, 1976), and *Christianity Today* (January 5, 1979), pp. 34–35. See also Chapter VI.

Do evangelicals and liberals need each other? Are they at a point in their mutual histories when they can hammer out a new middle? Before we attempt to answer these questions we must take a closer look at the changing climate and the historical roots that gave birth to liberalism and evangelicalism. Richard Quebedeaux is certainly correct when he writes that evangelicals on the left have gone beyond a one-way ecumenism (getting liberals saved) and find themselves willing to engage in dialogue with and act alongside Christians of different persuasions. The same is true for the other side of the coin: liberals are displaying a more open and positive attitude toward a liberated evangelicalism. Quebedeaux is even willing to foresee a "tidal wave of true ecumenism" emerging from a rippling that is beginning to pulsate.[31] Coalition may be the best term to describe what Quebedeaux and I are referring to as a new attitude—certainly not a new denomination nor an independent movement, but a continued searching on the part of scholars and practitioners to evolve a theology that is biblical, true to experience, and redemptive in the fullest sense.

HISTORICAL ROOTS

Evangelicals and liberals are who they are because of their historical roots. Many others have written extensively about the American religious experience and our purpose is merely to provide a historical context for the theological issues raised in the latter part of this book. History, of course, can be written from almost any perspective. The focus I have chosen is one that highlights the continued struggle between religion and culture, because the church today in its most enlightened expressions is critically assessing the manner in which it has become a servant of a corrupt society. Also critical is the period of dissent and reaction between the Civil War and World War I. Sidney Ahlstrom, the respected historian of American religion, is fully justified in noting that "no aspect of American church history is more in need of summary and yet so difficult to summarize" as this particular

[31]Quebedeaux, *The Worldly Evangelicals,* pp. 135–141.

period.[32] The spiritual foundation that had served for a general consensus was breaking apart and conservatives and liberals began to separate both culturally and religiously. If there is an opportunity to reverse these two debilitating trends, we must necessarily understand why they started and where they gained their impetus.

During the colonial period in America there were political conservatives and liberals, but no one would have thought to divide Christians along these lines. It may be an overstatement to say there was just one evangelical Christianity, but it is not unfair to agree with Martin Marty that the terms "Protestant" and "Evangelical" can be used interchangeably for all practical purposes until the Civil War.[33] There were many factors that contributed to this broad religious consensus, but primary among them was the belief among the settlers that God had called them out and gave them a new land (made a covenant) and would bless them in their efforts to establish a righteous empire. The origins of such a belief lie in the European/English Puritan movement which essentially sought to amplify the reformers' rediscovery of a biblical testimony to Yahweh's calling forth a new nation of Hebrews. Only in North America, though, did this divine call become translated into an unwritten blending of the religious and the civil. An ethic of personal freedom, individualism, and personal regeneration was perfectly matched with a doctrine of laissez-faire capitalism and global expansionism. The Protestant ethic of hard work, thrift, and personal piety would win you a desired place in heaven as well as in the American socio-economic structure. A theology that was essentially dualistic coupled with a Christocentric doctrine of election and judgment naturally resulted in a missionary zeal that was both religious (convert the world) and nationalistic (every nation ought to embrace democracy and capitalism).

It would be misleading to picture the seventeenth and eighteenth centuries as a homogeneous evangelical empire. A

[32]Sydney E. Ahlstrom, *A Religious History of the American People* (New Haven: Yale Univ. Press, 1972), p. 823.

[33]Martin E. Marty, *Righteous Empire* (New York: Dial Press, 1970), Foreword.

broad consensus did exist, reaching its glory in the middle of the nineteenth century, but this consensus had to continually be defended against waves of immigration and new blood, the rising tide of Roman Catholicism, and numerous Protestant fringe groups such as the Mormons, Shakers, and the Millerites. Divisions from various substrata were beginning to take shape. Black/white, north/south issues were only a prelude to issues of religious orthodoxy and social action. A faint outline of two distinct parties can already be traced: one more accommodating to a changing world and the other maintaining its established achievements. The great revivals of the first half of the nineteenth century were not the only sign that America needed to be "awakened," but a pretense that the Puritan crisis between sinful man and a transcendent God was being lost to an established civil religion.

The Civil War proved to be a point of no return. Marty notes that "the failure to mend and heal in the 1860s and 1870s shaped the destiny of Protestantism for the ensuing century."[34] The socio-economic issues were not solved but intensified by new waves of immigrants, urbanization, great shifts in population, and the scientific-technological explosion. It became increasingly difficult to identify where the center of this new era lay, but by the turn of a new century it was no longer possible to straddle the fence.

Thus, one group broke off to the left and were known as "modernists" or liberals, while the other broke off to the right and continued to be known as conservatives and later as fundamentalists. While one segment was busy with Bible conferences and revivals, another segment was turning its attention to the problems of industrialization and corporate profits. But the lines of division ran through to the very heart of one's view of the world. The liberals believed God was at work in the very structures of history and society. Their eschatology was optimistic and progressive because God was inherently present in the evolution of all matter. Biblical criticism was not a destructive force but an ally of a historical method that stripped away subjective interpretations and penetrated to the very core of truth. Faith became

[34]*Ibid.*, p. 134.

both personalized and historicized at once. The Incarnation was necessitated more by God's purpose to unite himself with man than by man's sin.

Just as firmly as liberals believed a new alliance had been struck between Christianity and modern thought, conservatives refused to accommodate themselves in any way. If they were to continue their identity it would have to be as a subculture rooted in the absolute teachings of Scripture and the doctrinal tenets of the church. They rejected the optimistic postmillennialist eschatology that was characteristic of nineteenth-century Protestantism and instead developed a dispensational premillennialism based upon the literal fulfillment of biblical prophecies. In general, they accepted the world as getting worse and worse until only the second coming of Christ could set it right. The 1860s and '70s gave rise to the Seventh Day Adventists and Jehovah's Witnesses with their predictions of the "end time," and the Darbyite dispensationalists, with their focus on the secret rapture of the true believers, dominated the American millennial movement in the latter part of the century.[35] The accent on the individual and his salvation out of this world through the supernatural action of God in Christ was an ideal barricade from which to defend against the enemies of modernism and all of its evils.

The period from 1910 to 1925 was one of real turmoil as liberals and conservatives moved to consolidate their positions and memberships. In 1910 a group of men, financed by two wealthy Los Angeles oilmen, proposed to begin distributing *The Fundamentals* (12 pamphlets) free of charge to "every pastor, evangelist, missionary, theological student, Sunday school superintendent, Y.M.C.A. and Y.W.C.A. secretary in the English speaking world, so far as the addresses of these can be obtained."[36] Even-

[35]Ernest R. Sandeen has made a valuable contribution in helping us understand how Darby and the other millennialists formed a crucial linkage with the history of fundamentalism. See his *Roots of Fundamentalism: British and American Millenarianism, 1800–1930* (Chicago: Univ. of Chicago Press, 1970).

[36]*The Fundamentals: A Testimony to the Truth* reached twelve small volumes and was published between 1910 and 1915. The story of how *The Fundamentals* came to be published is told by Stewart G. Cole in *The History of Fundamentalism* (New York: Richard R. Smith, 1931), pp. 52ff.

Much confusion, however, has resulted from Cole's mistaken

tually, 3,000,000 copies were distributed throughout the world—an indication of how strongly fundamentalists felt about the need to return the church to the basic Christian faith. By 1920 the term "fundamentalists" became roughly equivalent to militant conservatives. Almost simultaneously a group of people, known later as supporters of the Social Gospel, were gaining formal recognition by most of the major Protestant denominations and by their representative association, the Federal Council of Churches of Christ in America. When Walter Rauschenbusch stood on the platform of the Taylor Lectureship at Yale in 1917 to present in mature form *A Theology for the Social Gospel*, it could truly be said that "the social gospel is no longer a prophetic and occasional note" but "has become orthodox."[37] *Christianity and Liberalism* (1923), by respected conservative scholar J. Gresham Machen, was perhaps the best commentary on this period. Here he defined the situation as a test between two logically incompatible religions.

It seemed to most people that World War I brought the bitter controversy to an end. In theory, at least, it was thought that religion and science could coexist. But in 1925 the truth was revealed. What began as a simple test trial concerning the teaching of evolution in a small town in Tennessee soon attracted worldwide attention as the Scopes or Monkey Trial. The trial revealed that the theological questions had not been settled but had only gone underground for a period.[38]

---

identification of fundamentalism with a five-point creed adopted at Niagara in 1895 which supposedly included verbal inerrancy of Scripture, the deity of Christ, the virgin birth, the substitutionary view of the atonement, and the physical resurrection and bodily return of Christ. The very expansive nature of *The Fundamentals* included a much broader doctrinal basis than five points. See, e.g., Sandeen, *Roots of Fundamentalism*, pp. xiv, 140.

[37]Charles Howard Hopkins, *The Rise of the Social Gospel in American Protestantism 1865–1915* (New Haven: Yale Univ., 1940), pt. IV: "1900–1915, Maturity and Recognition."

[38]Norman F. Furniss, *The Fundamentalist Controversy 1918–1931* (reprint; Hamden, Conn.: Archon Books, 1963), p. 10: "In another way the Scopes trial was more disturbing than mystifying; it opened the eyes of newspaper readers to the fact that thousands, even millions, of Americans espoused a faith leaving no room for acceptance of the remarkable achievements of the past half-century."

Through the 1920s and '30s the debate raged passionately and consumed an enormous amount of time and energy. One characteristic event was the exodus of Professor Gresham Machen and his followers from the Presbyterian Church in the U.S.A. and their subsequent establishment of a rival seminary and independent Foreign Missions Board, and finally the Orthodox Presbyterian Church in 1936.[39]

By 1925 a new liberal consensus had been virtually achieved. The fundamentalists, sensing they were being reduced to minority status, had launched a fierce attack on the modernists, but lost. Whereas in the 1920s fundamentalism had been a movement within American Protestantism aspiring to control the churches and shape the culture, by the 1940s it had become a sectarian movement outside the mainstream. Whether by choice or by necessity evangelicalism resisted assimilation into the melting pot and preferred to build its own subculture with mores, social values, and institutions uniquely its own. Viewed in the shorter perspective, American evangelicalism had become an eccentric, separatist movement. On the other hand, viewed from the angle of a few centuries, evangelicalism embodied some of the most deeply rooted traditions and characteristic attitudes in American culture. Recognizing this paradox, George Marsden, Associate Professor of History at Calvin College, comments that "at times evangelicalism appears as a beleaguered sect; at other times it still poses as the religious establishment."[40] It is really only possible to understand contemporary evangelicals when this ambivalent attitude of rejection and acceptance of American cultural values is considered. Obviously this period from around 1926 to World War II was one in which an "immigrant mentality" proved useful in a culture that seemed to have turned from God. Marsden is entirely correct when he concludes that the tensions within the new evangelical upsurge are a reflection of this dual

[39]See Edwin H. Rian, *The Presbyterian Conflict* (Grand Rapids: Eerdmans, 1940); and Ned Stonehouse, *J. Gresham Machen* (Grand Rapids: Eerdmans, 1954).

[40]George M. Marsden, "From Fundamentalism to Evangelicalism: A Historical Analysis," in *The Evangelicals*, ed. David Wells and John Woodbridge (Nashville: Abingdon, 1975), p. 123.

legacy of separateness that had been developed in its fundamentalist phases, and its older heritage of shaping the culture.[41]

In the years following World War II, a new generation of evangelicals began to come to terms with the weaknesses inherent in a reactionary theology in a complex and scientific age. Some of these new leaders had studied at such well-known universities as Harvard, Yale, Basel, and Zurich, and consequently were able to see other theological traditions more objectively and appreciatively than their predecessors did in the 1920s, and to deal responsibly with these theologies from the standpoint of their own presuppositions.[42] The new evangelicalism that emerged never thought it departed from the "fundamentals" of the faith. It did seek, nevertheless, to move beyond the excesses of fundamentalism and to formulate a positive approach to the twentieth century. In the preface of *The Uneasy Conscience of Modern Fundamentalism* (1947), one of the first books that represented the feelings of the new evangelicals, Carl F. H. Henry clearly stated the purpose of their reform:

> Those who read with competence will know that the "uneasy conscience" of which I write is not one troubled about the great biblical verities, which I consider the only outlook capable of resolving our problems, but rather one distressed by the frequent failure to apply them effectively to critical problems confronting the modern mind. It is an application of the faith, for which I plead.

While evangelicals were struggling to overcome the handicaps of a period of isolation, liberals were coming to terms with having to strengthen weak spots in their theology as they tried to remain relevant. Since the driving concern of liberal theologians of the nineteenth century was to make viable the historic Christian faith in an age of Enlightenment, neoorthodoxy found it necessary to drive a transcendent wedge between Christian faith and modern culture in order to free the biblical message from

[41] *Ibid.*, p. 129.

[42] Arnold Hearn, "Fundamentalist Renascence," *The Christian Century*, vol. LXXV, no. 18 (April 30, 1958), p. 528.

being lost in the immanence of human experience. What were cornerstones in the theologies of Ritschl and Schleiermacher—the rational and moral perfectibility of man—became liabilities in the theology of Karl Barth. The autonomy of the scientific method and self were scourged as incompatible with the sovereignty and all-sufficiency of God. Throughout, dialectical theology was intent on contrasting the Word of God with that of man, the transcendent, wholly-other God with that of sinful man, and the reception of faith in Jesus Christ with that of the ordinary secular experience. Neoorthodoxy was not exactly pessimistic in the way fundamentalism was, but it made the most of the absurdity of the liberal confidence in historical progress after two world wars.

Today neoorthodoxy is generally assessed as being more successful in its exposure of the inadequacies of nineteenth-century liberalism than it was in providing lasting solutions. The post-liberal theologies of Bultmann, Tillich, Bonhoeffer, and the Niebuhrs are seen as new beginnings necessitated by a radical secularism. The basic premise of this neoliberalism is that "no assertions are to be judged true, unless, in addition to being logically consistent, they are somehow warranted by our common experience, broadly and fairly understood."[43] The extent that contemporary liberalism swims in the backwash of neoorthodoxy is due entirely to the feeling that neoorthodoxy seems illogical and unrealistic precisely because of its separation of faith and its language from ordinary experience. The newly defined task was to break loose from those language forms that were no longer meaningful: mythological (Bultmann), supernaturalistic (Tillich), religious (Bonhoeffer), the optimism of idealism (R. Niebuhr).[44]

[43]Schubert M. Ogden, *The Reality of God and Other Essays* (New York: Harper & Row, 1963), p. 20.

[44]Much of post-Bultmannian German theology, spearheaded by Ernst Fuchs and Gerhard Ebeling and the prior contributions of Heidegger and Dilthey, can be understood as pressing the issue of authentic language forms even further over against inauthentic ones. Not only does man give birth to language, he is born out of language; and that is why Bultmann did not go far enough in his program of demythologizing. For a fine summary of the movement see "New Frontiers in Theology," vol. II of *The New Hermeneutic*, ed. James M. Robinson and John B. Cobb, Jr. (New York: Harper & Row, 1964), pp. 39ff.

Writing about the American liberal tradition, Lloyd J. Averill delineates seven themes that presently lead the way. These include efforts to unfold a theology of social change (Harvey Cox), the quest for a "religionless" interpretation of Christianity (Bonhoeffer and his disciples), renewed interest in human experience as a legitimate source of our knowledge of God (Langdon Gilkey), fresh interest in natural theology (Alfred Whitehead and process theologians), a new mood of optimism concerning the creative possibilities open to secular man (William H. Hamilton), a fresh emphasis on love as the sufficient norm of ethical behavior (Joseph Fletcher), and a reaffirmation of the lordship of Jesus and his call to discipleship.[45]

This description, while being accurate for the 1960s, is neither a blueprint of where liberals find themselves in the '70s nor where they would like to be in the '80s. Averill's survey does point out, however, that the breakdown in neoorthodoxy has resulted in a return to the principles of classical liberalism.[46] The liberalism of the 1940s and '60s was a clear reaction to a theology that had removed God from the historical, cultural, and ordinary experience into sheer transcendence. Did not the great liberals of the nineteenth century try to create an alternative language form that opposed the transcendent dualism of orthodoxy, and did they not seek to locate God in the course of human history and make intelligible God-language in terms of modern philosophy? While recognizing the ways in which recent liberal theology reflects some of the major themes of classical liberalism, it must also be noted that names like Bultmann and Tillich do not enjoy the status they once did, and that other figures such as Harvey Cox, Bishop John A. T. Robinson, and Langdon Gilkey have signifi-

[45]Lloyd J. Averill, *American Theology in the Liberal Tradition* (Philadelphia: Westminster, 1967), pp. 133ff. Also useful accounts of the liberal tradition include Kenneth Cauthen, *The Impact of American Theological Liberalism* (New York: Harper & Row, 1962); and Wilhelm Pauck, *The Heritage of the Reformation* (Boston: Beacon Press, 1950).

[46]For a more complete analysis of the dissatisfaction of present-day liberals with neoorthodoxy see Ogden, *Reality of God,* pp. 1–20; and Langdon Gilkey, *Naming the Whirlwind,* pp. 73–106, 184ff. These two theologians are especially conscious of the manner in which their proposals are a return to, yet distinct from, classical liberalism.

cantly modified their positions.[47] It would be just as unfair to identify neoevangelicalism with those ancestors who sought to establish a righteous empire under a banner of zealous nationalism as to think contemporary liberals accept uncritically their theological ancestors. Both groups have much to affirm about their respective heritages while still acknowledging the excessive reactions that took place. Historical roots are just that—inspirational sources to which one returns again and again in order to grow new limbs and branches. The most encouraging sign that a new middle course might be forthcoming is the uniquely new willingness to confess the shortcomings of the past and the folly of believing one tradition possesses the whole truth.

There have been numerous signs of this new willingness to confess and to look beyond one's own narrow and particular religious tradition. The two outstanding events have been the Hartford Appeal and the Chicago Call (not to be confused with the Chicago Declaration of Evangelical Social Concern in 1973). The Hartford Appeal is not only an implied confession of certain contemporary heresies, but an attempt to forge a new starting point that battles both the reaction from the right and accommodation from the left. George Lindbeck, in his reflection on the Appeal, is certainly correct when he writes that "the cause of truth is not a *via media* between extremes, between thesis and antithesis, but is rather something fundamentally new, a synthesis in which the old reactions and progressivisms are both abrogated and *aufgehoben*."[48]

In May, 1977, a small group of evangelicals gathered and drafted a document known as "The Chicago Call: An Appeal to Evangelicals" (see Appendix for full text). Confessional in style also, this Appeal was intended to call evangelicals back to their historic Christian roots. The drafters were of a consensus that contemporary evangelicalism could mature only if it could broaden and deepen its understanding of the Christian faith. Robert

[47]If one simply reads the books of these authors in chronological order, it becomes clear that each has become dissatisfied with the rather nineteenth-century liberal stamp that characterized their earlier writings. See, e.g., Cox, *The Seduction of the Spirit* (1974) and *Turning East* (1977); Robinson, *Reading the New Testament* (1976); Gilkey, *Reaping the Whirlwind* (1977).

[48]*Op. cit.*, p. 23.

Webber, one of the moving forces behind the Call, underscores the growing desire among evangelicals to be able to trace the beginnings of their faith roots beyond the establishment of a particular denomination or church which may have arisen out of a split over this or that doctrine, or perhaps even a personality clash between two strong leaders.[49] Associated with this recognition that evangelicals are for the most part a people without roots is an acknowledgment that American evangelicalism became an expression of Christianity different from the shape of historic Christianity, in part because of its overemphasis on scholastic theology, pietism, and apocalypticism.[50] Perhaps the Chicago Call best expressed the sentiment among both evangelicals and liberals when its signers wrote—"but we cannot be fully evangelical without recognizing our need to learn from other times and movements concerning the whole meaning of that Gospel."

THE CHANGING CLIMATE

The situation today between liberals and evangelicals is marked by rapid social and theological shifts. Liberals, but especially evangelicals, are discovering the truth of this generalization. Among the most important factors that have shaped the course of events is the decision by evangelicals not only to enter the world but to change it. Quebedeaux describes the reversal:

> Evangelicals decided to enter the world to change it—a world that could no longer take the message and lifestyle of fundamentalism seriously, if it ever did in the past. They began to affirm the Christ who *transforms* culture. The evangelicals knew that to influence the world for Christ they would have to gain its attention in a positive way. In a word, they would have to become *respectable* by the world's standards.[51]

[49] *The Orthodox Evangelicals,* ed. Robert Webber and Donald Bloesch (Nashville: Thomas Nelson Inc., 1978), pp. 35–36.

[50] Robert E. Webber, *Common Roots: A Call to Evangelical Maturity* (Grand Rapids: Zondervan, 1978), p. 16. Even the title of this book is significant, because it is another sign that "maturity" is the key word in the evangelical reform movement.

[51] Quebedeaux, *The Worldly Evangelicals,* p. 13.

It would be difficult to find a statement more portentous than this, because entering the world is as dangerous as withdrawing from it.

It is only in the last decade that mainline Protestantism has recognized evangelicals as a new majority, and if not as a new majority at least as a third movement alongside Judaism and Roman Catholicism. Whether or not we can demonstrate the numerical plurality of evangelicals is beside the point. Illinois Congressman John Anderson, addressing an audience of the National Association of Evangelicals in 1974, spoke for many conservatives when he said:

> It was *they* [the liberals] who denied the supernatural acts of God, conforming the gospel to the canons of modern science. It was *they* who advocated laws and legislation as the modern substitutionary atonement for the sins of mankind. . . . It was *they* who were the friends of those in positions of political power. *They* were the "beautiful people," and we—you will recall—were the "kooks." We were regarded as rural, reactionary, illiterate fundamentalists who just didn't know any better.
>
> Well, things have changed. Now *they* are the "kooks"—and *we* are the "beautiful people." *Our* prayer breakfasts are so popular that only those with engraved invitations are allowed to attend. *Our* evangelists have the ready ear of those in positions of highest authority. *Our* churches are growing and theirs are withering. . . . *They* are tired, worn-out 19th century liberals trying to repair the pieces of an optimism shattered by world wars, race riots, population explosion, and the specter of worldwide famine. *We* always knew that things would get worse before the Lord came again.[52]

Although some of Congressman Anderson's audience may have been too overjoyed at the prospects of breaking out of an

[52]Quoted from Martin E. Marty, *A Nation of Behavers* (Chicago: Univ. of Chicago Press, 1976), p. 92. George H. Williams and Rodney L. Peterson believe that "evangelicals had outgrown their minority paranoia" in 1953—the year that President Eisenhower received a delegation from the National Association of Evangelicals, and signed a document calling for 'a national reaffirmation of faith in God . . . repentance from sin. . . . ' " See *The Evangelicals*, p. 225.

emigrant-minority subculture to detect something of "the pride that goeth before the fall," others are keenly aware of the burden inherited with social respectability. Donald G. Bloesch, for instance, asks whether this evangelical renaissance is rooted in a spiritual awakening or in the counter-reactionary mood of middle America against the vagaries of the once predominant liberal left.[53] His question is a good one and it leads to another: Are evangelicals trying to have the best of both worlds? In other words, are they taking advantage of an ephemeral mood to offer converts a subculture that provides meaning, belonging, and identity, *and* at the same time an establishment status as one of the "beautiful people"?

On the positive side, resulting from this newly gained respectability, evangelicals are much more open and less defensive. We have already noted an atypical willingness to be self-critical. Carl F. H. Henry believes that "the real bankruptcy of fundamentalism has resulted not so much from a reactionary spirit—lamentable as this was—as from a harsh temperament, a spirit of lovelessness and strife contributed by much of its leadership in the recent past."[54] One might argue with Henry that it was a temperament and not primarily fundamentalism as a theology which brought the movement to a standstill, but certainly a new openness is now the predominant attitude. This new pervasive attitude has recently been translated into a new aggressiveness. Evangelicals are now offensive-minded, and the effects are manifested everywhere from the "Jews for Jesus" movement to the establishment of a multimillion-dollar Christian Broadcasting Company. It is no wonder that premillennialism is no longer flaunted as a test of orthodoxy, but instead there is renewed interest in the here and now. Of course evangelicals are "fascinated by the great, noisy, aggressive world with its big names, its hero worship, its wealth and garish pageantry" (A. W. Tozer), but for the first time in over a century they are struggling with making it all work for the Lord and discovering, as the liberals did, the burdens involved.

[53]Donald G. Bloesch, *The Evangelical Renaissance* (Grand Rapids: Eerdmans, 1973), p. 18.

[54]Carl F. H. Henry, *Evangelical Responsibility in Contemporary Theology* (Grand Rapids: Eerdmans, 1957), pp. 45ff.

As the evangelical renaissance continues to pick up momentum, it is natural that it also experiences a broadening effect. Groups that had been traditionally excluded by the conservative establishment are presently demanding their right to use the title "evangelical." Among others, these include Pentecostal, charismatic, black, feminist, Roman Catholic, Episcopal, Wesleyan, and Lutheran. The argument given to those seeking entrance is that one's lifestyle, ethnic background, race, or political beliefs do not matter as long as they accept the authority of the Bible over their lives, are born again, and share the enthusiasm to spread the gospel. It is quite true that it is not safe to assume that all evangelicals are Republican or were supporters of Richard Nixon and the war in Vietnam. Some of the formal barriers and prohibitions against drinking, smoking, movies, and dancing have fallen into disrepair. Consequently, many evangelicals share the same lifestyle as other mainline Protestants and no longer feel alienated.

Richard Quebedeaux goes so far as to distinguish an evangelical left over against an evangelical establishment,[55] and justifiably. The establishment is composed of white, middle-class Americans who identify themselves with the cultural ethos of revivalism and a theology epitomized by Billy Graham. The chief symbols of this establishment have been the National Association of Evangelicals, the Evangelical Theological Society, Dallas Theological Seminary, and *Christianity Today*.

On the other hand, the young or left evangelicals take pride in rejecting status symbols. Many of them were involved in the civil rights struggle and the student counterculture of the '60s, and have been deeply influenced by such liberal writers as Bonhoeffer, the Niebuhrs, Karl Barth, Thomas Merton, and to a lesser extent by liberal German scholarship. Though often not openly admitted, they use the critical-historical method rather than a literal, static method of interpretation. To use Quebedeaux's phrasing, this "vanguard of younger liberals" constitutes a comparatively small group, but one which is highly literate and therefore influential. It remains to be seen if Quebedeaux is correct in his prognosis that the evangelical establishment is collapsing because

[55] *The Worldly Evangelicals*, pp. 18–24, 83–100.

it can no longer speak for a "growing number of evangelicals who affirm the full authority of the Bible, the need for conversion to Christ, and the mandate for evangelism," but who also accept "biblical criticism, evolution, the scientific method, and broad cultural analysis, while rejecting the cultural taboos and the ethos of modern revivalism."[56] What is certain is that evangelicalism is a much broader movement than it was twenty years ago.

Another way to describe the changing climate is to concede that a division lies between older and newer leadership. This situation is characterized by the division between one group who is interested in defending and maintaining the gains made by evangelicalism and another group that is troubled by those gains and wants to forge ahead. The more established leadership is fearful that evangelicalism will forfeit its doctrinal basis and thereby lose its identity. To them, liberalism is still the ultimate threat. In contrast is one group of evangelical leaders who sees racism, sexism, apathy, increasing fragmentation, isolation, and accommodation to cultural standards as the enemy. This latter group, for the most part, has some kind of liberal education, did not partake in the fundamentalist-modernist controversy, harbors no ill feelings against "enlightened" liberals, and willingly considers the contribution of different traditions.

One of the more pressing issues debated among evangelicals is how tolerant to be toward those moving to the left. In more theological terms, it is a question of how tolerant Christian fellowship can be until the issue of truth is compromised. In a book by Harold Lindsell, the former editor of *Christianity Today,* entitled *The Battle for the Bible* (1976), he thinks it is time for evangelicals to stand up and declare themselves rather than hide behind ambiguous statements. Lindsell speaks for many who believe evangelicalism has become as inclusive as it dares. Carl F. H. Henry is a moderating voice. For many years as the guiding light behind the success of *Christianity Today,* and now as a lecturer and writer, Henry has warned against increasing fragmentation and the price paid by ignoring the solid scholarship of others. In a modest volume entitled *Evangelicals in Search of Identity* (1976), he sees the movement as being in grave danger of wasting its

[56]*Ibid.*, pp. 163–164.

potential over less than crucial theological issues. Inerrancy, for example, in his opinion should not be used as a polemical weapon, and yet it is a theological tenet that gives evangelicalism a sense of identity. Clark Pinnock, who established himself as one of the new leaders with solid credentials with the publication of *Biblical Revelation* (1971), not only finds the specter of polarization sadly disturbing, but challenges those who "are closed to dialogue and insensitive of their need to learn from others as well."[57] Richard J. Mouw, Professor of Philosophy at Calvin College, echoes those sentiments in the same issue of *Theology Today*.

> As it turns out, many of the "neo-evangelical" leaders of the 1940's and '50's have been unwilling to depart from a virtual fundamentalism on this issue; and they are committed to the "control and limit" tactics which Pinnock describes. Large numbers of the evangelical rank-and-file are willing to follow them in this strategy.
>
> The break-up of the evangelical coalition will not be a pleasant experience for many of us, especially those of us who are convinced that the "evangelical" label does designate a significant theological option (p. 50).

Professor Mouw's statement implies that it is difficult to determine the number of evangelicals who are happy neither with strict neoevangelicalism as it is defined by men like Lindsell nor with the usual liberal treatment of biblical authority and similar issues.

It is always quite dangerous to categorize people, but it may be helpful here to mention a few names for the sake of the neophyte. Some of the more prominent leaders of the evangelical left include Richard V. Pierard, a historian at Indiana State University and frequent author on the subject of civil religion; black evangelists Tom Skinner (*If Christ is the Answer, What are the Questions?*), founder of Tom Skinner Associates, Bill Pannell (*My Friend the Enemy*), John Perkins (*Voice of Calvary*), and Rufus Jones, director of Conservative Baptist Home Mission Society;

[57]Clark H. Pinnock, "Evangelicals and Inerrancy: The Current Debate," *Theology Today*, vol. XXXV, no. 1 (April, 1978), p. 69.

Jim Wallis, founder of Sojourners and The People's Christian Coalition of Washington, D.C.; Fred Alexander and Al Krass, major contributors and leaders of the bimonthly magazine, *The Other Side,* and a communal type community in Philadelphia; Lewis B. Smedes, a signer of the Hartford Appeal; Paul K. Jewett (*Man as Male and Female*); Jack Rogers, who with Smedes represents the neoreformed evangelicals; Paul Henry (*Politics for Evangelicals*); David A. Hubbard, the president and professor of Old Testament at Fuller Seminary; Paul Rees, a nationally known leader in such organizations as World Vision and Billy Graham Crusades; Ronald J. Sider (*Rich Christians in an Age of Hunger*), organizer of Evangelicals for Social Action; Bruce Larson (*The Relational Revolution*); Richard Mouw; and Robert Webber, editor-in-chief of Creation House.

Contrasting different fields of expertise is another way to look at the contemporary scene. A considerable distance lies between Norman L. Geisler and George E. Ladd in biblical studies; Jack Rogers and Francis Schaeffer in theology and philosophy; John Warwick Montgomery and Gordon H. Clark vs. Paul Jewett and Clark Pinnock in systematic theology; and Vernon C. Grounds and David O. Moberg. Others like Bernard Ramm, J. I. Packer, and Carl F. H. Henry are staunch expositors of orthodox Christianity, but have a conciliar attitude toward those who represent another viewpoint. Interestingly enough, such well-known scholars as Helmut Thielicke, John Yoder, G. C. Berkouwer, Jacques Ellul, William Stringfellow, and Bruce Metzger, and popular writers like Elton Trueblood and William Barclay not only defy classification, but also represent the best hope for a new middle course that is truly ecumenical in a positive sense.

When evangelicals decided to enter the world and change it, rather than withdrawing into a distinct subculture, they automatically established a link with American liberalism. Their new status, among other reasons, has made them less defensive and less interested in drawing lines of demarcation. Their search, however, for identity or the meaning of a holistic evangelism is not theirs alone; it is also the search of contemporary liberals. Something is happening within the changing climate of mainstream Protestantism. The Christian knows a new period of evangelical-liberal relations is dawning when Richard Mouw casually states "there are growing opportunities for a healthy three-way conversation among chastened evangelicals, chastened Catholics and chastened liberals."[58]

There have been many significant changes in American liberalism since 1972, but none so telling as the fact that liberals can no longer ignore what evangelicals write and say. In short, liberals can no longer claim a stranglehold on theological integrity. The change is not merely one of coming to grips with the growing evangelical presence, but is due to a reexamination of their own religious roots. Dean M. Kelley's book, *Why Conservative Churches are Growing* (1972), helped the liberal establishment realize that their churches were not providing what people needed or wanted. When the model of ecumenicalism, social activism, dialogue, and theological faddism had almost been played out only a few asked why it had failed, and many wondered if it wasn't time to try a different approach. Bishop Pike's dream for a super church (COCU—Consultation on Church Union) failed to materialize for various reasons. The architects were too occupied with form, structure, and organization to consider the priority of building up the fellowship of Christians and making church unity work at a local level. Liberals were so confident that they knew how to transform society that when the fires began to burn low, so did the commitment to reorganize the church along more socially just patterns. Little did anyone foresee the problems that were to engage the "churches back home"—the energy crisis, the clergy-laity split, financial woes, and a general disillusionment. It was several years later that liberals began to understand that the charismatic renewal movement signaled the spiritual starvation of the people in the pew. And, of course, a price was to be paid for ignoring the silent evangelical majority under every rock and behind every door.

Simultaneously, a vast theological vacuum was taking its toll of church leadership and diffusing the energy of the laity. For a few decades neoorthodoxy provided a foundation from which liberals could rebuild their faith in a loving God and a tran-

[58]Richard J. Mouw, "Evangelicals in Search of Maturity," *Theology Today*, vol. XXXV, no. 1 (April, 1978), p. 51.

scendent will for their lives. When the 1950s and '60s brought new shock waves of race riots, urban decay, and unexpected prosperity, a new formula had to be found. Digging around in the reservoir of nineteenth-century liberalism or resurrecting some themes from the Reformation proved to be futile because Christians needed to hear a message that was not only good news but one that was spoken with authority. Liberalism entered a period of theological faddism, and as one experiment was rejected a new one was proposed. This was the time when movements arose out of the ashes of their predecessors—biblical theology, death of God, the new hermeneutic, the new quest for Jesus, process theology, the secular city, long prolegomenas analyzing our cultural context, Eastern religions, theology of hope, and liberation theology.[59] It is not surprising that clergymen were confused about what was "the" theology or even whether the Jesus of history could be reconciled with the Jesus proclaimed by the early church. Given sufficient sophistication the trained pastor could create his own cohesive, meaningful theology; but while he was working on this, the parishioner was subject to a smorgasbord of indigestible jargon couched in a language that left him bewildered. Theological relativity could be justified on philosophical grounds, as did Bultmann, but it could not be translated into practical results. The two overriding issues of biblical criticism and evangelism were simply passed over. Writing about the inspiration of Scripture or the mandate to preach the judgment and grace of God on a personal level was tantamount to crossing over into the evangelical domain. The liberal can see all of this in retrospect. And although he does not have the answers, he is better prepared to formulate the questions.

Theologically, American liberalism is still in a state of flux. Some are still hoping that a dominant figure will arise who will gain such respect that we can all rest content. To a certain extent that has happened with Roman Catholicism with the writings of Hans Küng, Karl Rahner, and Edward Schillebeeckx, but even here the Catholic believer becomes lost in a torrent of

[59]You can trace the zigzag course of the new theologies by reading each succeeding volume of the series entitled *New Theology*, edited by Martin Marty and Dean Peerman (The Macmillan Co.).

words. The real prospects for the future, it seems, lie in renewing the interest in setting biblical criticism in a theological context, laying a foundation for biblical authority, defining the mission of the church so it incorporates social justice and personal regeneration, and developing unified theological themes that are biblically grounded. In general, liberals are lagging behind their evangelical counterparts, but then it has been only in the last few years that liberalism has willingly looked beyond its own well-groomed hedges toward its roots in Puritan pietism and the German Evangelical experience.

On a more pragmatic level, mainline liberalism has taken some resolute actions. All of the major denominations have put together systematic programs on evangelism to be instituted at the local level. This does not mean that every pastor or layperson knows what to do with them. Thus, there are small beginnings toward inviting evangelicals to share their know-how. The National Council of Churches and the World Council of Churches have been in the forefront in including evangelical input before writing position papers. A policy paper adopted by the National Council of Churches Governing Board in March of 1976 was heavily influenced by Al Krass, coeditor of *The Other Side* and author of *Five Lanterns at Sundown: Evangelism in a Chastened Mood* (1978). Significantly, a statement in that paper reads: "The task of evangelism today is calling people to repentance, to faith in Jesus Christ, to study God's word, to continue steadfast in prayer, and to bearing witness to Him. This is a primary function of the church in its congregational, denominational and ecumenical manifestations" (see Appendix). While not naming evangelism as the primary task of the church, it does describe a growing phenomenon within liberal churches. Among the more popular courses and programs are those dealing with prayer and spirituality. Bible study groups are springing up in the most unexpected places; and for a change these Bible studies are taking Scripture more seriously than the latest commentary. Liberals are still very new at all this, but there is a genuine desire to feed the spiritual nature of their humanity.

The demise of the social action committee has meant a reordering of priorities. Laymen are now being employed on committees concerned with mission and outreach and are struggling to understand the meaning of those words. Ministers are often heard muttering "Whatever happened to social justice?" For the first time in many, many years people are asking the hard questions about how to invest their time and money so that it is truly redemptive. Liberals are eagerly reading books about the Church of the Saviour in Washington, D. C., by Elizabeth O'Connor because she probes deeply into what it means to be a missionary church.

The last few decades have had a sobering effect on churches that considered themselves middle-of-the-road. They thought they knew what it meant to be involved in the world and how to transform society. Now second thoughts have occurred. During 1975–1977, the United Church of Christ, which has the reputation of being one of the more secular denominations, initiated a program whereby prominent left evangelical leaders could be introduced to UCC ministers. At most of the regional meetings attendance was very good, but in some instances the conferences fell through due to the lack of a regional sponsor. This dual reaction is very symbolic of the changing climate in which we live. Some liberal leaders thought it was time to begin building bridges, and pastors came because they felt they had something to learn from their evangelical brethren, yet others were either intimidated or victims of stereotypes left over from the heyday of fundamentalism.

HOW DO WE DIVIDE?

In 1970 there would have been considerable discussion whether such terms as "liberal" or "evangelical" had much validity, and if Protestants could really be divided into these two categories. The terminology is as elastic now as it was then, and each of us in his or her own unique way is a mixture of both. Nevertheless, I am more convinced than ever, in spite of the difficulties inherent in any generalization, that "liberal" and "evangelical" are identifiable traditions that help us map the religious scene of today.

In recent years there has been a renewal in mapping American religious life. In the first chapter of *A Nation of Behavers* (1976), Martin Marty gives a brief review of how historians have categorized religious America. Perhaps the two best known attempts have been in terms of Jew, Roman Catholic, and Protestant by Will Herberg, and along social and economic lines by H. Richard Niebuhr (*The Social Sources of Denominationalism*). More recently is the proposal by Jeffrey Hadden to highlight the crisis between clergy and laity (*The Gathering Storm*, 1969). Since then numerous studies have tried to demonstrate that race, education, age, income, or denomination are the critical factors, but a strong feeling among historians is that the true nature of the American divide is hidden beneath these indicators. One can point to a unanimity among certain authors such as Sidney Ahlstrom, Martin Marty, David Moberg, and Dean Hoge. They argue that American culture has reflected two dominant viewpoints: one religious and confessional with its home in the church, and the other scientific and humanistic with its home in the academe. One might say America possesses two cultures which it inherited from a seventeenth- and eighteenth-century world view. This does not mean that the scientific and religious were always opposed, any more than the university and the church were always at odds. But a vast majority of people felt more at home in one world view or the other.

In particular, Marty argues that the deepest division within Protestantism was not doctrinal or denominational, but between two comprehensive views or parties. One "private" party, which later adopted the name "evangelical," accented personal salvation, individualistic morals, free will, fulfillment in the afterlife, a body-soul dualism, biblical authority, and a supernatural transcendent God working out his purposes through divine providence. The other "public" group stressed belief in evolution and progress, commitment to institutional change, theological relativism, the brotherhood of mankind, the Kingdom of God as man can bring it into this life, and a divine Being who is continually at work within the created structures. The word "social" usually found its way into the designation of the latter—Social Gospel, social services, Social Realism.[60]

The many books of Marty underscore from different perspectives the tendency of previous historians to miss the forest

[60]Martin E. Marty, *Righteous Empire*, ch. VI.

because of the trees. By the turn of the twentieth century the delineation of the two-party split in America became starkly clear—a division deeply rooted in their distinct and common past. This does not rule out, however, the persistent solidification of subgroups. It would not be inaccurate, for example, to speak of six religious clusters—as Marty does—on the American scene today: mainline Protestantism, evangelicalism and fundamentalism, the Pentecostal-charismatics, the new religions (Eastern, etc.), ethnic religion, and civil religion.[61] We miss the point if we do not see that these seemingly independent clusterings are in reality reflections of the culture in general, and that the culture itself is aligned via humanistic/scientific vs. transcendent/supernatural directions.

In his sociological study of the United Presbyterian Church, in part an attempt to verify Marty's thesis, Dean Hoge discovered that the tensions along the lines of age, race, education, clergy-laity, and religious backgrounds proved to be symptomatic of the culture in general and specifically of the two theological positions. "Our point is," he states, "that the total culture is divided, and as part of it the churches are also divided."[62] Further along in his study Hoge concludes: "Like most main-line Protestant denominations, the United Presbyterian Church contains two distinct theological parties with quite different assumptions and commitments. And what is more important, there is no theological middle that unites or synthesizes the two—but merely the appearance of one in politically balanced documents crafted to achieve denominational unity" (p. 120).

David Moberg (*The Great Reversal,* 1977) indulges in oversimplification when he finds American Protestantism divided over two basic approaches to Christian involvement: one generally concerned for each person as a person but apathetic about persons as members of larger groups, and the other convinced that social structures shape the individual for good or evil. In this book I will present at least five fundamental theological issues

[61]Martin E. Marty, *A Nation of Behavers* (Chicago: Univ. of Chicago Press, 1976), *passim.*

[62]Dean R. Hoge, *Division in the Protestant House* (Philadelphia: Westminster, 1976), p. 45.

that divide liberals and evangelicals, which suggests that it will take more than a great reversal in the personal evangelism vs. social-reform debate to restore a middle ground that never existed in the first place. In a very real sense so much has happened between the first and second edition of Moberg's book (5 years) that it is passé to characterize either evangelicals or liberals in such caricature form. The "two parties" must enter into deeper dialogue on many fronts, but no issue has received as much attention as defining the mission of the church. What has been lacking to date is serious study of the other theological issues that always arise to meet us as soon as we discuss the practical points.

The question of how we divide is also the question of what unites us. This fictitious middle ground that is often referred to is nothing more than a pervasive civil religion shared by both liberals and evangelicals. Strong accusations by conservatives assert that liberalism has fallen under the spell of cultural subversion; and liberals make similar charges concerning the sellout of establishment evangelicalism to political conservatism.[63] We are thankful that Robert Bellah revealed the existence of a civil religion in America with its own institutions, rituals, deities, sacred texts, and priests.[64] Bellah rightly makes the distinction between a civil religion that is identical to nationalism and one that acts as a pervasive and dominating influence within the sphere of church and religion. By and large, civil religion has not been the worship of the American nation, but an understanding of the American experience in the light of specific Christian symbols. On the other hand, early American history must be read as a period when religion did not function to give the individual an identity distinct

[63]Among the most recent works documenting the ties between political and religious conservatism are: Richard V. Pierard, *The Unequal Yoke: Evangelical Christianity and Political Conservatism* (Philadelphia: J. B. Lippincott, 1970); and Lowell D. Streiker and Gerald S. Strober, *Religion and the New Majority: Billy Graham, Middle America, and the Politics of the 70s* (New York: Association Press, 1972).

[64]Robert N. Bellah, "Civil Religion in America," *Daedalus* (Winter, 1967); and more recently, "American Civil Religion in the 1970s," in *American Civil Religion*, ed. Russell E. Richey and Donald G. Jones (New York: Harper & Row, 1974), pp. 255ff.; and his latest book, *The Broken Covenant* (New York: Seabury, 1976).

from national ideals. To be an evangelical Protestant was synonymous with being an American. Now, both liberals and conservatives are confronted by the same issue, namely, is the individual conscious of the sources that shape his identity and does he distinguish between those which are civil and those which are religious?

Is there a common enemy that unites evangelicals and liberals? Jim Wallis, throughout his stinging attack in *Agenda for Biblical People* (1976), does not always tell the reader what groups are the object of his scorn, but they are not hard to identify. The important distinction is not one's denomination but whether one is a supporter of establishment Christianity or a practitioner of the biblical faith. The real test of biblical faith, likewise, is not in concise doctrines but in the disciplined lifestyle of the committed Christian. Since the mainstream church, whether it is Protestant or Catholic, evangelical or liberal, is wedded to the mindset of the American status quo, commitment to the biblical faith transcends traditional and conciliar lines.

James Smart has made similar observations in his book, *The Cultural Subversion of the Biblical Faith* (1977). Here the principal issue is the confusion, rather than the merger, of biblical and patriotic faith.

> Is there a split personality in many Christians: an earnest Christian faith operating in one sphere of their existence while civil religion is operative with an equal earnestness in a second sphere, the two merging where they have common elements, so that the Christian is not even conscious of the split in his being?[65]

In either case, then, the Christian has the option, whether he is aware of it or not, of choosing his ideals and ritualistic reinforcement from a variety of sources.

Although this theological-ethical dilemma is nothing new, Smart, Wallis, and others would argue that the choice is a critical one because the stakes are especially high. The arms race and its relationship to budget priorities, hunger, global and national poli-

[65]Smart, *The Cultural Subversion of the Biblical Faith*, p. 34.

tics, for example, is an issue with such grave consequences that it is tragic if individuals cannot discern their loyalty to the government and their pocketbook from their loyalty to Jesus Christ and his Kingdom. To make matters worse, Dean Hoge, in his study of the United Presbyterian Church—a denomination which is possibly the most typical of the mainline churches—concluded that when people are in danger, the strongest middle-class commitments are to the family, the career, and the standard of living. "*For the typical Protestant church member these interests are so strong that church commitment is largely instrumental to them and contingent on whether the church appears to serve them.* As a result, many local churches tend to become instruments for achieving middle-class interests, whether or not these interests can be defended in New Testament terms."[66] If Hoge is correct, and I have no reason to think otherwise, the division within Protestantism is a division that runs right through Christianity. The crisis at hand is the same as it has always been—its nature being so fundamental that evangelicals and liberals, charismatics, fundamentalists, and radicals face a common enemy that is so injurious that it demands finding a common ground.

THE PARTICIPANTS

It has been my contention throughout this chapter that evangelicals and liberals constitute two groups sufficiently cohesive to define their boundaries. Since the first edition of this book considerable diversification has occurred, especially among evangelicals. Yet today it is easier to accept these labels as useful, so long as we understand that there is a wide spectrum within each group.

In speaking of a critical dialogue between evangelicals and liberals, I assume the risks involved in any generalization. Nevertheless, the task is not as difficult as it seems. There are certain basic characteristics which unite evangelicals, just as there are certain criteria by which liberals identify themselves. In certain sections I have found myself drawing upon the writings of some

[66]Hoge, *Division in the Protestant House,* p. 120.

of the more radical liberals, but in no sense should this be interpreted to mean they are representative. Rather, a segment of their thinking has been chosen because it seems to express best what most liberals think. On the other hand, the more liberal element of evangelical scholarship may have been selected where it is more engaging than the more conservative approach to a particular topic. In subsequent chapters the specific issues which separate the two participants will be taken up. Here it may be helpful to set down those features which constitute the inner fiber of liberalism and evangelicalism, features which may serve as a convenient measuring rod to identify evangelicals and liberals.

The evangelical enters into dialogue from a heritage which has consistently emphasized: (1) a living faith in a personal God and Savior, (2) a vital witness to Jesus Christ, and (3) a deep concern for biblical and orthodox Christianity. The adjective "personal" has a special place in evangelical thought and life. Faith is not only a very personal matter; it is directed toward a personal God. Conversion means the radical reorientation of the individual's life so it is rooted and sustained by a personal relationship with God through Jesus Christ. For the evangelical, God is not an abstract principle but a personal, caring being; Jesus Christ is not an ethereal, formless spirit but a living person to whom he can relate much as one relates to a fellow human being. A person's perspective is completely altered because Christ becomes the focal point of life. Consequently faith does not change just one's sociopolitical outlook but all of one's personal relations. The question that fills the evangelical life is, What would Christ have me do in this situation? Because faith is woven into the very pattern of life, the evangelical regards a routine of prayer and meditation, and the fellowship of the church, as essential. Nowhere else is the personal and consuming nature of faith more evident than in the home, where the individual's Christian witness is allowed to mature in an atmosphere of warmth, deep concern, and unusual closeness.

Historically evangelicals are known for their emotional revivals and dramatic conversion experiences. Such phenomena appear to be fading, but in reality the vitality of a deeply emotional faith still persists. Conversion is no longer believed to be so radical or automatic, but it is still seen as that moment when a man begins to recognize his sinful nature and is willing to open the door to communion with God. *The evangelical today stands more convinced than ever that faith can be deeply experiential without being sentimental, that it can be extremely personal without leading to an exaggerated individualism.* Faith in a personal Savior does not imply provincial narrow-mindedness any more than it implies anti-intellectualism, even if it has in the past. What it does mean for the contemporary evangelical is a different pattern of life emanating from a personal and conceptual commitment to the living Christ.

Evangelicalism has also distinguished itself by its vital witness to Jesus Christ as Lord. It has taken literally Christ's charge to make disciples of all nations. Their very choice of the designation "evangelicals" implies their understanding that evangelism, preaching the "good news," is their primary mission. While other theologies have swung from one emphasis to the other, evangelical theology has remained highly Christocentric. It may be a dangerous oversimplification to say "Christ is the answer," but in truth this is what evangelism comes down to. Christ, the evangelical proclaims, is the answer to life's deepest and most pressing questions. When one finds the source of profound satisfaction and spiritual confidence, he wants to share it with others. This undoubtedly accounts for why conservative and evangelical churches have sent the greatest number of missionaries to foreign countries, in proportion to their membership, of any group of churches.

Evangelicals do not see their theology leading to tension between soul-saving and social action. Such a problem arises only when conversion is seen as an end rather than as a starting point to a life of service. Evangelical history of the nineteenth and early twentieth centuries demonstrates that social reform is the natural consequence of redirected lives. Some of the greatest evangelists were also the most active social reformers, for they saw that only changed lives could bring lasting social change. In England, William Wilberforce (1759–1833) typified the spirit when after his conversion he led a movement against deplorable prison conditions, slave trade, and other social ills. Contrary to popular opinion, American evangelicals such as William Booth and

Charles M. Sheldon were as involved in social reform as were their more liberal brethren. In *Revivalism and Social Reform in Mid-Nineteenth-Century America*, Timothy L. Smith has dismantled the myth that the quest for moral perfection ran counter to rising concern for poverty, workingmen's rights, slum housing, and racial bitterness.[67]

The real danger is that social action may be taken out of the context of evangelism, for Christianity would then be in danger of losing its agent of change, Jesus Christ. The most effective social change comes from the winning of men's hearts and minds so they will have a continuing commitment to social justice, not just a temporary change of mind. The evangelical points to the history of the Social Gospel in America as confirmation of what can be expected when evangelism becomes secondary: social activism becomes an end in itself, the transformation of institutions becomes more important than the sin that produces them, and agitation for an economic revolution is substituted for spiritual awakening. The evangelical freely admits that his social conscience has not always been as broad or as deep as it should have been, and he is ready to amend that fault—not by neglecting the priority of preaching Christ but by giving fuller witness to the gospel's concern for the whole man.

The third characteristic of evangelicals has been their insistence upon a faith which is orthodox and biblical. In a time when relevance is at a premium, evangelicals believe as they always have that faith must remain true as it is reinterpreted. Orthodoxy implies not rigidity but flexibility within certain historical bounds. To be biblical means not literalism but fidelity to the essential truths laid down by Christ and recorded in the Bible. One does not need to read many books or hear many sermons by evangelicals to know of their persistent concern to measure every new theo-

[67]Timothy L. Smith, *Revivalism and Social Reform in Mid-Nineteenth-Century America* (New York: Abingdon, 1957). While the author has a very valid observation concerning the interrelationship between the quest for perfection and compassion for the poor, the Social Gospel marked a different period in American Protestantism by its emphasis on corporate sin and corporate action versus personal sin and personal action. In developing his thesis Timothy Smith neglects the unique character of the Social Gospel movement.

logical formulation against the principles inspired by the Reformation and the early church fathers.

One of the most prominent features of evangelical theology is the balance it has kept between personal and propositional revelation. The evangelical can speak of faith as both a personal relationship with Christ and a conceptual belief in the fundamentals of the Christian religion. From liberalism he feels he has learned not to turn faith into an arid intellectualism without personal commitment or into a spiritual encounter devoid of any objective knowledge of God; and from fundamentalism he has learned to avoid fossilizing faith into irrelevant dogma with narrow commitments or into pure emotionalism encased in obscurantism. It is by no accident, then, that the evangelical finds himself in a middle position.[68] The evangelical hopes to offer the Christian a faith which includes enthusiasm (*en theos*, possessed by God) as well as a definite content, a witness which is both socially aware and rooted in the power of the preached word, a theology which is informed yet nonetheless grounded in the biblical verities.

For the benefit of the uninitiated liberal it is worthwhile to name some of the recognized leaders and theological spokesmen for the new evangelicals. Among many persons, these come to mind: G. C. Berkouwer, Donald G. Bloesch, Geoffrey W. Bromiley, F. F. Bruce, Gordon H. Clark, Donald Dayton, Frank Gaebelein, W. Ward Gasque, Carl F. H. Henry, Morris Inch,

[68]According to Ronald H. Nash, *The New Evangelicalism* (Grand Rapids: Zondervan, 1963), evangelicals see themselves as occupying a middle position between fundamentalism and liberalism (see pp. 174–177). In *The New Evangelical Theology* (Westwood, N.J.: Revell, 1968), Millard Erickson likewise states that one of the prime objectives of the new evangelicals has been to bridge the gap between fundamentalists and liberals (see pp. 219, 224). This appears to be the case, as we find that evangelicals are criticized from both the right and left. For an example of criticism from the left see Daniel B. Stevick, *Beyond Fundamentalism* (Richmond: John Knox, 1964), who consistently chides neo-evangelicalism for not really moving beyond fundamentalism. Robert P. Lightner, however, complains that evangelicals have moved too far to the left and have broken with the fundamentalists. See Lightner, *Neo-evangelicalism* (Findlay, Ohio: Durham, 1962). The situation has remained unchanged since the '60s, except that now the arguments have been refined.

Kenneth Kantzer, Harold Lindsell, Richard Lovelace, John Warwick Montgomery, Harold John Ockenga, Bernard Ramm, Francis Schaeffer, and Donald Tinder (see also pp. 34–35).

In describing the contemporary American liberal we must be careful not to identify him with nineteenth-century liberals in Europe. To be sure, threads of continuity exist, but American liberalism has developed a distinctive style all its own. Nor can the typical American liberal be identified with neoorthodoxy. He may accept the corrective insights of this creative theological movement which reacted so sharply against nineteenth-century liberal theology, namely, the fresh discovery of the unique witness of Scripture, the transcendent and other-worldliness of God and his Word to us, the centrality of Christ, and the reassertion of man's sinfulness and his tendency to equate what is human with what is divine. The liberal today, however, has the distinct feeling that neoorthodoxy managed to dodge some of the crucial theological questions. Those powerful voices of the 1920s and '30s seem strangely silent in relation to our peculiar American scene of the '70s and '80s. This does not mean the liberal rejects the contribution of these theological giants; rather, he also includes in his thinking the added insights of contemporary thinkers such as Bonhoeffer, Tillich, the Niebuhrs, and many present-day American theological leaders such as Gregory Baum, Robert McAfee Brown, John Cobb, Jr., Harvey Cox, Leslie Dewart, Avery Dulles, Langdon Gilkey, Van H. Harvey, Paul Lehman, Martin Marty, Michael Novak, Norman Pittenger, Schubert Ogden, and Rosemary Ruether.

Many traits could be cited but three stand out as distinguishing the liberal: (1) his search for truth, (2) his zeal for relevance, and (3) his acceptance of the critical-historical approach to the Bible. If some think that the liberal's motto is, "Truth first and God second," they assume an antithesis which the liberal himself does not draw. To be sure, there have been times when the pursuit of truth seemed to have set faith and reason in opposition, but the liberal is willing to live in uncertainty as to which is right because he believes that ultimately there can be no conflict between truth and God. Moreover, liberal Protestantism has been strongly influenced by the conviction that faith is much more than reason and objective proofs. The liberal tradition is filled with names like Lessing, Strauss, and Bultmann, thought by many to be destroyers of faith, who exemplify for liberals that faith has to fear reason only when it is made dependent upon historical conclusions and scientific findings. It has been the very search for truth which has taught the liberal that faith must be faith in God, not faith in what man can know about God.

Through the centuries liberal Protestants have shown a certain willingness to accept the new discoveries of science and the social sciences. One important reason why has been opposition to authoritarian barriers which hinder the search for truth. Charles Davis, author of *A Question of Conscience* (1967), interestingly criticizes the Roman Church for not being a zone of truth because it uses words not to communicate truth but as a means of preserving authority without regard for truth. The liberal tradition has resisted any presuppositions which would place authority before truth, whether they have to do with an infallible Pope, supernaturally revealed doctrines, miraculous events, the inspiration of the Bible, the finality of the canon, or the preservation of the text. Similarly, the liberal has reacted against the idea that "religious" truth can be separated from other kinds of truth. Liberals have accordingly maintained a positive and open attitude toward science, psychology, sociology, secular literature, the theater, and the arts, believing that God's truth may be revealed anywhere and through many religious traditions.

God's truth must not only be sought; it must also be interpreted and reinterpreted. One of the driving concerns of liberal theology has been to make the Christian faith meaningful in the light of man's historical situation. Friedrich Schleiermacher, for instance, wrote his *Speeches on Religion* in the hope of winning back to Christianity those who had come to consider the gospel completely irrelevant. The extent to which we today are conscious of the problem of reinterpretation is due to the long liberal tradition which raised the problem in the first place and continually tried to match positive Christian answers to deeply analyzed human questions.

The liberal now realizes that the act of interpretation involves many more problems than he first thought. He is more aware that in his zeal for relevance he has not always avoided the danger of accepting current philosophies too readily as a means of updating the gospel, and in the extreme even confusing these human systems with the biblical message itself. Nevertheless, the liberal's concern for relevance has intensified over the years. Biblical theology, followed by the new hermeneutic, were two movements devoted to making God's revelation of himself understood.[69] Some of the best known names today in the liberal camp are engaged in study of hermeneutical problems such as demythologizing, language and speech, the meaning of history and historiography, process theology, a nonreligious interpretation of biblical concepts and symbols, and the technological politico-social revolution. It would not be too far off the mark to say that the whole of liberal theology has been cast and recast in terms of hermeneutics—the discipline of interpreting Scripture so that it can be understood by secular man.

Although evangelicals are beginning to accept a critical-historical approach to the study of Scripture, the irreversible and total decision of liberal Protestants to incorporate the method into their theology sets them apart.[70] Only as the absolute Copernican picture of the world began to collapse did man begin to understand himself as a historical and evolutionary being. Simultaneously, Christianity became aware of the time-conditioned character of its creeds, doctrines, and history. Once the critical spirit of man had been aroused, no limits could be set, and it was only a matter of time until historicism was applied to the sacred books themselves. The rise of the study of comparative religions and the application of archeological procedures strengthened the growing conviction that the biblical testimonies did not come

[69]The two best sources explaining and evaluating these two movements have already been mentioned—*The New Hermeneutic*, ed. James Robinson and John Cobb; and Brevard Childs, *Biblical Theology in Crisis*.

[70]Gerhard Ebeling spelled out in no uncertain terms the implications of the decision of liberal Protestants to accept the critical-historical method. Almost everything he says in reference to Roman Catholicism applies equally as well to conservatives, the more so in the light of recent changes in the Roman Catholic Church. See his extremely important article, "The Significance of the Critical Historical Method for Church and Theology in Protestantism," in *Word and Faith* (Philadelphia: Fortress, 1963), pp. 17–61 (esp. pp. 52–55).

directly from God but have their own history of human development. The full acceptance of the critical-historical method, therefore, implies something much more basic than the acknowledgment of historical, archeological, and philological methods as a means of better understanding Scripture. It means the acceptance of the historical nature of man's existence and his progressive understanding of God, the historical development of Scripture, and a positive attitude toward the truth contained in other religions and other written traditions.

Unfortunately, since the phrase was first used, the critical-historical method has received generally a negative connotation. The liberal does not see the method in that light. The critical-historical method has not destroyed his faith but has given it new life and integrity. It has proven to be an indispensable tool for interpreting the Bible in its original context. It has given us untold insights into primitive Judaism and Christianity, unknown in all previous centuries. It has kept biblical research in step with modern methods of inquiry and so prevented the gap between religion and science from becoming intolerable. Because of its disclosures we have a fresh appreciation of the Bible as a real book written by real men with a real message. The critical-historical principle has made comprehensible to contemporary men how God revealed and reveals himself in past and present times—namely, indirectly, through men and natural events which bear witness to something divine.

DO EVANGELICALS AND LIBERALS NEED EACH OTHER?

In 1965 Edward J. Carnell, one of evangelical Protestants' most gifted and creative minds before his sudden death in 1967, asked this question and his answer was negative.[71] He based his reply on the presupposition that no essential mutual need existed (Do palm trees need icebergs?). We ask ourselves if Carnell's response would be the same today. The question is certainly worth further discussion.

[71]Edward J. Carnell, *The Case for Biblical Christianity*, ed. Ronald H. Nash (Grand Rapids: Eerdmans, 1969), p. 32.

Which one ranks higher: Christian truth or Christian unity? If the former ranks higher, then "it is better to be divided by truth than to be united by error."[72] Even though this was Carnell's opinion, it could very well have been the feeling of most liberals since World War II, since both conservatives and liberals believed they possessed the truth, and therefore thought that entering into dialogue about Christian unity was useless. No essential mutual needs exist! But two important differences have arisen since 1965 when Edward Carnell wrote those dogmatic-sounding words. The first is that we are all more aware of the pain and suffering, along with the wasted energy and competitive witness, caused by our divisions. Carnell is aware that the church has become divided primarily because individuals and groups believe they have a monopoly on Christian truth. Even though confessions mirror the times and naive conservatives presume that their particular interpretation of Scripture is infallible, truth is used as a divisive force. It is clear that Carnell has in mind a truth that transcends doctrinally formulated expressions of that truth. Without making light of the very real and basic differences separating evangelicals and liberals, each side is at least looking critically at its own past and questioning whether pettiness and superficiality were not at work too. If we compare *then* with *now*, we are more sensitive to the effects of a divided house.

Secondly, Carnell could only see dimly, but we can see more clearly the possibility of a middle ground between liberals and evangelicals. In this chapter and in the following ones, I have set forth the central issues but also indicated where areas of mutual concern and prophetic thinking are beginning to overlap. The difference between *then* and *now* is one of perspective, namely, a perspective that grows out of a feeling that much unites the liberals and evangelicals. It is hard to think of two more divergent outlooks than those held by Karl Barth and Cornelius Van Til. Both men were headstrong and thoroughly convinced of the rightness of their approach to theology. Yet, every Sunday morning Professor Barth, while he was alive, went to the Basel, Switzerland, jail to visit the prisoners and preach to them. Every Sunday afternoon Professor Van Til, who is still alive, went to the

[72] *Ibid.*, p. 27.

hospital in Chestnut Hill, Pennsylvania, to visit the sick and share the gospel. If discussing theology, they would have disagreed on many important issues, but when they went from cell to cell or from bed to bed they shared a mutual sense of mission and Christian responsibility.

Which ranks higher: Christian fellowship or Christian doctrine and form? It was Carnell's belief that form and doctrine ought to be the servants of fellowship. "The scandal of Christendom," he writes, "is not the plurality of denominations, but the manner in which believers seek status in doctrine and form, rather than love."[73] This conclusion does not mean that we become indifferent to right doctrine and unite around the least common denominator, because then we would become indifferent to what makes our fellowship unique. On the other hand, history demonstrates the consequences when Christians exclude others because they do not accept a particular church doctrine or creed. After all, religious absolutism has its own dangerous way of making us indifferent to any truth but its own. Carnell seems to be saying that love can transcend all barriers if given a chance, but too often theological doctrines and ecclesiastical forms have unnecessarily become virtual road blocks. Yet, we must be on the watch that we do not become so anxious about church unity that we compromise our commitment to the basic truth of Scripture.

Truth ranks first, fellowship second, and doctrine and form last. Even if we came to this rather crass, static conclusion, we would have passed over the most important question—What is the dynamic relationship between truth and fellowship? On the one side, we do not want to so circumscribe truth by way of doctrines and confessional statements that fellowship with other Christians becomes intolerable. But on the other side, we dare not make entrance into Christian community so open that issues of belief and theology become frivolous. Fellowship is a broader concept than unity or church union, and therefore possesses greater parameters. Consequently, the structures that surround church union are different from those when Christians simply want to explore their theological differences. The very nature of Christian fellowship is that we erect no barriers that might

[73] *Ibid.*, p. 22.

give evidence of a love that judges or excludes. The same cannot be said of such rites as baptism, church membership, or entrance to the Lord's Supper. Here the individual is asking for formal recognition that he is prepared and willing to make a particular commitment at a particular time in a particular way.

At one time there was considerable resistance to dialogical study between evangelicals and liberals. The former were hardened by the idea that until there was agreement on basic matters of truth, fellowship with others was dangerous. The latter simply thought they could ignore evangelicals and assumed dialogue was irrelevant. The conservative still tends to be apprehensive about any situation that might compromise his position. But liberals have likewise been reluctant to do any more than meet with evangelicals over an occasional lunch because they, too, hesitate to be challenged.

It must be stressed to both liberals and evangelicals that their misgivings are largely unfounded. Sincere dialogue, for example, does not necessitate compromises or require that either party give up its claim to truth. In a sincere dialogical relationship each person (group) "seeks to give himself as he is to the other, and seeks to know the other as he is. This means he will not attempt to impose his own truth and view on the other."[74] In a monologue, communication is likely to become three things: parasitical when each participant is not really concerned to learn from others but uses them to confirm his own views, anxious if it is afraid of personal encounter and tolerates only agreement, and uncreative when each party is closed to new insights and seeks to present his position as the final one.[75]

True dialogue, therefore, requires a certain maturity. That maturity has been developed over the last half decade. The beauty of beginning with Christian dialogue, rather than with Christian unity, is precisely *this freedom* to unconditionally accept each other in the exploring and understanding of Christian truth. It is false to assume that dialogue weakens Christian belief or dilutes one's identity. Dialogue often strengthens the partici-

[74]Reuel L. Howe, *The Miracle of Dialogue* (New York: Seabury, 1965), p. 37.

[75]*Ibid.*, p. 36.

pant's understanding of his own beliefs while simultaneously deepening his appreciation of another way of seeing the same theological problem and answer. Many who took part in Roman Catholic-Protestant-Jewish dialogue groups have experienced this. Likewise dialogue does not presuppose that I forfeit my personal commitment to truth. What it does ask is that I do not *judge* my brother (Matt. 7:1–2). I may hold up God's truth to him (as I see it) so he can judge himself, but to actually pronounce the judgment that he does not belong in Christ's fellowship is not my personal prerogative.

Further, successful dialogue requires the desire to understand what is *at the heart* of our distinctive ways of grasping and expressing the Christian faith. It is not enough simply to know that someone holds a certain position, such as, "The basic mission of the church is the conversion of individuals"; we must also know *why* he believes what he does. The evangelical speaks about an experience with Christ, the inerrancy of the Bible, or the objectivity of God's revelation, and the liberal has no real idea what he means. And too frequently the evangelical does not make himself explicit because he has never taken the time to examine the meaning beneath his language. The liberal accuses the evangelical of disregarding the historical nature of Scripture, reducing faith to an individualistic experience, thinking the preaching of Christ will solve all our social ills, and being moralistic about the wrong issues. Meanwhile the evangelical accuses the liberal of not believing in a personal God or in the supernatural character of revelation, confusing Christian social action with humanism, and reducing the transcendence of God to a worldly immanence. These statements, however, are only half-truths, and as long as both participants continue to pass along half-truths, general misconceptions will hold sway. Even more important, we will not get to the real issues.

Above all, we cannot allow ourselves to think that second-hand or paper acquaintance with the issues will alter deeply seated attitudes and feelings. If we are planning to wait for doctrinal accord before we engage in firsthand personal contacts, we face an indefinitely long wait. The dialogue which really counts is the dialogue that takes place around the shared life of prayer, discussion, worship, and common service for Christ. When these avenues are open, mutual understanding and trust will take root among Christians of different persuasions. Out of this the fruits of the Holy Spirit follow: sympathy for varying doctrines and presuppositions, a willingness to put Christ before self, and a Christian experience of fellowship which extends beyond narrow confines and familiar boundaries.

DISCUSSION QUESTIONS

1. Do you agree with the statement by Jim Wallis to the effect that the most important distinctions in theology are no longer between evangelicals and ecumenicals (p. 4)? If you do concur, do we then conclude that in the present religious situation there are overriding issues which draw liberals and evangelicals together?

2. What significance do you see in the fact that conservative evangelicalism has at least lost its minority image and has in part become the new religious majority?

3. Richard Mouw comments that "there are growing opportunities for a healthy three-way conversation among chastened evangelicals, chastened Catholics and chastened liberals" (p. 36). Do you believe this to be true and what do you think he means by "chastened"?

4. What are the implications of the statement that "we cannot be fully evangelical [or liberal] without recognizing our need to learn from other times and movements concerning the whole meaning of that Gospel" (the Chicago Call)? Is there a common past shared by liberals and conservatives that serves to broaden out their theological roots?

II. THE HEART OF THE MATTER: *God as Personal: Jesus and Faith*

Is Jesus in the garden or on the street corner? The dilemma of the modern Christian is tied up with how and where we meet Jesus Christ. The evangelical expects to find Jesus in a personal relationship, in an atmosphere of solitude and meditation, while the liberal looks for Christ in a social context of worldly involvement. The rift this has caused is all too apparent. When the evangelical looks at liberal theology he sees a vague speculation which has lost the centrality of Christ, when he looks at liberal churches he finds that they have lost their mission to witness to Christ, and when he looks at the individual's Christian life he sees a shallow personal faith. The liberal, in contrast, feels evangelicals are so comfortable in their self-centered relationship with Christ that they are not pulled to step outside the community of faith into the secular world.

Whenever evangelicals criticize liberals, or vice versa, there is about as much misunderstanding as truth. The evangelical-liberal split within the church has made it imperative that we begin to separate truth from misunderstanding so that valid criticisms may be heard and biased ones erased.

Perhaps we may begin by eavesdropping on the following conversation:

L. I might be able to agree with you if we were talking about a living person, someone I can talk with and see, but we're talking about the historical person Jesus who lived nearly two thousand years ago.
E. Don't you believe in the Resurrection?
L. Yes, but I don't see how that makes any difference. I be-

lieve that Jesus appeared to the disciples and others after his crucifixion in some form of a "spiritual body," but then his appearances ended except for an occasional appearance to a saint in a vision.

E. So you don't believe that Christ is still present with us as a living Spirit?

L. He may be present, but not in such a way that I can enter into a personal relationship with him.

E. But you don't understand. My relationship with Jesus is not as if I enter into communion with a formless spirit floating around someplace. The Spirit of Jesus has a personality, a character, even an individuality, which we know from the New Testament.

L. Then according to you our relationship with Christ is dependent upon a certain image we have of him, but, as you said, not one that we dream up but one which we know from the Gospels.

E. How could it be otherwise? Our relationship with him, roughly speaking, is with his eternal Spirit clothed with certain historical-human traits.

L. There is that word "historical," and here is where we certainly differ. The one sure result of biblical criticism has been to show that historical investigation is only capable of yielding approximate results about Christ. And secondly, I am not sure it would make any difference to my faith if we didn't know for certain the details of Jesus' life.

E. Yes, this is where we do part. If you believed Scripture to be the infallible Word of God, then you would trust its description of Jesus. And you seem to forget that if we did not know what Jesus said and did, then we could never be sure about what we should say and do.

L. If you want to tie your faith to the accuracy of particular historical details, that is your choice, not mine. All I need to know is the fact of Christ's sacrificial love on the cross. This one act tells me how I should live my life.

E. How do you live your life? You may be involved in the world, but Christ is at best only an example to be followed.

L. And I suppose you expect me to believe that your kind of faith will give me a supernatural power for my life. But how do I know it isn't a psychological trick—this "experience" of Christ?

E. Well, if it is a psychological trick, then explain how thousands experience daily the power of Christ in their lives!

HOW DO WE EXPERIENCE CHRIST?

In this brief dialogue some very important theological problems are raised. The liberal is not able to dissuade the evangelical from his belief in a personal experience of Christ, because the evangelical knows Jesus as the power in his life. The evangelical is not able to erase the liberal's doubt about the validity of a personal encounter with Christ because he has never had such an experience and would not trust one if he did. A stalemate? Not entirely, because we can learn something from our different perspectives.

Very often the evangelical is not clear about what he means by a "personal conversion" or a "personal experience of Jesus Christ," and when the phrases are unpacked we find that he has in mind more than a tingling sensation or a warm glow. Christian faith often begins for the evangelical with an emotional, momentary experience, but this experience is only the beginning of a sustained relationship with the person of Jesus. Faith in a personal God commences in those moments in life when the sense of communion is so real, and the feeling of another personal reality so overwhelming, that the only way to describe it is to say that one has been confronted by another, independent "Thou."

To experience Christ may mean, as in the case of St. Paul and others, a sudden and dramatic confrontation with Jesus himself, but more often than not it means gradually entering into a personal relationship with Christ, usually through prayer. There may be that initial gripping experience we associate with the Pentecostals, but true conversion for the evangelical must also include the formation of a sustained relationship with Christ. Otherwise the individual will have nothing to hold him from returning to his old, unconverted self.

Bernard Ramm gives an excellent description of what it means to have a personal relationship with Jesus.

> *There is in Christian experience a wonderful daily walk with God.* There is the experience of comfort in hours of sorrow; of courage in times of discouragement; of spiritual vitality in times of physical sickness; of guidance in times of decision; of inspiration when surrounded by difficulties and problems. Thousands of Christians in every land, in every generation, will bear witness to the blessedness, sweetness, and delight of a daily Christian life with all the benedictions of spiritual graces given by a heavenly Father.[1]

It is more than coincidence that the language used by evangelicals to describe their faith is based upon the analogy of meeting and knowing another person. They speak of "accepting Jesus Christ" as one would accept another person, "winning someone to Christ" as one is won over to somebody's side, and "knowing Jesus" as one personally knows another person. The same idea of a personal relationship is reflected in many gospel hymns, such as, "What a Friend We Have in Jesus," "Held in His Mighty Arms," "I've Found a Friend," "While Jesus Whispers to You," and the familiar refrain, "And He walks with me, and He talks with me. . . . "

Once this central point is understood, the whole complex of evangelical theology and practice comes into focus. The evangelical is primarily concerned with bringing the individual into a personal relationship with Jesus, because this is the way God is known to him. A decision for Christ means a willingness to take the first step toward accepting Jesus as one's personal Savior, in other words, toward entering into a personal relationship with him. It is important, therefore, for the believer to know what kind of person Jesus is, for otherwise a personal relationship with him is meaningless if not impossible. For this reason Christian preaching and education is aimed at building up an image of the historical Jesus. Most sermons deal with the life of Christ directly, all sermons at least indirectly. One of the main purposes of Sunday school is to help the child form a picture of Jesus so that he can later accept and know him as Lord.

[1]Bernard Ramm, *Protestant Christian Evidences* (Chicago: Moody, 1953), p. 223.

It is understandable that a historically accurate picture of Jesus is important for the evangelical. Either he is following a true picture of Jesus or he is patterning his life after a false model. It is clear why "situation ethics" is such a bad word. Its very name indicates that it is the situation, not the person of Jesus Christ, which determines the ethical decision. For the evangelical everything relates directly to Christ, whether it be his attitude toward sex or his community involvement, because Christ is the model and the inspiration for the Christian life. Apart from Christ, God would be only an abstract principle and life would lose its meaning and motivation.

The liberal usually feels apprehensive about talk of an experience with Christ. His uneasiness spreads to the whole realm of religious experience. If you approach a liberal with a theological query, he will consider it thoroughly. But if you approach him with a religious experience, he panics. Liberals have taken the position that deep religious experience is not worthy of a mature person. That is not a theological position but rather a social and psychological stance.[2] Nevertheless, when the liberal considers his relationship to Jesus, he raises two basic problems: (1) historically it is not possible to know Christ as he *was*; and (2) even if we did have a completely reliable account of his life, it would be a psychological construction to enter into a personal relationship with the spirit of a man who is no longer physically present.

In the nineteenth century, liberal theology was devoted to the historical person of Jesus. No earlier movement was so assured that the methods of historical science could uncover the true Jesus of history. But even before the twentieth century arrived a host of biblical critics cast a large shadow over the "objectivity" of historical research and over the Bible as an objective historical record. Albert Schweitzer's chronological survey of the

[2]A heritage of suspicion is still with us from the tradition of pietism, the period of early American revivals, and Pentecostalism. Roman Catholics inherited this suspicion from the era of John of the Cross and Teresa of Avila, many of whose contemporaries claimed to have had religious experiences but later proved to be either dupes or imposters. For a searching analysis by a Roman Catholic of the validity of visions and prophecies, see Karl Rahner, *Inquiries* (New York: Herder and Herder, 1964), pp. 88–188.

many "lives of Jesus" (*The Quest of the Historical Jesus* [1906]) seemed to leave no doubt that every age paints its own picture of Jesus, consciously or unconsciously, according to its presuppositions and needs. Rudolf Bultmann set the pattern for later liberalism when he rejected the possibility of a personal relationship with Jesus for the reason that such a relationship would only be based upon an image built on the quicksand of historical research (*Jesus and the Word* [1926]). More recently Ronald G. Smith has stated that "the time of the historical approach to the life of Jesus is past. It has proved to be a cul-de-sac. There is no way of reaching a picture of the facts which is objective in the sense of being unassailable, unproblematic, and generally accepted."[3]

The second objection usually raised by liberals is the feeling that a psychological trick is involved, a trick which can't be trusted. It may seem like a psychological projection to the liberal because he fears his picture of Jesus may not be a mirror image of the historical Jesus. The liberal also asks himself how a personal relationship can be formed with a person who is not physically present.[4] In the dialogue above the evangelical explained that he was referring not to a ghostly or bodily presence but to a spiritual presence which has a definite form. An analogy can be drawn to

[3]Ronald Gregor Smith, *Secular Christianity* (New York: Harper, 1966), p. 80. The same basic conclusion was reached by Martin Kähler in 1896: "I regard the entire Life-of-Jesus movement as a blind alley." Yet he continued, "In other words, we cannot reject this movement without understanding what is *legitimate* in it" (italics mine). See Martin Kähler, *The So-Called Historical Jesus and the Historic, Biblical Christ*, trans. Carl E. Braaten (Philadelphia: Fortress, 1964), p. 46. Ruth Robinson more explicitly draws the implication when she says, "So it is not to the individual, the man called Jesus of Nazareth, that I am committed. Such a man is unknown to me. It is true that a picture of him has been built up in my mind from various sources, but this is largely imaginary and unverifiable. I can never know for myself what he was like as a person, nor am I really concerned to know, apart from natural curiosity. I have no more to do with an individual who lived 2000 years ago than he with me." See Ruth Robinson, *Seventeen Come Sunday* (Philadelphia: Westminster, 1966), p. 46.

[4]Bultmann set the pace when he declared that a personal relationship with Jesus was possible only in Jesus' lifetime and is no longer possible today. See Rudolf Bultmann, *Glauben und Verstehen*, vol. I (Tübingen: Mohr, 1964), p. 106.

the passing away of a close friend or relative. He (she) is no longer present in the flesh, but in some almost indescribable way it can be said that he (she) is still present as a spiritual person. The relationship is maintained as long as the memory image of the deceased does not fade away. The relationship may even change if new information comes to light about the person. A personal relationship with Jesus is different insofar as we will never have the opportunity to know him in his earthly existence. The relationship must therefore be formed on what we can learn about Jesus secondhand rather than by a firsthand experience; but this is no different from forming a personal relationship with someone by correspondence.

How do we experience Christ? The pat answer to this question has been that the liberal does not really experience him (except perhaps indirectly), but the evangelical knows Jesus through a direct spiritual relationship. As true as this generalization may be, it dodges the real issue, for both liberals and evangelicals experience Christ through a historical image of him.

The evangelical is mistaken if he thinks he has a completely unmediated relationship with Christ, unless Jesus is thought to be present as a ghost or some indefinable spirit within us. The phrase "historical image" in no way implies that Jesus is not real or alive but reminds us that as human beings we must be confronted by Jesus through some medium or picture. For example, although we pray to Jesus as a spiritual rather than a physical presence, the reason we are able to pray to him in the first place is that we have a mental image of what he is like. Certainly one of the primary purposes behind the Gospels was to give early Christians a mental picture of the kind of person Jesus was.

The liberal is mistaken if he thinks a spiritual relationship with Jesus is impossible since historical research cannot guarantee the details about his life.[5] It is one thing to say that our picture of

[5]This is the unwarranted conclusion Bultmann and others draw. Their reasoning is that since the picture of Jesus Christ cannot be verified historically or expected to remain the same decade after decade, a personal relationship with him would be a relationship built upon an illusion or a deception. This has been one of the main reasons why liberal theology since Bultmann (and before) has rejected the idea of a personal identity or relationship with the person of Jesus.

Jesus has no historical basis, quite another to say it is not now verifiable in all of its particulars. There is no agreement among evangelicals, much less among liberals, on just how historically correct our image of Jesus must be before we can trust it. Most liberals are probably in accord with evangelicals to the extent that they believe the essential facts, events, and character of Jesus' life are determinable and certain. Even if, as the liberal claims, our picture of Jesus is a changing one, allowing every age and individual to interpret Jesus in a slightly different manner, it by no means follows that a personal relationship with Christ is no longer legitimate or desirable. A relationship with Jesus is a psychological deception only if there is no resemblance between Jesus as he actually was and the image we have of him. As long as there is a basic continuity between the two, our relationship is not a figment of the imagination.[6]

Evangelicals and liberals are misled if they believe Christianity can get along without a picture of Jesus.[7] Christianity's power to transform human life lies in part in Jesus' giving to his

[6]The "new" quest for the historical Jesus must be mentioned in this context. Only the most radical liberal denies the existence of a *basic continuity* between the historical Jesus and the first image of him proclaimed by the early church. There also seems to be little reason to think we have since lost that continuity. On the contrary, modern historical methods have tended to restore our confidence in the ability of the community of faith to preserve a reasonable facsimile. See, for instance, the essays in *The Historical Jesus and the Kerygmatic Christ*, trans. and ed. Carl E. Braaten and Roy A. Harrisville (New York: Abingdon, 1964).

[7]The extreme to which denial of the need for a picture of Jesus can be carried is well illustrated by a passage from one of the death-of-God theologians, Thomas Altizer: "Confronted as we are by a new and revolutionary moment of history, we can accept our destiny only by acknowledging the loss of all our traditional Christian images. No sacred images whatsoever are present upon our horizon. The original form of Jesus has disappeared from view. . . . May we hope that the time has at last arrived when the Christian faith can transcend the language of images?" See Thomas J. J. Altizer and William Hamilton, *Radical Theology and the Death of God* (Indianapolis: Bobbs-Merrill, 1966), p. 128. The idea that Christianity has outgrown its need for religious symbols and pictures, however, has been soundly rebutted by the work of Mircea Eliade and many others. See, for example, Paul Ricoeur, *The Symbolism of Evil*, trans. Emerson Buchanan (New York: Harper, 1967).

followers the image of a new possibility of self-understanding. Christianity is like other religions in that it is dependent upon certain dominant images by which its adherents orient themselves to the present and future. As these images or models prove helpful in relating the person or the community to reality, they become immortalized in story, song, and myth.[8] For Christians it is the picture of Jesus that becomes the model for one's style of life. Paul Tillich describes the process very well:

> The power which has created and preserved the community of the New Being is not an abstract statement about its appearance: it is the picture of him in whom it has appeared. No special trait of this picture can be verified with certainty. But it can be definitely asserted that through this picture the New Being has power to transform those who are transformed by it. . . . And it was, and still is, this picture which mediates the transforming power of the New Being.[9]

There exists therefore a common denominator between evangelicals and liberals: both are dependent upon a mental picture of Jesus to experience his presence. For the evangelical, Christ is present through a conscious and deliberate act based upon a personal image, while for the liberal this picture tends to be more abstract and less conscious. The evangelical also depends upon a historically conditioned picture of Jesus. But what really divides liberals and evangelicals is how this image or model of Jesus becomes central to Christian faith. Not only does Jesus serve as a different kind of model for the liberal and evangelical; faith itself takes on a different meaning for each.

JESUS AS MODEL

As we move toward the heart of the matter we find that Jesus serves as the model for Christian faith in contrasting ways for

[8]Van Austin Harvey, *The Historian and the Believer* (New York: Macmillan, 1966), pp. 258ff.

[9]Paul Tillich, *Systematic Theology*, vol. II (Chicago: University of Chicago, 1963), pp. 114–115.

evangelicals and liberals. It cannot be said fairly that Jesus is more central for the evangelical or for the liberal. But we need to clarify in what way he is central.

In two principal respects Jesus functions as the model for evangelicals: as the obedient and trusting Son of God and as the morally perfect person. Central to evangelical theology is the conviction that Jesus Christ came reconciling man to God (see II Corinthians 5:18) by atoning for man's sin on the cross. In other words, Jesus came to restore the original relationship between man and God that was lost through the pride of Adam and Eve. The history of mankind has since proved that man cannot restore this relationship by his own effort. God's own chosen people repeatedly broke the covenants which he had initiated as the model for their relationship. The divine law given to Israel through Moses was subverted and petrified into an impersonal legalism. Even the words of the prophets were disregarded. So God decided to give the world the perfect revelation of what the divine-human relationship should be by sending his son. Never before had anyone dared to forgive sins, and never before had anyone entered into such a personal and intimate relationship with God. He even dared to speak to God in the most personal way, calling him "Dad" (*Abba*).[10] As the disciples came to know and trust Jesus they discovered a new relationship with God. More amazing was that their relationship with Jesus did not end with his death but took on a new dimension with his resurrection and the testimony of the Holy Spirit. Thus Jesus' relationship of perfect trust and obedience with his Father became the model for our relationship with God.

Generally, when the evangelical speaks of the atoning sacrifice of Christ, the liberal does not see its connection with daily Christian living. The missing link is that man would never have been able to enter into a *new* relationship with God if Christ had not broken the willful and self-righteous pride of men. And the way that Jesus broke it was by the completely unselfish death which he suffered for our sin. Consequently we are freed from our sinful pride when we are willing to accept what Christ has done for us—not what we do for him—for it is the very act of

[10]Joachim Jeremias, *The Central Message of the New Testament* (New York: Scribner's, 1965), pp. 17–30.

submission in obedience and trust that opens the way for our acceptance by God.

The moral perfection of the earthly Jesus is a constant model for the evangelical Christian as he seeks to live a holy life. Sheldon's book, *In His Steps,* has become a classic for a century of readers and still rings true for those who would follow Jesus. True regeneration will be manifested in the conduct, attitudes, and morals of the individual. The born-again Christian has found a new power in his life which helps him break the bondage of sin that previously held him fast (see Galatians 5:16ff.). For the first time he is able to acknowledge a law other than his own wishes, a truth other than his own personal gratification. Suddenly he is more conscious of how he spends his time and uses his material possessions. His life is no longer his own, for now he looks to another, Jesus Christ, for guidance and direction.

Within this context it is easy to see the important role played by the *person* of Jesus Christ. A mental picture serves as a model on which the individual can pattern his own life, and a personal relationship with Jesus provides the strength needed to sustain that way of life. The historical and the spiritual Jesus are closely tied together, and each complements the other. Once the historicity of Jesus is dissolved, the relationship between Jesus and the believer becomes an abstraction. Once the spirituality of Jesus is lost, the relationship becomes academic. But the evangelical knows a personal relationship with Christ, based upon the living Jesus.

When the liberal looks to Jesus as his model his approach is from a different angle. To be a Christian is not so much to believe as to act, not so much to defend orthodoxy as to follow a style of life. Christian faith, then, is not so much a relation to Jesus as a "place to be," specifically, in the world alongside the neighbor in love.

If we begin with this approach to faith, the revelation of God in Jesus Christ has a different significance. Jesus is not the bearer of a new ethic, a molder of personality, or the founder of a new social order.[11] Instead Jesus is the model of what we should

[11]Cf. Rudolf Bultmann, *Jesus and the Word* (2nd ed.; New York: Scribner's, 1965), p. 105: "Here it is again made plain that Jesus is not interested in character building, personality values, and the like."

be, and so he shapes our style of life. He loved the world, served it, stood beside its needy persons, and finally suffered at its hands out of love. This pattern is our pattern, and we should become like him. Paul van Buren uses the same basic concept when he interprets Jesus as the only truly free man, free from the anxiety of justifying himself before God and thus free to serve his brother. Those who follow Jesus, as did his disciples, come to share this same freedom to be for others.[12] On the other side, the liberal mind feels a reduction is involved when Jesus becomes simply the model for a personal code of ethics. If his message is examined carefully it will be seen that the thrust of Jesus' preaching was not to formulate new precepts but to lay before man the clear-cut choice between being for himself or being for God.[13]

Since Jesus serves less as a model for personal morality than as an example of "where to be," it is understandable why less significance is attached to the historical Jesus. Details about his personality and conduct, the precise words he spoke, the veracity of his miracles, and the chronology of events all fall into the background. The liberal does not thereby fall into complete historical skepticism. Rather he asserts that the historical features required for faith are plain to all.

> Of him [Jesus] we know something; not enough to satisfy, not enough to provide answers to our ethical problems, but enough to be able to say what was characteristic of him and his way with men.[14]

[12]Paul M. van Buren, *The Secular Meaning of the Gospel* (New York: Macmillan, 1963), pp. 133–134, 137–139, 142.

[13]Bultmann's study of the New Testament led him to believe Jesus could not have preached both an eschatological and a moral message. See *Jesus and the Word*, p. 130: "So long as we speak of an ethic of Jesus in the usual sense, we cannot understand how the teacher of a system of ethics can at the same time preach the imminent end of everything in the world." Also pp. 130–131: "Every ideal of personality or of society, every ethic of values and goods was repudiated. The one concern in this teaching was that man should conceive his immediate concrete situation as the decision to which he is constrained, and should decide in this moment for God and surrender his natural will."

[14]William Hamilton, *The New Essence of Christianity* (New York: Association, 1961), pp. 89–90.

It is only the historical details about Jesus' life which the liberal finds irrelevant, certainly not the model of Jesus as "the man for others."[15]

The evangelical experiences God as personal through his relationship with Jesus Christ. The liberal also believes in a personal God because of his revelation in Christ, but Jesus serves as a model in a different way. By his actions and words Jesus demonstrated the true meaning of the word "personal." When Jesus confronted the woman caught in adultery, his first concern was not to condemn her sin, as did the scribes and Pharisees, but to restore her personal dignity, rebuilding the personal dimension in all her relationships. Jesus' ministry revealed that at its deepest level reality is personal and that in personal relationships as nowhere else we touch the final meaning of existence. Following Christ is thus translated by the liberal to mean enacting Christ's

[15]With perhaps a few exceptions like Altizer, who presumes the historical figure of Jesus to be irrelevant to modern faith, liberals have remained steadfast in their conviction that the historical Jesus is essential to the gospel. The new quest for the historical Jesus has taken many different forms, but each makes some connection between Jesus the historical man and Christ the preached Savior. Ernst Käsemann, who reacts mildly to Bultmann, concedes to both the necessity and the possibility of centering the gospel in the historical Jesus. While we are not justified in reconstructing a biography of Jesus, the biblical witnesses are sufficient for us to distinguish "certain unmistakable traits of Jesus' individuality." See Käsemann, "Blind Alleys in the 'Jesus of History' Controversy," *New Testament Questions of Today* (Philadelphia: Fortress, 1968), pp. 23–65.

Wolfhart Pannenberg, on the other hand, has been one of the principal liberal figures to challenge Bultmann's argument that faith must be satisfied with the kerygma (the church's preaching about Jesus), and not ask for the security of "objective" facts. Pannenberg's main thrust has been to demonstrate the "unity of fact and meaning" that is already present in the nexus of historical events. See Pannenberg, "Kerygma and History," *Basic Questions in Theology* (Philadelphia: Fortress, 1970), vol. I, pp. 81–95.

One explanation to this paradox of liberalism—intense interest in Jesus of Nazareth coupled with a general skepticism about recovering the historical details of his life—seems to be the feeling that Christ can be the center of faith even though we do not have more than a general outline of his life.

readiness to heal and renew the world around him, showing personal concern for every human being.

Thus the liberal does not look to a special kind of personal experience with Christ to meet God but to the very human experiences of personal involvement in the joys and sorrows of other persons. His faith does not rest upon a psychological relationship with Jesus. Nor does he have the feeling of being "invaded by an invisible Presence, personified as an extension of Christ's human personality, who is thinking my thoughts or acting on my conscience."[16] The liberal's experience is rather the feeling of being united with Christ, he in us and we in him, as we engage in similar acts of self-surrender to others in love. It begins to be clear that the very movement of faith is different for the evangelical and the liberal.

THE MOVEMENT OF FAITH

In evangelical theology the basic movement of faith is from the vertical to the horizontal: from God to the individual to the neighbor. The inward relationship between God and the individual takes priority, in time and significance, over the outward man-to-man relationship. We may illustrate the movement graphically:

In liberal theology, on the other hand, the basic movement of faith is from the horizontal to the vertical: from the individual to the neighbor to God. The outward relationship between the individual and the neighbor takes priority over the inward divine-to-human relationship. Graphically the movement may be represented thus:

[16]Ruth Robinson, *Seventeen Come Sunday*, p. 53.

We are speaking here of a dominant movement, not an exclusive one, because evangelicals and liberals certainly experience both kinds of movement. We are consciously oversimplifying in order to highlight a contrasting tendency between evangelicalism and liberalism.

The evangelical claims that true faith begins when we are confronted by God in Jesus Christ, not when we experience love, forgiveness, or mercy through human relationships. Priority must be given to our relation to God; otherwise man will never transcend his own limitations and sin. When the movement is reversed deception creeps in—the deception that deeds of unselfish suffering for someone else can be substituted for a living relation with Christ, that man has seen God when he has only seen his own reflection. To experience God is to experience the totally Other, not a deeper dimension of human reality. God, the absolute, is known through a relationship that transcends and supersedes the finite, for it is only God who exists above and independent of all other relationships.

Theology must likewise begin with the objective revelation God has given of himself to man, the evangelical insists. If we began with man's reaching out to understand God, we would have to settle for a philosophy based upon human insights conditioned by time and place. The study of God can be a nice pastime for some, but the serious Christian wants to know more than what a few intelligent men think is true about God. This is why the movement must always be from what Scripture states to what theologians say, from what the church fathers and Reformers wrote to what contemporaries think is true of God. *One's starting point makes all the difference.* It determines whether one accepts the Bible as the authoritative witness of man to what God said and did or as the authoritative Word of God which man has inscribed. It determines whether special revelation validates natural theology or human reason validates God's once-for-all acts of revelation. Only when the movement is from God to man can we have any hope of being able to distinguish his ways from our ways, his Word from our thoughts.

The evangelical insistence that conversion be the first step in the Christian life may seem antiquated to some, but for evangelicals it is still a sound principle. Man must be reconciled to God before he can be an agent of reconciliation between men, because a man-centered foundation can do nothing to alter basic human nature. Love of God is the starting point for our love for man. If the movement is reversed the almost inevitable outcome is the delusion that horizontal reconciliation between man and man, group and group, race and race, is the answer to society's problems, and that this can be accomplished without God. But when Christ is made the center, then the Christian cannot forget that his motivation for serving the world is God's love for him. He knows that the trouble with society is man, not vice versa; and the trouble with man is that he is separated from God. There, the evangelical believes, and only there, is the right starting point.

On the other side, the liberal stands convinced that God is encountered in the horizontal relations common to our worldly existence. Dietrich Bonhoeffer set the tone for contemporary liberal theology when he wrote, "Our relationship with God is not a 'religious' relation to a supreme Being, absolute in power and goodness . . . , but our relation to God is in 'being there for others,' in participation in the being of Jesus."[17] According to the liberal's interpretation of the New Testament, we can expect to experience God most poignantly by participation in the self-giving existence of Jesus. Just as Christ himself discovered the fullness of God's love and power in human relationships, we also come to know the real meaning of divine forgiveness and mercy as we forgive and unconditionally accept our fellowman. A Jewish commentator puts it succinctly: "God dwells in our togetherness." And Bishop Robinson states, "For the eternal *Thou* is met only *in, with and under* the finite thou, whether in the encounter with other persons or in the response to the natural order."[18] The end of Matthew 25 confirms that the neighbor, "the least of these," is the bearer of the worldly Jesus.

Behind the liberal's belief that God can best be known through horizontal relationships is the theological view that God is already present in the world, as is Christ. The peculiar nature

[17]Adapted from Dietrich Bonhoeffer, *Letters and Papers from Prison* (New York: Macmillan, 1953), pp. 237–238.

[18]John Robinson, *Honest to God,* p. 53. The whole of Robinson's third chapter is a good example of how the liberal sees God as being met in a horizontal movement of faith, as are his third and sixth chapters in *Exploration into God* (Stanford: Stanford Univ., 1967).

of faith is to reveal a divine dimension in the ordinary. William Hamilton explains why faith can begin with an outward, horizontal movement.

> First, Jesus may be concealed in the world, in the neighbor, in this struggle for justice, in that struggle for beauty, clarity, order. Jesus is in the world as masked, and the work of the Christian is to strip off the masks of the world to find him, and finding him, to stay with him and to do his work. In this sense, the Christian life is not a longing and is not a waiting; it is a going out into the world.[19]

Liberal theology is filled with the idea that there is no special time and place to experience God; his presence is anywhere to be shared. With this in mind, Father Michel Quoist reminds us in his book of *Prayers* that we can meet Christ in the "Gospel of daily life," if only we have the eyes of faith to see each person and event as a token of God's love.

In the last decade liberals have been returning to the nineteenth-century liberal assumption that theology should begin with man and move to God. In a culture where relativity and secularism have triumphed, the only natural starting point for theology is the ordinary experience of man. Theology cannot go on presupposing an ultimately fixed order from which man draws his meaning and standards for life, because in reality ultimate meaning and coherence have disappeared. If faith must begin with beliefs about God, it must begin with objective statements about his nature. This will never do, the liberal argues, because there is no possible way to verify such statements. And statements which cannot be tested seem unreal and irrelevant to modern technological man. The fallacy of trying to begin with statements about God was brought home by the early collapse of neoorthodoxy, as Langdon Gilkey explains:

> Apparently what has happened has been that the transnatural reality that neo-orthodoxy proclaimed—the transcendent God, his mighty acts and his Word of revelation—became more and more unreal and incredible to those who

[19]William Hamilton, *Radical Theology* . . . , p. 49.

> had learned to speak this language. Younger enthusiasts began to wonder if they were talking about anything they themselves knew about when they spoke of God, of encounter, of the eschatological event and of faith. Do these words point to anything, or are they just words, traditional symbols referring more to hopes than experienced realities?[20]

Theology must begin where it can, and today faith is founded not so much on the experience of eternity as on those moments here and now where the grace and power of God are evident. The task of theology is therefore to uncover and thematize those aspects of everyday life that contain elements of transcendence and permanence, hidden and neglected as they are by the modern secular spirit.

Since the horizontal movement of faith precedes the vertical movement, it follows according to the liberal pattern that commitment to Jesus' style of life can precede belief in his divinity. Christian faith in general requires commitment before belief, not belief before commitment. Creeds and confessions should not be used as fences over which people must jump in their minds before they can call themselves Christians. "Beliefs take their place not as material to be swallowed before the way is taken, but as along-the-way expressions of the experience of whose who walk."[21] The disciples, like Christians thereafter, had to make their decision to follow Jesus before all their questions were answered, before all the facts were in. If they had waited in their boats to weigh carefully what they knew about Jesus against what they didn't know, he would have long been gone. So ascription to doctrine or dogma must not be made a prerequisite to discipleship. The liberal even goes so far as to say it does not matter what you believe; what matters is how you live your life.[22]

[20]Langdon B. Gilkey, "Secularism's Impact on Contemporary Theology," in *Radical Theology: Phase Two*, ed. Christian and Wittig, (Philadelphia: J. B. Lippincott, 1967), p. 21.

[21]N. Bruce McLeod offers a classic liberal exposition on the relationship between commitment and belief in his sermon, "Faith to Follow," *The Princeton Seminary Bulletin*, vol. LXIII, no. 1, pp. 53–59.

[22]The relation between assent to creeds and Christian discipleship is no abstract issue. It is beginning to assume a prominent place as the

In addition, it is obvious that evangelicals and liberals have contrasting Christologies. Evangelicals emphasize the superhuman qualities of Christ that made him one with God; the liberal stresses the human qualities of Jesus that made him one with man. The evangelical is more comfortable speaking of Christ's healing powers, miraculous deeds, sinless life, pre-existence, supernatural birth, and resurrection; the liberal more at ease when referring to his simple style of life, his concern for the poor, his freedom to laugh and enjoy life, and his challenge of the status quo. In evangelical theology Christ's transcendence is the basis for our relationship with him, while in liberal theology his immanence is made the basis. The liberal looks to a *kenosis*[23] Christology which puts the accent on Jesus' emptying himself of his distinctively divine qualities in order to exemplify true servanthood. The evangelical tradition underlines Jesus' glorious ascension into heaven as well as his atoning death for the sin of mankind, which only the Son of God could accomplish. For the liberal, Jesus is Lord because the divine shone through the human. For the evangelical, Jesus is Lord because humanity shone through the divine.

Two divergent movements of faith cannot help but produce two diverging doctrines of God. No one would be justified in saying evangelicals and liberals have radically different conceptions of God, but contrasting tendencies are evident. Evangelical theology is basically Apollonian in character: its God is one of

question of church union arises. Harold Lindsell, former editor of *Christianity Today*, wrote in the first of a two-part critique of the Consultation on Church Union: "The union will mark the end of adherence to creeds and confessions as we have known them (or their use to determine orthodoxy). . . . Rather than hastening the reunion of churches based on biblical truth, the Church of Christ Uniting is likely to be an affront to bodies like the Lutheran Church-Missouri Synod, the Southern Baptists, and the smaller denominations in the National Association of Evangelicals." See *Christianity Today*, Oct. 9, 1970, p. 5. There is a deeper philosophical and theological issue involved here which concerns the question of whether conceptualization, as, for example, in creeds, proceeds out of, precedes, or is an integral part of the experience of faith. The heart of the issue is taken up in Ch. III.

[23]A term from the second chapter of Philippians, where Paul speaks of Christ's self-emptying.

reasonableness, order, discipline, balance, and moderation. The Apollonian tradition depends upon a clear distinction between God and man, good and evil, the permissible and the impermissible, that which belongs to eternity and that which belongs to mortality. Its God must epitomize the absolute qualitative difference between Creator and creature. God must therefore be a Being, transcendent and separate from his creation, and he must not be confused with the world or any part of the world. In order to maintain this absolute distinction, boundaries need to be laid out separating sacred from profane, revelation from human thought.

Liberal theology has at its center a Dionysian view of God and man. The Dionysian way exalts ecstasy over order, freedom over security, creativity over stability, the new over the traditional. Its theism has come to speak of a God whose perfection is in process, whose life is not isolated from the relativities of relations. God is not a timeless absolute who stands above or beyond history but a promising power who drives history forward toward new horizons. One does not find him coming to us out of the past as much as one senses his presence beckoning us onward to a new future. Boundaries only serve to restrict the individual and prevent him from sharing the divine power which pervades all experiences and relationships.

Apollonian theology, with its assumption that the decisive acts of revelation took place in a sacred past, becomes a "theology of the Word" oriented around the hearing and preaching of the word in which the witness to God's acts is preserved. The ear is the organ of religious perception, and Scripture, the inscribed memory of the divine in-breaking, is the instrument of revelation. It is after all only a monarchical God, supernatural and transcendent, who must occasionally make himself known by way of special acts and words. Under the omniscient eye of the Absolute, man always stands under judgment and scrutiny.

On the other hand, Dionysian theology, with its assumption that God is always present in history as the source of life and wholeness, becomes a "theology of the Spirit" oriented around feeling and doing. The believer seeks the fullest possible participation in the present moment in order to penetrate to the abiding dimensions of meaning and value already there. Scripture is illustration, important to the contemporary Christian insofar as it helps him to understand his purpose and direction in life. God is God, in fact, because of his utter freedom to give himself and incarnate himself in nature and human history. To accept the Dionysian way is to be willing to dance and challenge, to accept the risks that freedom and revolution inevitably invite.[24]

The respective differences between an evangelical and a liberal doctrine of God might be summarized in this way:

EVANGELICAL *(Apollonian)*	LIBERAL *(Dionysian)*
God is a supernatural Being: timeless, absolute, immutable.	God is a personal power: ever new, becoming, moving.
Based on a static analogy: pure actuality, essence, substance.	Based on a dynamic analogy: energy, process, forward movement.
Transcendence highlighted: God reveals himself objectively by breaking into history via special acts.	Immanence highlighted: God reveals himself indirectly as a creative power within history.
A theology of the Word: hearing and speaking, preserving, past, pessimistic, theocentric.	A theology of the Spirit: sensing and doing, exploring, present, optimistic, anthropocentric.
Traits engendered: nurturing, stability, standards, orthodoxy, traditional.	Traits engendered: suffering, risk, freedom, tolerance, novelty.
Image of God: father, judge, repressive, protector.	Image of God: spirit, enabler, permissive, urger.
Tendency toward: Manichaeism, dualism, Neo-Platonism.	Tendency toward: pantheism, pluralism, universalism.

[24]The Dionysian-Apollonian dichotomy is taken from the stimulating article by Sam Keen, "Manifesto for a Dionysian Theology," in *New Theology No. 7: The Recovery of Transcendence*, ed. Martin E. Marty and Dean G. Peerman (New York: Macmillan, 1970), pp. 79–103.

MUTUAL CRITICISM

The history of theology in America suggests that evangelicals and liberals have each been reacting against the imbalance they see in the other's theology and consequently creating a lack in their own theology. For instance, we find liberals who are beginning to sound like evangelicals of thirty years ago with their talk about feeling and experience, while evangelicals who warn of the danger of humanism and the necessity of maintaining the transcendence of God sound like the neoorthodox of thirty years ago. It is also ironic that while liberals are moving to define God as passionately involved in the sufferings of this world, they still pray to a God who is unable to respond in a personal manner. Evangelicals, on the other hand, define God as the changeless transcendent Being but pray to him as one who can act upon the smallest request. There are innumerable similar comparisons, and all point to the need for fair and accurate criticism and for the willingness to see in a different tradition a strength which complements one's own weaknesses.

A. Evangelical against Liberal

Evangelicals echo and re-emphasize the words of Langdon Gilkey when he said of liberalism, "faith has collapsed into love, and theology into action for the modern secular Christian community."[25] And the paradox of present-day liberal theology is that Jesus is robbed of the power to bring about the self-giving model he inspires. Jesus has been reduced to a paradigm of the human excellence that can be achieved by humanistic faith, and he is therefore a universal possibility for man even without God.

The real criticism of evangelicals is not that liberals fail to recognize the centrality of Jesus to faith,[26] but that in attempting

[25]Gilkey, *Naming the Whirlwind,* p. 167.

[26]At times evangelical criticism is too broad and accuses liberal theology of denying the centrality of Christ. Such a criticism, however, does not take into account liberals' common and constant Christological preoccupation, from Schleiermacher and Ritschl to Shailer Mathews and Walter Rauschenbusch, not to mention Barth's Christologically based *Church Dogmatics,* Bonhoeffer's Christ-centered theology, and Bultmann's dependence upon the unique event of Jesus Christ. Cf. Lloyd J. Averill, *American Theology in the Liberal Tradition* (Philadelphia: Westminster, 1967), pp. 77ff., 95ff.

to reinterpret the meaning of Christ for today they have annulled the supernatural work of Jesus. The liberal argues, convincingly enough, that Jesus is the rightful lord of man's existence. Above all other men he is the one who gives us our stance in life and stands as the model for a truly concerned style of life. But this Lord of life is *only* a supreme paradigmatic model, who can influence our lives *only* as one who stands in the past. Since the historical Jesus cannot transcend natural time, the only way we can know him is through historical inquiry or through the Christian community that preserves his memory. We relate to Christ, then, as we would relate to any other historical figure such as Mahatma Gandhi.

The liberal's relation to Jesus, therefore, is totally dependent upon man's power of memory and ability as historian. We are the active ones, Christ the passive one; for he is dead except as we can resurrect him through the exercise of our wills. He serves as the model for us to follow, but he cannot give us the power to enact that picture by some transcendent grace. Gone is his mysterious power to transform us in a way in which we cannot change ourselves. We are left quite alone without any possible help from a living Lord whom time cannot contain.[27]

In this important respect the liberalism of today is reminiscent of nineteenth-century liberal theology, and evangelicals have been announcing the return right along.[28] Liberal theology has historically dissipated the supernatural power of Christ by turning him into a kind of moralistic principle. The liberal, complains the evangelical, is still guided by a theory that Christ can "influence" but not transform. His death on the cross was instructive, as the perfect example of love, but not atoning. This has led the evangelical to criticize liberal theology for being rid-

[27]Cf. Gilkey, *Naming the Whirlwind*, pp. 150–151, 160–161.

[28]Among others see Kenneth Hamilton, *What's New in Religion?* (Grand Rapids: Eerdmans, 1968), esp. pp. 55, 127–139; Carl F. H. Henry, "Cross-Currents in Contemporary Theology," in *Jesus of Nazareth: Saviour and Lord*, ed. Carl F. H. Henry (Grand Rapids: Eerdmans, 1966), esp. p. 9; and Cornelius Van Til, *The New Modernism* (Philadelphia: Presbyterian and Reformed, 1946), who is the most radical in his assertion that there exists an essential continuity between Schleiermacher and Barth. Gilkey, *Naming the Whirlwind* (pp. 73–80, 185–189), and Averill, *American Theology . . .* (pp. 118–149), agree only in part and raise some important distinctions.

dled with "adoptianism," the belief that Jesus was not God in himself but was only adopted by God to reveal his truth. Bernard Ramm makes this one of the important issues in contemporary theology which divide evangelicals and liberals into two continents:

> Schleiermacher's Jesus as the model example of God-consciousness is adoptianism; the Ritschlian version of Jesus as the model example of filial piety is adoptianism; Tillich's Christology of the man Jesus surrendering himself to the Christ of the new being is adoptianism; Bultmann's Christ-event as the perfect existential example of dying to the world and rising to openness to the future is adoptianism; the new hermeneutic with Jesus as the perfect example of "the word" of existential communication is adoptianism; and all the recent expressions of young theological Turks who destroy traditional Christology but still find some kind of mystique in Jesus are adoptianism.[29]

What the liberal gives us, then, is a Christ who revealed what man should be, but not a Savior who frees man from sin so he can become what he is not. The understanding of salvation that emerges from this theology has the undertone, to evangelical ears, of a "do-it-yourself" activity which overestimates the power of man and underestimates the power of sin.

The second major criticism leveled by evangelicals has been liberalism's heavy reliance on a vague, indefinite definition of God which ultimately depersonalizes him. Liberal theology has made a deliberate effort to find a new way of expressing the personal nature of God. The liberal may think he has solved the problem by using the word "personal" when he describes God as "the divine personal principle" (Bishop Robinson), or by using metaphors of human relationships such as "the absolute ground of any and all personal relationships" (Schubert Ogden), but the evangelical does not see these as a satisfactory solution if God is no longer described as a supernatural Person who exists independently of the world. All of the major liberal theologians have

[29]Bernard Ramm, "The Continental Divide in Contemporary Theology," *Christianity Today*, Oct. 8, 1965, p. 16.

offered suggestions, if not entire philosophies, and to each the evangelical critic has made about the same response. Carl F. H. Henry rather succinctly summed up the evangelical attitude when he entitled his review of *Exploration into God* (1966) by Bishop Robinson, "God in the Mists."[30] The end result of locating God in the heart and depth of all things is an ephemeral deity. The biblical witness to a transcendent personal Being is reduced to a philosophical abstraction—an abstraction which can move the universe as an inherent power but cannot communicate conceptually or act in a directly personal way.

The liberal says he distrusts the subjective nature of a spiritual relationship with Christ, but seldom does he have misgivings about the subjectivity of a sense of the divine in a particularly meaningful human relationship. It is clear that the liberal's uncertainty about a God "out there" beyond ordinary human experience has driven him to search for God within the man-to-man relationships, but P. R. Baelz asks whether this encounter with God is "merely a metaphorical way of talking of an uprush of the unconscious or a release of psychological power."[31] The evangelical wonders if the real reason why God seems so remote and nebulous lies not only in the secular world in which we live but also in the condensation of the living God to rational principles and human encounters.

The evangelical also believes that the liberal's interpretation of God is always dangerously close to pantheism.[32] Even granting that the liberal is aware of the danger and does not, strictly speaking, end up with a pantheistic conception,[33] he does evaporate away the transcendence of God until it is uncertain whether we are referring any longer to a supernatural, self-

[30]Carl F. H. Henry, *Christianity Today,* Jan. 19, 1968, pp. 28–29.

[31]P. R. Baelz, "Is God Real?" in *Faith, Fact and Fantasy* (Philadelphia: Westminster, 1966), p. 64.

[32]Pantheism is the reduction of God to everything: God is everything and everything is God. In its modern form it is the belief that God is not a person but that all laws, forces, and objects of a self-existing universe *are* God.

[33]See John Robinson, *Exploration into God,* pp. 25–26, 88ff., for his qualifications; and Ogden, *The Reality of God,* pp. 61ff., for his qualifications.

existent God. Bishop Robinson, for instance, admits the inherent tendency toward depersonalization within pantheism:

> In its familiar forms, whether of Eastern religion or of Western intellectualism, pantheism tends toward an aesthetic, impassive, impersonalistic view of life in which the individual loses his significance. It makes for an unhistorical quietism, without political cutting edge or involvement with the neighbor. And it plays down evil and suffering as partial or illusory. In sum, it depersonalizes and dehistoricizes.[34]

If this is the result pantheism brings to our human relationships, then why shouldn't it have the same effect on our relationship with God? The evangelical sees an obvious tendency toward pantheism which makes it increasingly difficult to believe in a God who is personally involved in history and the lives of individuals. The crucial question is whether a conception of God which sees him "dwelling *incognito* at the heart of all things," or "shining forth from the depth of every event, every element," can do justice to the clear biblical testimony to a God who is able to confront us as a *person*. A depersonalized God cannot help but be a pale image of the real God who is known through a personal relationship.[35]

B. Liberal against Evangelical

One side of the evangelical critique of liberal theology is directed against the abandonment of the redemptive power of the living Jesus to transform and sustain a new life. The liberal reverses the criticism by pointing to the inadequate picture of Jesus that the evangelical holds up to faith. From the liberal perspective, a basic misunderstanding of the gospel message comes to the fore in the way in which Jesus becomes the model for life. Probably nothing has made the liberal react more negatively toward the idea of a

[34]John Robinson, *Exploration into God*, p. 90.

[35]John Robinson has asked the right question (*ibid.*, p. 91): "Can we, in fact, depersonify God but not depersonalize?" A related question is whether God's transcendence can be maintained apart from a supernaturalistic world view. To both questions the evangelical registers an emphatic "No" and the liberal an emphatic "Yes."

personal relationship to Jesus than the prevalent evangelical picture of Christ. The Jesus who is our friend, comforter, anchor, and rock; who brings peace and quietness; who becomes our hiding place, shelter, and home; and who redeems us by his blood is scarcely the one who activates us and leads us out of the comfort of selfishness into a new life of self-sacrifice. Whatever a personal relationship to Christ may be, it must not be the kind of relationship which encloses a person in individualistic piety and self-concern. The picture of Jesus that leaps out of every page of the Gospels is that of a person who was uniquely able to live for others. His faith clearly drove him more deeply into the world, not away from it. If the liberal model of Jesus lacks power, then the evangelical model falls short of being biblically sound.

The liberal also accuses the evangelical of moralizing about Christ. Too often Jesus' moral perfection is made the central feature. As a result the primary goal of the Christian life becomes the achievement of the same kind of perfection by imitating Jesus. The model of Jesus is constructed so narrowly that every issue becomes a clear-cut question of right or wrong. The primary task of the Christian thus becomes directed too narrowly toward the development of moral character. And in the process, far from being freed to develop our individual gifts to the fullest extent, we become less free and are burdened with more guilt. In the New Testament Jesus' concern for others was not primarily toward making the leper (Luke 17), the woman caught in adultery (John 8), Zacchaeus (Luke 19), the demoniac (Mark 5), or the rich young man (Mark 10) more moral. Rather, he freed each from his own personal hangup—enslavement to self—so they could love God, their neighbor, and themselves more fully. Gordon Cosby, minister of the Church of the Saviour in Washington, D.C., sharply defines the two ways of seeing our Christian mission:

> We are not sent into the world in order to make people good. We are not sent to encourage them to do their duty. The reason people have resisted the Gospel is that we have gone out to make people good, to help them do their duty, to impose new burdens on them rather than calling forth the gift which is the essence of the person himself.[36]

[36]Elizabeth O'Connor, *Journey Inward, Journey Outward* (New York: Harper, 1968), pp. 36–37.

At the heart of the liberal's critique is whether there is some intrinsic reason why evangelical theology leads to individualism. The evangelical is certainly more aware today than he was a decade ago of the dangers of individualism, and as a result he is gaining more and more a social awareness. Yet a strong heritage holds the central mark of Christian faith to be how *I* live *my* life. By being concerned first about how closely his life conforms to the life of Christ, the evangelical naturally becomes more self-concerned. By its very nature a personal relationship with a spiritual Person who exists outside of and separate from other human relationships tends to isolate the individual from the world and encourage him to withdraw into himself. The liberal asks how Christ can be the one who drives us to unselfish concern for the world if we must enter into a special relation with him which displaces us from our historical existence. For all the dangers in liberal theology's placement of Jesus in the other person, it has the important strength of a built-in movement away from the ever-present "I" of self.

The traditional evangelical emphasis on the individual's decision for Christ has brought with it a dangerous tendency to turn salvation into a personal reality. The salvation the Bible speaks of is related not simply to the individual but to the salvation of the world. Whenever salvation is turned inward, the ideals it seeks to realize are internalized. Even the hope for justice and peace is narrowed to apply only to the home and the individual. This internalization, says the liberal, actually advances the evils of technological society, for it unburdens and stabilizes the society but in no way disturbs it.[37]

When Carl F. H. Henry asks why we do not see a dynamic and committed minority of evangelicals assuming the lead in the social arena, confronting modern man with a fresh option for personal meaning and worth, the liberal suspects part of the answer lies in the evangelical's image of Christ and his conception of faith and salvation. By their own admission, evangelicals often fail to live up to a lifestyle in accord with Christ's own life. Liberals would probably agree with the letter to the editor in which Mrs. Hamilton asked:

[37]Jürgen Moltmann, *Religion, Revolution and the Future*, trans. M. Douglas Meeks (New York: Scribner's, 1969), pp. 113–115.

> Could it be because there has been such a credibility gap between our statements as evangelicals and our actual behavior, such an unrighteous acceptance of the fact that our *inner* lives and attitudes are so contrary to what Jesus taught, that we now find ourselves in the position of having little left to say with any effectiveness or authority?[38]

The liberal may admit that much of his language is taken from the culture we live in, but he wonders if the evangelical is really sensitive to the difficulties Christian faith encounters in a secular society. The liberal frequently feels the evangelical is insisting that we return to another era in order to make belief possible. The evangelical's language and conceptual framework seem to be hangovers from the prescientific age, preserved as though they were essential to the gospel. The evangelical has a valid point when he sees liberals capitulating too readily to the spirit of our culture, but the liberal scores a point when he complains that evangelical theology has failed to express the gospel in language that is relevant and familiar to its hearers. This liberal criticism seems to fall most clearly on how evangelicals define the nature of God.

At a time when no one feels himself to be part of an eternal order, evangelicals are declaring as indispensable the view that there is a supernatural realm which determines and gives coherence to the natural order. While children are beginning to feel at ease with a universe stretching further than we can imagine in all directions, God's transcendence is nevertheless being defined in spatial metaphors such as "up there" and "out there." There comes a time, and it seems to be here, when God's separateness from man and his supernatural distance seem like indifference. The danger of an evangelical picture of God who directs people and the world from afar, watching some suffer and bestowing blessings on others, is no less than that of a liberal conception of God who dwells incognito within the world. If for no other reason, the liberal asserts, a personal relationship with Jesus is needed by evangelical theology in order to overcome the feeling that God is unreachable. The liberal agrees that there is an essen-

[38] *Christianity Today,* Nov. 6, 1970, p. 40. The statement by Henry is in the same issue, p. 41.

tial meaning behind the terms "transcendence" and "supernatural" but disagrees that God must be isolated out in space to preserve that meaning.

The evangelical acts as if he can hold together by mere pronouncement a supernatural Creator who is both self-existent and unchangeable *and* personally involved in the world. The evangelical gives the impression that there is no problem in reconciling the classical attributes of God—pure actuality, impassivity, aseity, immateriality, immutability—and the fact that they "all entail an unqualified negation of real internal relationship to anything beyond his own wholly absolute being."[39] The inherent contradiction which the evangelical passes over is that God's perfection is the very reason why he must by definition remain untouched by that change, suffering, novelty, and growth which so characterize the reality we experience. It does not seem to have made an impression on evangelicalism that "almost every significant aspect of the modern spirit—its sense of contingency, of relativity, of temporality, and of transience—moves in exactly the opposite direction from the concept of a necessary, self-sufficient, changeless, unrelated, and eternal being."[40] The result is an evangelical theology based upon a traditional theism which hinders more than it helps modern intelligence to understand the one who is wholly other and personal.

CONCLUSION

In this section of each chapter our purpose will be to come to some conclusions concerning the particular topic. Because of the many complex questions involved, these conclusions can only be suggestions. We should set out to find not a compromise that is entirely satisfactory to both evangelicals and liberals but the biblical truth as it is found in these two Christian traditions.

[39]Ogden, *The Reality of God,* p. 49. Ogden also points out how Hellenism involved theology in the endless discussion, "How can the Absolute be understood as personal?" rather than, "How can the eminently personal One be appropriately conceived in his absoluteness?"—thus reversing the emphasis of Scripture (p. 66).

[40]Gilkey, *Naming the Whirlwind,* p. 54.

I hope the reader will discover in the concept of a "journey inward" and a "journey outward" a unifying theme which takes into account the positive contributions of both liberal and evangelical theologies.[41] The journey inward is the road taken by means of meditation, introspection, and prayer grounded in Scripture in order to know our true self and the true God. No one can know God who does not know himself, and no one can succeed in knowing himself unless he seeks to know God. The journey outward points us away from ourselves toward others and is taken as we actively engage the world. As the inward journey compels us to surrender ourselves to God, the outward journey compels us to divest ourselves of self-interest in order to be with the brother in need. Those on the inward journey can better see God, and those on the outward journey can better see the neighbor. It is a crucial mistake for either the individual or the church to assume that the fullness of the Christian life is possible unless one journey complements the other.

There must always exist a creative tension between the two journeys, for otherwise the one will dissolve into the other. Perhaps there will always need to be the same kind of creative tension between evangelicals and liberals within the Christian church. It is tragic that the tension which is present now is more destructive than beneficial. The wholeness that could be ours is largely lost because of the lack of meaningful dialogue between those who represent the journey inward and those who represent the journey outward. Surely there is something the liberal can learn from the evangelical and vice versa, so that we will not have to choose between a God who is isolated from the contemporary experiences of man and a God who loses his identity in the fabric of life. The evangelical needs the liberal's emphasis on God the creative power within history as much as the liberal needs the evangelical's emphasis on God the transcendent Being beyond.

[41]See Elizabeth O'Connor, *Journey Inward, Journey Outward*, and its companion book, *Call to Commitment* (New York: Harper, 1963). See also the "postscript" in Mary Bosanquet, *The Life and Death of Dietrich Bonhoeffer* (New York: Harper, 1968); she concludes that Bonhoeffer's life was a continuous effort to hold in balance his outward identification with the world and his inward identification with the power that could deepen and sustain Christian life.

Why can't we look to Christ as the model for both our relationship with God *and* our relationships with our fellow humans; as the one who reveals both what God is *and* what man should be? The differences that presently divide us could serve to tie us together. Whether that will happen depends upon whether we are open to receive what others have to offer. It depends upon our recognizing that when some are unable to move out beyond themselves, others who know how to engage the world can lead the way. And when some of us have lost our way in a confusing world, there will be those who can teach us the beauty of the inward journey.

It can almost be said that evangelicals and liberals are divided because each stresses one side of Jesus' summary of the law to the exclusion of the other: "You shall love the Lord your God with all your heart, soul and mind. And you shall love your neighbor as yourself." The evangelical believes the movement is always, or at least primarily, from a personal relationship with God in Christ to a personal relationship with the neighbor. Love God; then you can love your neighbor. The liberal's major emphasis has been on the movement from love of neighbor to love of God. Only as you love your neighbor, whom you can see, can you love God, whom you have not seen. It is important that the basic presupposition is the same for both: Jesus Christ is the most personal revelation of God. Different paths are taken, however, when we inquire further how Jesus brought men into this new personal relationship with God: by leading men to believe in him as the son of God, or by showing men how to love their neighbors as children of God.

The division between liberals and evangelicals would not be so intractable if both positions did not have sound biblical roots. The liberal can appeal to a strong theological tradition running through the New Testament which indicates that the new personal relationship to God is based upon a self-sacrificing concern for others. Consider some examples:

—Jesus' teaching about the meaning of discipleship (Mark 8:34–38): "If any man would come after me, let him deny himself and take up his cross and follow me. For whoever would save his life will lose it; and whoever loses his life for my sake will save it."

—Jesus' warning about how we will be judged (Matthew

25:31–46): "Truly, I say to you, as you did it not to one of the least of these, you did it not to me."

—St. Paul's teaching about the life in Christ (II Corinthians 4:7ff.): "But we have this treasure in earthen vessels, to show that the transcendent power belongs to God and not to us. We are afflicted in every way . . . ; always carrying in the body the death of Jesus, so that the life of Jesus may also be manifested in our bodies."

—St. John's teaching about love (I John 3:11–18; 4:7ff.): "By this we know love, that he laid down his life for us; and we ought to lay down our lives for the brethren. He who does not love does not know God, for God is love. If we love one another, God abides in us and his love is perfected in us."

Likewise the evangelical finds in Scripture justification for his conviction that the Christian's relationship with God is based upon a direct relationship with Christ:

—Jesus' own personal relationship with God (Mark 14:32–42): "And they went to a place which was called Gethsemane; and he said to his disciples, 'Sit here, while I pray.'" Note also his words on the cross: "*My* God, *my* God, . . . "; "*Father,* into thy hands . . ." (italics added).

—Jesus' statement that he is the way to the Father (John 8:19; 14:6ff.): "He who has seen me has seen the Father; how can you say, 'Show us the Father'? Do you not believe that I am in the Father and the Father in me?"

—St. Paul's encounter with the resurrected Christ (Acts 9:1–7; Galatians 1:11–16; I Corinthians 15:3–11): "Last of all, as to one untimely born, he appeared also to me."

—St. Paul's description of the Christian life (Galatians 2:20; 3:26–29; II Corinthians 5:17): " . . . it is no longer I who live, but Christ who lives *in me.* Therefore, if any one is *in Christ,* he is a new creation; the old has passed away, behold, the new has come" (italics added).

This does not mean that the New Testament is unclear as to how love of God and love of man are related; but it does illustrate that we must be guided by the whole of Jesus' life and not rely on isolated incidents or texts. Jesus was the Savior because he gave himself unreservedly to God and man. Christ's singular ability to be "the man for others" was not something he possessed independently of God. His love of God, his obedience, and his readiness to profess his faith in a Being greater than himself were first steps in breaking the grip of pride. His relation to the Father was the avenue by which Jesus became free to love every human being as he was and for what he could become. The uniqueness of Christ's relationship to men is that he had no need to prove himself at the expense of another. He was able to meet the deepest need of each individual without demanding anything in return. He did not find it necessary to condemn a man for his sin, and yet he did not condone it; he so poured himself out that the individual knew his true worth. In short, Jesus perfectly demonstrated the same relationship with his fellowman that he had with his Father.

The gospel, therefore, is centered precisely at the point where Jesus' relationships to God and to man coincide—the self-surrender of the "I" for the other. One cannot really surrender his life to God without being turned outward toward those in need. Likewise, one cannot be totally involved in the world's suffering and not be turned inward to find a strength of spirit and purpose.

So we who confess Jesus as Lord must be willing to commit ourselves in faith to God, for this is the absolutely necessary condition for a real commitment of love to our fellow human beings. The liberal tends to think that as long as he is involved and concerned in the world his relationship to God will somehow fall into place. He is aware of the danger of humanism but excuses himself by declaring that God is really a divine power underlying all things. *What he fails to understand is that when our relationship to Christ deteriorates, so does our commitment to others.* Christ is not simply the guide that keeps faith on the right track but the transcendent power who lives *in* us and lifts us out of our self-preoccupation. The person who does not care about the transcendent is not bound to care about anything beyond his immediate interests. He may, perhaps, care for others out of a sense of social responsibility; but for how long and through how much suffering will this sense carry him?

Just as our service to mankind is headed toward bankruptcy without a personal relationship with God, so our personal relationship to God is unbalanced without an involvement in the social and political upheavals of our society. At this level the evangelical needs to listen more carefully to the liberal. The personal relationship with Christ which remains on an individualistic, isolated plane cannot help but drift soon into aimlessness or stagnation. What is more, the "I" of self is bound to creep in again, until faith is no longer a vital relationship with God but an ego-satisfying or illusion-fulfilling relationship with oneself. A relationship with God which truly surrenders the self cannot stop with God but must flow into human relations. *Concern for others is not only the fruit of a right relationship with God but also the means by which one's relationship with God is kept concrete.* For, as St. John asks, how can you love God if you cannot love your brother whom you can see? It is in this sense that God's forgiveness is experienced as we forgive someone, that God's grace is experienced as we pour ourselves out to support a falling brother. So it is that God is known in and through another human being.

Either our relationship to God or that to man can be absolutized or so emphasized that one or the other becomes inconsequential. Both evangelical and liberal are aware of the danger of a one-way journey, and this criticism should not be leveled at either. Yet each in his own way has traveled a road which upsets the delicate balance between love of God and love of man. If we were to draw a picture of the interrelationship between the inward journey and the outward journey it would look like this:

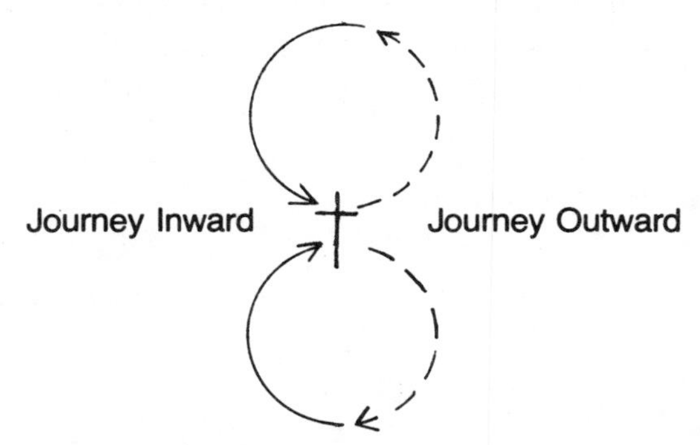

The inward journey feeds the outward journey, and the outward journey draws us inward again. Prayer must drive us into concrete involvement as well as open the way to communion with God. Our participation in civil rights issues, for example, must also lead us to seek a deeper dependency on the Father. If the inner dimension of our faith does not push back horizons so that we see neighbors we did not see before, then that faith is incomplete. And if our efforts to humanize political and social structures is not balanced by an equal effort to bring rebirth to the very lives who shaped those structures, then we are on a one-way trip.

There was nothing unique about Jesus' commandment to love God and neighbor, for these were two time-honored Jewish laws (Deuteronomy 6:5; Leviticus 19:18). The uniqueness lay instead in that Jesus dared to summarize the *whole* law at *one point,* namely, where the love of God and the love of man coincide. What differentiates two sound Jewish principles from the gospel is that the latter finds its unity and integration in Christ. We see in him what it means really to love our God and our neighbor, but, more important, we also see that we cannot really love God without our neighbor, nor love our brother in need without God. The Christian life must be as St. Paul testified: the life in Christ is a life of self-sacrificing love, and the life of suffering love is the life in Christ.

DISCUSSION QUESTIONS

1. From your own experience, when and where has God been most personal in your life? In a sudden individualistic experience, in a moment of really being with someone else at a time of crisis? Is God's presence something you experience directly or indirectly? Is God experienced differently depending upon the situation?

2. Describe your image of Jesus. How does this image or model of Christ influence your life? How important are the historical details of his life to your Christian faith?

3. What do you consider to be the primary strengths and weaknesses of the evangelical and liberal doctrines of God? What are the positive and negative points in a supernatural, transcendent Christology and in one which stresses *kenosis* and immanence (p. 77)? Can the two be combined in some way?

4. Study the following passages and ask how Jesus brought each person into a new relationship with God: Mark 5:1–13; 10:17–22; Luke 19:1–10; John 8:1–11. Was his method always the same? Did he attempt to bring about a direct confrontation between the individual and God? In what way was the individual's self-understanding changed?

5. How are the love of God and the love of man integrated in your life? Do you tend to emphasize one more than the other? Why? Is there anything unique about the Christian faith in the indissoluble bond between the journey inward and the journey outward?

III. THE HEART OF THE MATTER: *The Nature of Revelation: Absolutes vs. Relatives*

Thus far our dialogue has taken up the issue of the relationship between Jesus and faith. In this chapter we continue our attempt to get to the heart of the matter by comparing how the evangelical and liberal understand the nature of God's revelation. The question here is essentially *how* God reveals himself. Undoubtedly a great deal could be made about the difference in their understanding of *what* God has revealed, but I believe this would not prove to be the most profitable starting point. I intend not to make light of the doctrinal differences which exist but to emphasize that the way God reveals himself has deep implications for the content of his revelation. Let it not be forgotten that liberal and evangelical (as well as Roman Catholic) are in full agreement that God has revealed himself sufficiently for men to be saved. Furthermore, there is accord that Scripture contains in written form sufficient revelation for man's salvation. Just how important and basic the question of how God reveals himself is, subsequent chapters will show. A dialogue between a typical evangelical and liberal will be our launching pad.

L. In several conversations I have had with evangelicals I have received the impression that you believe God has revealed himself by speaking directly, such as to the prophets and apostles, and by performing objective miracles, such as the opening of the Red Sea.

E. That may be the popular view of what the evangelical believes, but I am not sure it is the most accurate picture. What we really mean by direct and objective revelation is that God has disclosed to us, as recorded in the Bible, truths which are timeless and universally valid.

L. Could you explain to me what you mean by timeless and universally valid? I have some trouble with these words.

E. Truth is timeless if it is unbounded by time or place; to be universally valid means that any rational being ought to agree with it. We would not deny that God communicates his truth to men who live in a particular historical situation and who express themselves in specific literary forms. The terms "objective" and "direct," however, point to our belief that our knowledge of God is independent of human reason, insight, or religious feeling. In a word, it is supernatural, that is, its source is beyond and above men.

L. In other words, you are saying revelation is not what man happens to think or feel about God but what he knows to be true because God has revealed himself objectively and directly.

E. Yes, and that is why we insist that Scripture is not simply a human response or witness to revelation, but revelation itself. It is also the reason we believe that there are certain truths, dogmas, propositions, and concepts which cannot be sacrificed or compromised.

L. This is where I begin to have misgivings, because I do not feel we are justified in making a simple identification between revelation and Scripture, or for that matter between revelation and any human formulation.

E. Then you're saying that revelation is little more than a personal encounter between you and God in which nothing is really communicated. Revelation, modern theology seems so fond of saying, is an I-Thou encounter which demands a decision, and faith is not a mental assent to truth but a blind response of trust.

L. I think that is a common conception of what the liberal believes, but it also is not the accurate picture. You have undoubtedly caught something of the apprehension the liberal feels when revelation is identified with objective and direct truths about God. I am not at all sure what an objective truth about God is—it sounds like it is a statement which has dropped from heaven. I cannot see any clear evidence that our thinking or speaking about God escapes the limitation of all human thought, namely, that it is historical and therefore relative and open to further development.

E. If you believe that, aren't you opening Pandora's box? Then propositions about God must necessarily be discussed as non-divine, inspiration is exchanged for enlightenment, authority is replaced by subjectivism, miracles are no more than mistaken ideas of what happened—the Bible is reduced to a fallible and subjective witness, and revelation cannot be distinguished from human reason!

L. I am not at all sure that everything you have said follows from my statement about the nature of revelation, because there seems to be a confusion here between the source of revelation, on the one hand, and the manner or "how" of God's revelation. You say that we reject the supernatural character of revelation, but that is true only in regard to the "how." We would say that revelation is supernatural, just as we would say Scripture is divinely inspired, in the sense that the origin is not simply human or the mere product of human deduction. In other words, man is not capable of his own salvation. What we reject, however, is the idea that this superhuman revelation is made known in a supernatural way, that is, in some way which makes revelation ahistorical, objective, or eternal.

E. If I understand you, you believe that God reveals himself to us only indirectly and through historical truths, yet sufficiently for our salvation.

L. That is right. We make no claim to a final or objective revelation which comes directly from God, only to an indirect revelation of God which must be understood and expressed in human—and therefore relative—concepts and words.

E. Very interesting, for you have spelled out our differences quite well. As evangelicals we believe that God has revealed himself directly through timeless truths about himself, while you believe God has communicated himself indirectly through conditional truths about himself.

The dialogue is by no means exhaustive, but it does serve to bring to the surface three different issues which need to be discussed:

(1) Should revelation be understood as direct and objective or as indirect and nonobjective?

(2) What are the limits and conditions imposed on conceptual thinking by a particular time in history? To what extent does the resulting historical relativity influence our understanding of the nature of revelation?

(3) What is the criterion by which the Christian faith may judge its truth? Does Christianity base its religious authority and truth on absolutes or on relatives?

The following chart summarizes the two positions:

	Liberal	Evangelical
the nature of revelation	indirect	direct
	non-objective	objective
	relative	absolute

THE EVANGELICAL POSITION

Let us first turn to the position of the evangelical on these three issues. What does he mean by objective and direct revelation? He will first of all point out that revelation is both event and interpretation, action and speech. In other words, the divine event without the corresponding prophetic word would be a bare historical occurrence without redemptive power; and likewise a divine word without the corresponding objective, historical event would merely be a subjective, nonhistorical interpretation.[1] When the words objective and direct are used, it should be remembered that they refer to both divine event and word.

Revelation as *divine event* is objective and direct first of all

[1]Among others see Bernard Ramm, *Special Revelation and the Word of God* (Grand Rapids: Eerdmans, 1961), pp. 77–83; Ramm, "The Evidence of Prophecy and Miracle," in *Revelation and the Bible*, ed. Carl F. H. Henry (Grand Rapids: Baker, 1958), pp. 256–263; and Henry, *Frontiers in Modern Theology* (Chicago: Moody, 1964), ch. IV.

For a summary of liberal treatments of revelation as the relationship between fact and interpretation see Van A. Harvey, *The Historian and the Believer* (New York: Macmillan, 1966), pp. 204–245; and the iconoclastic approach. . . .

because something actually happened. There is an objective, given reality to Israel's deliverance across the Red Sea, or the miracle of the loaves and fishes, or Ezekiel's vision. Because these divine events did take place in time and space, they are open to the same kind of verification as all other historical events. The nature of revelation therefore cannot be reduced to the inspiration of the biblical writers themselves. Secondly, it must be said that revelatory events are distinguished by being initiated by God for a specific purpose. This is not to deny that God is the author of all events but to emphasize that within the general course of nature and history God's particular actions are inserted for the purpose of salvation. Christ was not born at just any time, and Israel was not released from Egypt just for the sake of freeing a captive people. Because these particular events occurred as witnesses to a divine purpose, we are justified in understanding them as direct and objective revelations of God. The third distinguishing characteristic of revelatory events is their inner connection with each other. If God's actions in history were isolated incidents without shared meaning, it would become difficult to see them as objective and direct revelation of the divine purpose. Fortunately we are not overcome by an ambiguous, neutral universe, and God does make his will sufficiently clear by relating one event with the next to form a pattern of meaning—salvation history. Although biblical writers selected and omitted certain events, the coherent relationships between sacred events belong primarily to the objectivity of revelation itself rather than to subjective editing.

Revelation as *divine word* is also direct and objective in that God gives man certain truths about himself. The evangelical, in contrast to fundamentalists, is not claiming a kind of mechanical dictation or an ecstatic trance whereby God merely used a person's voice or hand. Although the biblical authors wrote and spoke from a particular historical perspective, the evangelical argues, their message and interpretation is God's, not man's. What prophets spoke was not a word about God but the Word of God. When it is asked how it is possible for a man to speak a divine word, the answer lies in the direct and personal relationship these men had with the living God. It is not by coincidence that the Old Testament prophets and St. Paul included in their preaching an account of their call or personal encounter with God.[2] The biblical writers were obviously aware of the distinction between their human thoughts and God's, or they would not have prefaced their speeches and writings with, "Thus says the Lord. . . ." The prophet or the apostle is not simply a passive instrument, for that would not explain the different literary styles, theological emphases, and historical backgrounds which we find among the biblical writers.

At the same time, however, we should not confuse the matter by thinking the infallibility of God's revelation to be dependent upon the perfectibility of the men he chose. These persons did not possess God's revelation as private individuals but only as they spoke and later committed to writing his divine word. Thus the authority of their interpretation rests in God and not in their human nature. Yet the reason God used them rather than other men was because of their personal relationship with him.

It is important to notice that the evangelical places particular emphasis on the interrelationship between the objectivity and the directness of revelation. Just as a historical event needs an interpretation (and vice versa), objectivity needs directness (and vice versa). It is erroneous to think that because God's revelation is objective everyone will recognize it as revelation. Many did not accept Jesus as the Son of God even though they saw the same man and heard the same words as the disciples. Likewise the Egyptians did not believe what happened at the Red Sea was a mighty act of Yahweh. In the language of the Bible, they saw and heard but their hearts were hardened and they did not believe.[3] Without the inner revelation of God men may misunderstand, misinterpret, or ignore what has happened. On the other side, men may be directly inspired, but this does not remove the necessity for something objective to have occurred. Without the historical objectivity of revelation the inspired word could be a witness to a series of meaningless aberrations just as well as to a divine intervention into time. Objectivity serves to root revelation in reality and history and thus make it verifiable.

[2]See, for example, Isaiah 6; Jeremiah 1; Ezekiel 2; Galatians 1:11–24.

[3]Cf. Exodus 14:8; Isaiah 6:9–10; Matthew 13:10–15; Mark 8:17–18.

Finally, it might be argued that the direct and objective nature of revelation depends upon a literal interpretation of the Bible. This, however, places the cart before the horse. The reason for understanding Scripture in a literal and straightforward sense (except at some obvious points where it would make nonsense) is not a prior assumption about its inerrancy. It is much more accurate to say that the Bible can be interpreted in this manner because God reveals himself objectively in history and directly to his human witnesses.

Since the nature of revelation is both objective and direct, it is likewise both propositional[4] and personal. *In fact, the interrelationship here forms one of the basic tenets of evangelical theology.* Revelation is personal insofar as God reveals himself through a direct and personal relationship. Revelation is propositional insofar as God reveals objective truths about himself. The Christian faith receives its necessary balance only when revelation is *both* objective and direct, personal and propositional. If the nature of God's revelation did not include the personal aspect, faith would become mere assent to a set of cold, impersonal facts. On the other hand, if it did not include the conceptual, faith would become merely an unverifiable, subjective experience. The objective norms which form the content of faith make it possible to distinguish a valid encounter with God from an encounter with the devil or with one's inner self. So the validity of our experience of Christ is dependent upon our objective knowledge of God, and our propositional knowledge of God is in turn dependent upon our personal relationship with Christ. The two are inseparable, because "revelation is event *and* interpretation, encounter *and* truth, a Person *and* knowledge."[5]

The acceptance of propositional truths, revealed doctrines, and an objectively inspired Bible naturally leads to an important

[4]A few evangelicals have preferred the term "conceptual revelation" to "propositional revelation." Ramm, for instance, finds the phrase "propositional revelation" an unhappy one, because it tends to reduce faith to a mental assent and picture God as "dictating Euclidean theological statements to the prophets and apostles" (*Special Revelation* . . . , pp. 154–160). The difference in tone and meaning between the two terms is significant and needs to be made explicit and brought into open discussion.

[5]Ramm, *Special Revelation* . . . , p. 160.

confrontation with the concept of historical relativity. The evangelical approach to this idea, as to the critical-historical method, is to accept it, but with "proper limitations."[6] A certain degree of relativism is necessary and beneficial in understanding the Bible and later theological reflection upon it. It would be foolish to think the biblical writers could be properly understood without relating them to their particular historical age. Likewise, the words of Scripture need to be seen in relation to their linguistic and stylistic usage. Relativism will also play a proper role in the representation of the gospel by contemporary theologians and preachers, since God's truth must continually be set in new historical contexts. The danger, however, of an unrestricted acceptance of relativity is that it erodes and levels all norms and absolutes. Relativity in this sense makes it impossible to distinguish between what belongs to God and what belongs to man, thereby nullifying divine authority. With a little creativity almost any dogma or biblical statement can be made to mean almost anything. The basic mistake made in this kind of blind relativity is the failure to distinguish between the historical form of revelation and its inner, objective substance. The external, mediated form of revelation will naturally reflect all the particulars of a certain historical age. But the essential or religious truth is supernatural in nature and origin and thus is changeless. Relativity applied to Holy Scripture must not overlook the possibility that the biblical writers, inspired by the Holy Spirit, were able to transcend their restricting cultural environment when speaking God's Word. The fact that it is *God* who is speaking *through* men confers a distinctive absoluteness to their words, an absoluteness which prohibits us from making them relative.

By inseparably joining the personal and conceptual aspects of revelation, evangelical theology offers a view of religious authority markedly different from that of liberalism.[7] A prominent theme of contemporary evangelical thinking is that neoorthodoxy or liberalism has opened the door to religious skepticism and subjectivity by neglecting the objective and direct nature of reve-

[6]Geoffrey W. Bromiley, "The Limits of Theological Relativism," *Christianity Today,* May 24, 1968, pp. 6–7.

[7]Compare Ronald H. Nash, *The New Evangelicalism* (Grand Rapids: Zondervan, 1963), p. 55.

lation. Once it is admitted that all of man's conceptual thinking is inescapably conditional and historical, then there is no way to test for error or to recognize a valid religious experience.[8] So the evangelical feels strongly that unless we possess an objective knowledge of God which can be trusted, theology is reduced to little more than mysticism and guesswork. The basis and justification, then, for the evangelical's belief in an inerrant Bible, revealed doctrines, the validity of universal truths, authentic ontological knowledge of God, and the intelligible and verbal character of God's revelation rests squarely on his confidence that revelation is direct, objective, and conceptual.

THE LIBERAL POSITION

It goes without saying that the liberal has been more radically affected by historical relativity. The whole of liberal Protestantism since the nineteenth century must be seen as a movement to accommodate and incorporate a historical approach to Scripture and faith.[9] Hence it is imperative that the issue of

[8]A predominant theme running through evangelical thought is the criticism that liberalism has no test whatsoever for error. See, for example, Carl F. H. Henry, *Remaking the Modern Mind* (Grand Rapids: Eerdmans, 1946); Henry, *God, Revelation and Authority*; vol. I: *Preliminary Considerations* (Waco: Word, 1976), pp. 70ff., 213ff.; R. A. Finlayson, "Contemporary Ideas of Inspiration," in *Revelation and the Bible*, pp. 224–234; and Edward J. Carnell, *The Case for Biblical Christianity* (Grand Rapids: Eerdmans, 1969), pp. 51–57, 119–121.

[9]As one traces the historical development of liberal theology from the nineteenth century, it becomes clear how this single question of the relation between faith and historical conclusions has determined the outcome. After such men as Gotthold Lessing, Friedrich Strauss, Martin Kähler, Albert Schweitzer, and Wilhelm Herrmann, it became common to assume that faith has its own certainty apart from historical research. And this is precisely what we see in various ways in dialectical theology, existential theology, the new quest for the historical Jesus, the new hermeneutic, the death-of-God theology, and the theology of hope. An interesting and fair treatment is H. M. Kuitert, *The Reality of Faith: A Way Between Protestant Orthodoxy and Existential Theology*, trans. L. B. Smedes (Grand Rapids: Eerdmans, 1968).

historical relativity be dealt with before the issue of the nature of revelation if we are to understand the liberal's position.

"We are in history as the fish is in water"—so the apothegm goes. The liberal simply does not allow for the exceptions claimed by the evangelical. All conceptual thinking, even our knowledge of God, is conditioned sociologically, culturally, and historically —and no exceptions can be made for dogmas, biblical propositions, or religious truths. At first this statement may seem too strong. It may seem strong, first of all, because it is still dawning upon us. The liberal himself has constantly tried to avoid this conclusion and frequently has unconsciously resisted accepting the inevitable. There exists a close analogy here with the idea of evolution, for it should be remembered that nearly every Christian at first resisted admitting the implications of biological evolution. Only as time passed could there be a definite distinction drawn between those Christians who fully accepted evolution and those who rejected it outright or accepted it only in part.[10]

The liberal Protestant and Roman Catholic find themselves in agreement over against the conservative Protestant and Roman Catholic on three points concerning historical relativity. The lib-

[10]Georges Crespy is undoubtedly correct when he writes, "Evolution is not only a scientific theory, though it may primarily be this; it is also a *mentality*, a mental attitude toward the problems posed by the understanding of the phenomena of matter. When one attacks the 'gaps' in the theory of evolution (and this is done rather easily, because in fact the theory of evolution is practically all 'gap'), one is actually attacking the evolutionist mentality without ever saying it, often without even knowing it too clearly." See Crespy, *From Science to Theology: The Evolutionary Design of Teilhard de Chardin*, trans. George H. Shriver (Nashville: Abingdon, 1965), pp. 14–15. Just how true this observation is can be seen by the public's reaction to the Scopes Trial of 1925. Norman F. Furniss comments, "People wondered why the controversy should have burst out so unexpectedly and irrationally after the end of World War I; why the country should have suddenly become involved in a bitter dispute over theology. Such questions revealed a mistaken analysis of the whole affair; for those who assumed that the conflict had broken like a summer thunderstorm . . . were unaware that events had been preparing the way for the phenomenon." See Furniss, *The Fundamentalist Controversy 1918–1931* (reprint; Hamden, Conn.: Archon Books, 1963), p. 10. The controversy surrounding evolution continues precisely because a mental mindset is involved.

eral, following the warning of Karl Barth, senses a double danger when claims of directness or absolutism are made, whether they be a direct encounter-experience or an objective support such as an infallible Bible or eternal truths. Once the Christian believes he possesses direct and objective knowledge of God, he has really only succeeded in making the transcendent God a captive of his own rational thought and his own inner emotion. Such claims also result in closing off further search for the truth, since it is assumed truth has already been obtained. Secondly, the liberal understands truth itself to be a progressive, growing entity rather than a static, unchanging collection of facts. Faith is continually in the process of development, because its content is constantly in the process of development and refinement. Thirdly, looking at history and at the continuing aggregation of his self-understanding, the liberal believes his knowledge of God is likewise becoming more perfect and objective. This implies that revelation is *progressive*, *open-ended*, and *partial* in nature.[11] Any particular revelation is an ongoing process having its determinative beginning during the biblical period but reaching its totality only at the end of history. Objectivity and directness must then await the future in anticipation of the return of Christ, when he will make all things known.

This brief summary of the liberal's attitude toward the question of historical relativity helps to make many of his statements about revelation more intelligible. For instance, here is a typical definition of revelation from the *Theologisches Wörterbuch zum Neuen Testament* (Vol. III, p. 575):

> Revelation is *not* the communication of supernatural knowledge and *not* the stimulation of numinous feelings. To be sure, revelation can become the occasion for the growth of knowledge, and the revelation of God is necessarily ac-

[11]A theme most consistently developed by Wolfhart Pannenberg. See Pannenberg, *et al.*, ed., *Revelation as History*, trans. David Granskou (New York: Macmillan, 1969), pp. 3–31, 123–158. Roman Catholic scholarship is also interested in the progressive nature of revelation and how it relates to doctrine and biblical inspiration. Compare Jan H. Walgrave, *Unfolding Revelation: The Nature of Doctrinal Development* (Philadelphia: Westminster, 1972), and Bruce Vawter, *Biblical Inspiration* (Philadelphia: Westminster, 1972).

> complished by religious feelings. But revelation does not consist of these; it is the peculiar activity of God, the unveiling of his hiddenness, his giving of himself in communion.

The definition states what revelation is not and what it is. Revelation is not the divine communication of absolute truths about God, because man cannot be delivered from his historical environment and his sinful nature for a moment in order to perceive utterly new and unknown divine truths. According to Reinhold Niebuhr there is no exception to the sin of pride:

> All human knowledge is tainted with an "ideological" taint. It pretends to be more true than it is. It is finite knowledge, gained from a particular perspective; but it pretends to be final and ultimate knowledge. Exactly analogous to the cruder pride of power, the pride of intellect is derived on the one hand from ignorance of the finiteness of the human mind and on the other hand from an attempt to obscure the . . . taint of self-interest in human truth.[12]

Nor can revelation be defined properly as the divine communication of a system of doctrine or of universally valid propositions, because this would define revelation too narrowly and consequently lock revelation into the thought patterns of a particular age. When the *primary* function of revelation consists in the giving of new information, whether moral or theological, then that information can never be superseded by fresh knowledge of the nature of God.

Rather, revelation is the divine self-disclosure which creates faith in man and establishes him in a new, living relationship with God. Revelation is God's communication of his living Spirit, transforming the way a person experiences life, understands himself, and relates to the world. In this personal encounter, God's Spirit touching man's spirit, the individual is not so much introduced to new truths as given a new self-consciousness which radiates out to illumine, and in some cases radically alter, his

[12]Reinhold Niebuhr, *The Nature and Destiny of Man* (New York: Scribner's, 1941), pp. 194–195.

understanding of all previous truth. For example, Christ did not bring a totally new law but a revolutionary understanding and application of the already existing Jewish moral law.[13]

It is essential to see that liberals in no way deny that revelation as a divine self-disclosure has a conceptual or intellectual content which faith can express in words. The point they emphasize is that the content of faith is not the immediate result of revelation but the subsequent verbal development of the believer's decision to commit his life to Jesus Christ. The response of man to God's disclosure of himself is his witness in words and deeds which have been uniquely and authoritatively preserved in Scripture and the apostolic church. This is why the liberal uses the phrase "the Word of God" in reference to the disclosure of God in his Son but not to the historical and human response to Jesus Christ. This is also why faith in its primary sense is to be distinguished from assent to certain statements about God. For the liberal, faith is an integral act of the entire self, placing one's trust in God rather than in the world or oneself.[14]

Revelation is best compared to a paradigmatic event which brings about a new orientation in thought and life. A modern example of a paradigmatic event may be found in the assassination of Martin Luther King, Jr. The dimensions of this event went far beyond the historical facts. His death awakened powerful feelings and questions about the meaning of existence—about the hatred, bigotry, intolerance, indifference, and violence in our nation and our world. The man and the event almost immediately became transformed into a universal symbol or myth (where "myth" does not mean a false story but an event which becomes objectivized and universalized in order to convey a significant and fundamental meaning into the future).

A revelatory event of self-disclosure is one that so captures the imagination of an individual or community that it alters their

[13]H. Richard Niebuhr, *The Meaning of Revelation* (New York: Macmillan, 1941), pp. 171–175. This book and the one cited above by Reinhold Niebuhr, both dating from 1941, represent the original and most important development of the liberal view of revelation in America.

[14]Schubert M. Ogden, "The Christian Proclamation of God to Men of the So-Called 'Atheistic Age,'" in *Is God Dead?* ("Concilium," vol. 16; New York: Paulist Press, 1966), pp. 89–98.

way of looking at the *totality* of their experience.[15] The crossing of the Red Sea (Sea of Reeds) for Israel and the resurrection of Jesus for the Christian community were such events. A community preserves the event, as did Israel and the church, by continually reinterpreting the event in light of its particular historical situation. The event thus becomes a continual source of revelation, each succeeding generation relating to these paradigmatic events in a new way. One can compare the way contemporary Jewry celebrates the Passover in reference to their exodus from the German repression to the promised state of Israel, and the way the modern church celebrates Easter in light of the hope it brings to suppressed and deprived people in American ghettos and the Third World.

The conclusion for the liberal is that God does indeed reveal himself, but he does so indirectly and nonobjectively. To illustrate what the liberal means by these two terms we might look at how he interprets one of the important "miraculous" or paradigmatic events. The account of the exodus from Egypt in Exodus 13 and 14 gives the general impression that God directly intervened to reverse and hold back the flow of the Red Sea. Within the text, however, there are certain hints of an older, more historical tradition of a military encounter in which Israel defeated the pursuing chariotry of Pharaoh. Based upon Exodus 13:17–18; 14:25, 30–31; 15:4, 21, the liberal thinks he can reconstruct what actually happened. Israel, pursued by Pharaoh's heavily armed men and chariots, decided to cross at the Sea of Reeds where the terrain would be in their favor. The alternate lengthy route along the Gulf of Suez would have enabled the Egyptians to overtake the Hebrews fleeing on foot. Crossing the muddy marshland at night, possibly aided by a "strong east wind," Israel lay in wait for the Egyptians to become trapped and immobilized by the mud. Panic set in, chariots became mired in the sand or mud, horses threw their riders, Hebrew archers (if there were any) found their mark, and in general the Egyptians were routed (14:27) by a people considered to be an easy prey. In time, out of Israel's enthusiasm to profess their faith in a powerful Yahweh, the water separation was attributed to Moses' outstretched hand

[15]Harvey, *The Historian and the Believer*, pp. 253–258.

(14:21) and God was pictured as holding back a great sea so the Hebrews could cross on dry land (14:22).[16] It was not long before the military aspect of the event became almost completely overshadowed by the miraculous intervention of God.

Leaving aside the accuracy of every detail of this interpretation, the liberal would see it as a good example of how God reveals himself indirectly and nonobjectively. From a scientific point of view there is nothing supernatural about the crossing at the Sea of Reeds, but for Israel at that particular time in her history the event was significant far beyond its overt meaning. For the Hebrews, this victory and escape were revelatory because they enabled them to understand their history and future in an entirely new light. Yahweh had confirmed his promises to Abraham of a new land and a strong nation. A people once in bondage with no future now had an identity and a hope. Even today the Jews view the Exodus as their beginning as a nation with a destiny.

The liberal would not insist that every reported "miracle" can be so interpreted, but he feels no compulsion to understand the actions of God as objective breaks in historical, natural, or psychological processes. God's revelation, because it is indirect and closed to objective, scientific proof, is hidden and equivocal. With the eyes of faith it is possible to see within the natural processes of life and history something of what God is and what is expected of us. The cross of Christ, for example, is an objective fact of history for everyone, but it is a saving act of God only for faith and for the man who makes it his own. The closed web of history seen by the objective observer is thus left undisturbed.

It might be tempting to conclude at this point that for the liberal truth is formless, faith groundless, and theology normless. It is more to the point, however, to say the liberal finds religious authority located in relatives rather than in absolutes. From his point of view Christian commitment is possible not because we have an unchanging dogmatic essence but because we have a

[16]Lewis S. Hay, "What Really Happened at the Sea of Reeds?" *Journal of Biblical Literature,* vol. LXXXIII (1964), pp. 397–403; Frank E. Eakin, Jr., "The Reed Sea and Baalism," *Journal of Biblical Literature,* vol. LXXXVI (1967), pp. 378–384. Geographical, archeological, and textual considerations must also be taken into account.

historical continuity which has proven sufficient for renewal and opposition to error.[17] If truth and revelation cannot escape the fact that they are historical, and if the doctrinal content of Christian faith could have been given only within the historical process, then our knowledge of God must have a *historical* norm. The foundation for our faith is the confidence that the ongoing process of revelation will lead to results which strengthen and confirm faith's historical basis.[18] This confidence is grounded in the fact that God has already given us authentic knowledge of himself in Scripture and in the teaching of the universal church. The key to the liberal's understanding of religious authority is the belief that truth can be relative and historical and still be of God. Relative truth is not complete or immutable, but it is sufficient for salvation and drives toward its fulfilment in the future. Consequently liberals find words such as "continuity," "faithfulness," and "development" more appropriate to describe truth and revelation than "constant," "eternal," or "unchanging."[19]

THE REAL ISSUES

For the most part the real issues between liberals and evangelicals have been clouded over with misconceptions and defined only in generalities. Areas of important agreement have also been

[17]Charles Davis, *A Question of Conscience* (New York: Harper, 1967), pp. 233–243. In his book, *Faith and the Vitalities of History: A Theological Study Based on the Work of Albrecht Ritschl,* Philip Hefner stresses the point that the norm for theology cannot be an abstract category, principle, or "essence" but must be historical, i.e., not restricted to one historical manifestation but open to the whole continuum of the Christian witness.

[18]According to Pannenberg, faith's certainty lies not in knowing that certain critical-historical conclusions are irrevocable but in knowing that God has a purpose for history (historical change) and that he is faithful to his promises. See Pannenberg, *Revelation as History,* p. 157, n. 15. Compare Jürgen Moltmann, *The Theology of Hope,* trans. James W. Leitch (New York: Harper, 1967), pp. 78–79, 92, 94.

[19]Roman Catholics have followed a similar line of thinking. Compare Leslie Dewart (see n. 22, 23); Walgrave and Vawter (n. 11); and Hans Küng, *Infallible? An Inquiry,* trans. Edward Quinn (Garden City: Image, 1972), where he develops the concept of "indefectibility."

neglected, resulting in mutual judgments which are wide of the mark. Much of the criticism on both sides falls away when we recognize the striking agreement concerning the twofold nature of revelation as historical and personal, event and interpretation. Liberals and evangelicals have recently shown that they also agree that faith involves the whole person and therefore includes both a personal act of decision and an intellectual act of assent. As we saw above, the liberal finds historical continuity to be a base sufficient to separate truth from error. He acknowledges in addition that faith has its own proper cognitive content. On the other hand, the evangelical has been grappling with the question of historical relativity and is beginning to realize the implications of affirming a supernatural revelation.

The real issues must therefore be formulated along different lines. For instance, the basic question is not whether faith has a particular content but whether it is received objectively or nonobjectively from God. It is an issue not of whether God acts and man interprets, but of whether God's action is supernatural in appearance and whether man's interpretation is received directly from God. There is no dispute that historical relativity is a pertinent issue. The disagreement is over whether the evangelical has minimized its implications or whether the liberal has accepted it blindly. It must also be asked whether historical relativity can affect the outer time-given framework without affecting the inner religious truth. There is no doubt faith must involve the whole person. Yet it is unclear what the precise relationship is between the content and the experience of faith. And we do need to ask what are the consequences when religious authority is based upon relatives or absolutes.

The heart of the matter can be expressed, "*Does God reveal himself in concepts and propositions which are direct and objective?*" Or from a different perspective the central issue might be worded, "*Can man formulate statements about God and his nature that are valid for everyone in all places and times?*" The evangelical answers an emphatic "yes" to both questions, the liberal an emphatic "no." Both questions are inextricably bound to the issue of historical relativity, and so it may be helpful to turn our attention to the contrasting evaluations evangelicals and liberals give of historical relativity.

In essence the evangelical argues that revealed truth, because it is supernaturally revealed, escapes the time-bound character of man's progressive knowledge. The liberal argues that revealed truth, even though it has its origin in God, cannot escape historical relativity and therefore is not different in form from human insight. If the evangelical wants to make a special claim for revealed truths, then he must be prepared to demonstrate their qualitative difference which distinguishes them from all other kinds of truth, whether religious or scientific. The dialogue would be more meaningful to him if he were willing to be more open to the liberal criticism at this point. The liberal, on the other hand, finds himself in a difficult position because he does not wish to make any special claim for divine revelation. The dialogue would be more meaningful to him if he were more open to the criticism of the evangelical at this point.

A. The Liberal's Criticism

The liberal's criticism may be divided into three parts. (1) The evangelical does not deny that revelation is given in historical forms—literary forms such as drama, poetry, parable, letter, short story, and chronicle, as well as cultural forms, for example a prescientific, geocentric view of the universe. But he argues that beneath these historical forms there is a religious essence which is valid for everyone in all places and times. (The similar classical Roman Catholic view is that dogma or revealed truth can change accidentally, in expression, for example, while remaining substantially or essentially the same.) Age does not invalidate the truth that Jesus is the Son of God or the commandment not to worship graven images. Revealed truths also have the distinction of being inspired in thought and idea as well as in the language in which they are cast. Quoting James Orr, Ronald Nash presents the contemporary evangelical position: "'Thought of necessity takes shape and is expressed in words. If there is inspiration at all, it must penetrate words as well as thought, must mould the expression, make the language employed the living medium of the idea to be conveyed.'"[20] To drive a wedge between verbal

[20]Nash, *The New Evangelicalism,* p. 41; cf. Ramm, *Special Revelation . . .* , pp. 41–42.

and conceptual revelation would be philosophically unsound in view of what is known about the development of language and theologically unsound because certain words or certain concepts would be held immutable but not both. This is why evangelicals insist that there are certain "primary words" *and* "basic concepts" such as "incarnation," "resurrection," and "virgin birth" which cannot be replaced or improved upon.[21] Their conclusion is that the biblical writers used both the right thoughts and the right words in setting down the truth revealed to them.

The liberal counters that truth cannot remain unchanged while it acquires different and more complex forms of expression and understanding. He agrees completely that the historical forms cannot be so easily peeled away from the inner core of truth. In fact it is interesting to see that evangelicals and liberals have moved toward an important theoretical agreement about the intrinsic relation between the experience of faith and its verbal expression.[22] The liberal, however, reaches the opposite conclusion. Since the inner consciousness of faith and its conceptualization are intrinsically bound together, neither can escape historical

[21]Walter Künneth, *The Theology of the Resurrection*, trans. James W. Leitch (St. Louis: Concordia, 1965), p. 56. Cf. pp. 67–68.

[22]The extent of this theoretical agreement is not completely clear because of the different terms employed by liberals and evangelicals. The liberal seems to be working on a deeper level, when he speaks of the intrinsic relation between the experience of faith and its verbal expression, the consciousness of faith and its conceptualization, than is the evangelical, who speaks of the interrelation between words and ideas, language and concepts, religious substance and pictorial representations. I see this area as an important one for further study, especially in regard to what will happen if the evangelical accepts the deepest level on which the interrelation operates. Leslie Dewart defines the central question dividing evangelicals ("traditionalists") and liberals as the way each understands the nature of truth and reality. He also deals with the issue of whether truth and error are mutually exclusive. See his book, *The Foundations of Belief* (New York: Herder and Herder, 1969), pp. 27–40, 313ff. In *A Survey of Catholic Theology 1800–1970* (Glen Rock, N.J.: Paulist Newman Press, 1970), Mark Schoof charts the history of Roman Catholic thought as the struggle to find an acceptable place for historical relativity. Although operating on a different level and concerning different specific issues, the same basic issue has determined the course of Protestant theology.

relativity. According to one liberal Roman Catholic, Leslie Dewart, the truth of faith can never be found in a state of "pure" experience. It can only be found as conceptualized, and once it is put into words and ideas the truth of faith is necessarily conceptualized under one cultural form or another. Since every cultural form is limited in some way by its historical boundaries, faith's truth must likewise be conditioned by the age in which it was formulated. It is a fallacy therefore to believe the substance of faith is not changed as the church sees more deeply into and draws out more fully the implications of the faith once given by God in Jesus Christ and written in Scripture.[23]

The evangelical finds that he must explain how revelation can be conceptualized without being subject to historical relativity. More specifically, he must demonstrate how revelation can be cast into human and historical forms which reflect a particular culture and still provide propositions which are universally valid. Evangelicals frequently point out that God needed to condescend himself by utilizing human modes of thought and speech in order to be understood by mortal men. And although these historical forms prevent us from knowing God totally, they do not falsify or misrepresent God in any way. But if revelation is not complete, then it must be partial and theoretically possible of improvement. The liberal's argument is precisely that partiality necessitates nonobjectivity and indirectness. It may be that the biblical authors did not substantially misrepresent God by the literary and cultural forms they used, but it does not follow that their forms or propositions are absolute or incapable of development. To maintain his argument the evangelical must disregard the onward thrust of human thinking and deny revelation the benefit of later inspiration which adds to the very core of divine truth new insight, precision, and understanding. The evangelical is also caught in the inconsistent argument that God accommodated himself by using historical forms but that certain men at certain times received God's word so perfectly as to transcend human and historical limitations.

To give a concrete example, the evangelical might argue

[23]Leslie Dewart, *The Future of Belief* (New York: Herder and Herder, 1966), pp. 102–118.

that "God is love" is as unchanging a truth as "1 + 1 = 2." The liberal would reply that this is an oversimplification on two accounts. In the first place, the developing mind of man now has a greater understanding of the equation, "1 + 1 = 2," than did the ancient man who first realized it. He understands more completely the logic behind such equations and the conditions under which they are true. Likewise, contemporary man brings a much greater breadth of knowledge concerning language, history, psychology, and philosophy when he interprets the phrase, "God is love." In both cases the increase in understanding does not make the statement or equation any more true, but it certainly does add *substantially* to its meaning. Secondly, the liberal would point out that statements like "God is love" or even "You shall not make for yourself a graven image" mean little until they are interpreted and elaborated. A golden calf may have constituted a graven image in Moses' time, but that is scarcely the threat of idolatry today. To say that interpretation does not affect the basic core of Christian truth overlooks the point that the greatest difference among Christians lies not over what are the basic biblical truths but over how they are to be understood. To know how the commandment "not to kill" applies to the war in Vietnam is neither incidental nor extraneous to knowing fully what God meant to reveal in that commandment. To support his view, the evangelical must show that the act of interpreting and reconceptualizing does not improve or alter substantially the content of faith.

There is one added problem that the liberal raises in regard to the evangelical position. If we grant Scripture the authority of being the most perfect human witness to God possible, how do we know which interpretation of Scripture is correct? Simply to appeal to the Holy Spirit or Scripture as providing its own internal standard does not help, because intelligent Christians differ widely on what is divine truth and what is merely human knowledge. There is, for instance, wide divergence about whether the virgin birth is a literal fact or a sign of the divinity of Christ. The evangelical seems to agree with the liberal that even though the apostles gave a normative interpretation of the redemptive events, we still have to interpret their interpretation. What the evangelical leaves unanswered is how we today can draw a firm line between relatives and absolutes when this secondary and later interpretation must be made by men who are fallible and prompted by personal interests.[24] Would the evangelical then assume that certain men since the biblical period have been so inspired as to be able to transcend their historical time? If so, which men—and are they liberals or evangelicals?

(2) It seems to the liberal that the evangelical depends upon an inner logic which is not necessarily valid to support his belief in absolute and timeless truths. The inner logic runs something like this: "Since God is a supernatural Being, revelations of himself will be supernatural in character. Truth, if it is divine in origin, can be expected to be timeless, eternal, and infallible." The danger that the liberal sees here is that of identifying the appearance of revelation, which is supernatural, with its truthfulness. As much is implied when the evangelical says, "Our faith is based, not on man-made dogmas and opinions, but on a divine revelation, *supernatural in its nature and miraculous in its effect.* The minute one begins to tamper with God's supernatural being and his manifestations *in supernatural and miraculous ways,* he is tampering with the foundational realities of the Christian faith."[25] The liberal finds this kind of logic unconvincing and unwarranted because he knows he can believe in an indirect, nonmiraculous manner of revelation and still believe in an absolute God. His own faith testifies that revelation can be from God without being confirmed by awe-inspiring acts. The liberal has argued again and again that the elimination of the supernatural and miraculous does not mean the end of Christianity. Does it really impugn the sovereignty of God, he asks, if one believes God chooses to reveal himself nonobjectively in the historical and natural processes of life without resorting to inexplicable interventions?[26]

[24]The evangelical admits that "variable error attends all biblical exegesis," because all theologians are sinners and prompted by personal interest. See Carnell, *The Case for Biblical Christianity,* pp. 170–173.

[25]*Christianity Today,* Feb. 28, 1969, p. 30. (Italics mine.)

[26]What has been said should not be interpreted by the liberal to mean the evangelical is oblivious to the danger of making revelation depend upon "a pyrotechnic display of power" for its credibility. Nevertheless, the evangelical maintains the miraculous character of revelation cannot be discarded because it serves to point to the power of God, authenticate his message, act as an antidote to the blindness and ignorance occasioned by man's sinful condition, and protect against human

Should the foundation of the Christian faith be made to rest upon the supernatural *manner* of revelation or upon the *veracity* of the content revealed? If the church's truth is divine in origin, then it is its content that will convince men, not testimonies to its superhuman entrance into the world.

(3) Third, the liberal asks if the evangelical does not depend upon a presupposition about the nature of revelation in order to prove something about revelation. The evangelical begins with the assumption that revelation is direct and objective, which leads to the conclusion that he has an objective and timeless standard inscribed in Scripture to test for false revelations. The liberal finds this to be a circular argument, proving nothing. The evangelical points out, however, that Christian theology cannot operate without some presuppositions, including, for example, the existence of God and the common rationality of men. Even scientific knowledge begins with assumptions about the regularity of the universe and the reliability of sense experience. Theological and circular arguments, the evangelical argues, are valid so long as they produce a metaphysical system of thought which offers a coherent and consistent picture of the world without logical contradictions.[27]

---

subjectivity. See Ramm, *Special Revelation . . .* , pp. 83–91. But from the liberal's vantage point these arguments are unconvincing because they all presuppose that revelation is direct and objective. The liberal, for instance, begins with the same sinful nature of man but concludes that this fact makes it impossible for man to receive direct revelations from God that are untainted by personal and cultural biases.

[27]Nash, *The New Evangelicalism,* pp. 118–120. It would be safe to say that most evangelicals are "theological presuppositionalists." The strongest proponents are: Edward J. Carnell, *An Introduction to Christian Apologetics* (Grand Rapids: Eerdmans, 1948), pp. 122ff.; Gordon Clark, *A Christian View of Men and Things* (Grand Rapids: Eerdmans, 1952), esp. pp. 29–34; Henry, *Remaking the Modern Mind,* pp. 223–233; Cornelius Van Til, *A Christian Theory of Knowledge* (Nutley, N.J.: Presbyterian and Reformed, 1969), pp. 25–40. This third objection falls heaviest on Van Til because he insists that the authority of Scripture is so inherently self-attesting that no evidence from the outside could be offered which would call it into question.

In Carl F. H. Henry's most recent book, *God, Revelation and Authority*, vol. II: *Fifteen Theses, Part One,* he characterizes his approach as "axiomatic" in order to show that all logically dependent theorems flow

The basic argument the liberal raises is not whether theology in the final analysis depends upon a few fundamental presuppositions, for he also depends upon theological assumptions. The liberal's concern is rather that theology not be contained in an enclosed system that insulates it from relevant experience outside the system. The tests for consistency and coherence are fine, but they verify truth only in terms of the logical relations of ideas. In other words, revelation must be judged by external as well as internal criteria before we can make claims about its directness and absoluteness.[28] From an internal criterion, the evangelical has argued that the Christian metaphysical system best unifies our ideas about the world and man and therefore must be based on objectively inspired principles. Most liberals would agree that the Christian faith presents the best interpretation of the meaning of life but would not accept the conclusion about the nature of revelation.

The real brunt of the liberal criticism is that revelation as it is defined by the evangelical does not meet the external or empirical test of being faithful to reality and true to the everyday experience of contemporary man. As Leslie Dewart sees it, one of "the most fundamental theoretical problems which challenges Christianity in the present age . . . is the problem of integrating Christian theistic belief with the everyday experience of contemporary man."[29] The critical issue for the evangelical, therefore, is not whether a system of thought is free of self-contradiction, but

---

from a few basic axioms. Henry is thus unwilling to depart from the traditional evangelical understanding of revelation as propositional. As a result he subjects his theological system to the same basic criticism, namely, he prizes logical consistency over historical empiricism (John Warwick Montgomery), empirical theism (Boyce Gibson), or critical realism (Étienne Gilson), and therefore believes philosophical reasoning can in some way guarantee a Christian certainty. Unfortunately, Henry does not answer the question whether an axiomatic approach ultimately relies on the dogmatic acceptance of certain truth claims.

[28]Frederick Ferré, *Language, Logic and God* (New York: Harper, 1961), ch. 2, 12.

[29]Dewart, *Future of Belief,* p. 7. In very much the same vein, Schubert M. Ogden, *The Reality of God* (New York: Harper & Row, 1963), p. 20; and Langdon Gilkey, *Naming the Whirlwind* (Indianapolis: Bobbs-Merrill, 1969) where he levels a similar criticism against neo-orthodoxy (pp. 15–21, 101–104).

whether a system of concepts relates to lived experience and makes a discernible difference. The liberal thinks the evangelical tends to posit a system of abstract, biblical-sounding propositions which are internally valid but out of touch with our common experience of reality. The consequence is a kind of religious schizophrenia in which the Christian thinks and lives in two entirely different structures of thought: the everyday world of work and play and the Sunday world of religious ideas. There is also the serious problem of having one standard of truth for religious propositions that are confirmed by faith, the scriptural Word, and a relationship with Christ; and another standard of truth for scientific and secular propositions that are verified by the experiences and observations common to every man.

The basic experience of men does not seem to support the presupposition that revealed truths are clearly distinguishable from other religious and secular truths. The evangelical offers many explanations of why all men do not accept the fundamentals of the Christian faith—that the hearts of men have not been changed, for example. While agreeing with the evangelical in part, the liberal still believes that the essential reason why it is difficult to distinguish divine concepts from human concepts is simply that God did not reveal himself in an obvious and direct manner. In a word, the liberal offers a serious challenge when he says the test of reality and everyday experience of man is on his side.

B. The Evangelical's Criticism

It would be well for the liberal to give his attention to evangelical criticisms of his position concerning revelation, for they are no less weighty.

(1) The principal criticism leveled by evangelicals is the liberal's reduction, almost elimination, of the conceptual dimension of revelation. He charges liberal theology with being antimetaphysical, meaning that the liberal rejects the belief that theology works with concepts, ideas, or notions that make sense for all believers in any age. Because of his antimetaphysical bias, the liberal has reduced revelation to some vague notion of "encounter" and faith to a pure act of believing divorced from any authoritative content. Even though the liberal does not deny a divine reality outside of man, he does reject the belief that we

can make universally valid statements about this supernatural or invisible world as we can make universally valid statements about the visible world.[30] Liberals would lead us to expect theological statements to tell us something important about man but very little about an objective reality which stands outside and beyond man. Ultimately even this antimetaphysical bias can be traced back to the liberal conviction that God has not revealed to us direct and objective truths about himself.

To a great extent the evangelical presents a very valid criticism of contemporary liberal theology. Some evangelicals, however, are carried to an extreme when they state that liberals repudiate rational thought, extol personal experience to the point of being anti-intellectual, and possess no test whatsoever for error. If these criticisms were accurate, liberalism could scarcely engage in rational discussion. Yet there can be no doubt that liberalism has not kept the balance between the personal and conceptual dimensions of revelation. Names like Schleiermacher, Bultmann, and Tillich are synonymous with the strong liberal tendency to reduce faith to the level of individual acts of commitment and at the same time minimize the content of Christianity.

Beginning with a theory that all knowledge is historically conditioned, revealed truths not excepted, it seemed necessary to the liberal to provide faith with its own certainty apart from any specific historical content. How one believes became much more important than what one believes. Revelation became something that happens existentially between God and man, not the communication of intellectual knowledge about God. The moment

[30]Kuitert, *The Reality of Faith*, pp. 23–25. Carl F. H. Henry makes the same indictment: "So dawns the end of an era in which Ritschl held that the validity of religious judgments can be known only through an act of the will, in which Troeltsch found himself unable to assert the universality of the Christian religion, and in which both Barth and Bultmann failed to vindicate the universal validity of Christian revelation apart from a miracle of personal grace or an act of subjective decision. But if the deepest truth of God is found in Jesus Christ, if the contention is to be credited that Christianity is a religion for all nations, bringing men everywhere under judgment and offering salvation of import to the whole human race, then it is imperative that the Christian religion reassert its reasoned claim to universality" (*Christianity Today*, Jan. 1, 1965, p. 337).

man discovers himself to be unconditionally given to his fellowman is much more important than theological truths about God. Rudolf Bultmann even proposed the almost indefensible position that the content of faith could be gained outside the life of Jesus Christ by philosophical analysis of man's experience. As a result of these conclusions liberal theology has worked itself into a corner where faith requires the rejection of external evidence, where faith is not interested in the historical actuality of the biblical events and the life of Christ. What is left is a formless and contentless belief, cut loose from its historical foundation.[31]

For decades the liberal has relied upon euphemisms which the evangelical has challenged. Could it be that all his talk about "encounter," "address," "I-Thou relation," "word event," and "existential decision" has been a way to convince Christians that commitment was possible without a system of doctrine? It was easy to speak about an existential encounter with God through the preached word in faith. But to experience this was another matter. One wonders how liberals could have been satisfied so long with so simple and vague a definition of revelation as "the self-disclosure of God," when no attempt was made to explain how God could reveal himself apart from historical truths and conceptual ideas. If revelation is defined as the disclosure of a person, how does God reveal himself without disclosing propositions about himself? At least from the analogy of human encounter, it is nonsense to talk about real encounter between persons divorced from mutual knowledge and understanding. "The richness of love between a happily married couple cannot be exhaustively reduced to a set of propositions; but that such a rich love could come into being independently of mutual knowledge is absolutely impossible."[32] Likewise, the liberal has yet to ex-

[31]Carl F. H. Henry, "Justification by Ignorance: A Neo-Protestant Motif?" *Christianity Today*, Jan. 2, 1970, pp. 10–15. Henry uses the theme of "justification by ignorance" to demonstrate how neoorthodoxy and existential theology perverted the Reformed doctrine of "justification by faith" into the idea "that revelational truths and revelational history are efforts at self-justification," and so sacrificed on the altar of scientific-historical positivism "the essential connection of Christian faith with intelligible and historical revelation" (p. 15).

[32]Ramm, *Special Revelation*, p. 159.

plain how the new self-understanding created by belief in Christ can fail to include new concepts and ideas.

If we accept the liberal definition of revelation, then Scripture is reduced to the mere recording of the new ways Israel and the church applied old codes and concepts to new situations as a result of their encounter with God or Jesus Christ. The liberal has acted as if revelation could be existential without being conceptual. But again the same question remains: Do we claim that revelation and Scripture are entirely devoid of any *completely new* insights (e.g., man as made in the image of God), concepts (God as a loving father), imperatives (love your enemy and pray for those who persecute you), or propositions (the unity of the human and divine in Christ)?[33]

(2) Because the liberal makes no special claims for revelation, he faces the opposite problem from the evangelical's. Just as the burden of proof is on the evangelical to show how Christian truths are essentially different because they are revealed supernaturally, the burden of proof is on the liberal to demonstrate how revealed truths can be distinguished from the merely human. Without a doubt liberalism suffers from a crisis of authority because it has neglected, or decided not, to draw any firm line between what comes from God and what comes from human reason. The liberal finds himself in the difficult situation of arguing that revelation is indirect, nonobjective, and progressive but still divine in origin. This is a difficult argument to maintain since revelation is attributed all the characteristics common to human conceptualization, while no special characteristics are posited for divine revelation. As a consequence of this leveling effect the

[33]The key phrase is "completely new," because the debate has raged whether any truth is ever *completely* new and whether the Bible is unique as a written document because it posits utterly distinctive truths or because its writers interpreted current ideas from a radical perspective. In either case we have been rather careless and vague about our use of words like "new," "absolute," "objective," and "relative." We need to begin to ask some hard questions: "Is there a difference between an absolutely new truth and a completely new truth?" "Was the imperative to love our enemies a new truth or a new interpretation of an old commandment?" Likewise, we need to ask what determines a revealed truth: is it newness at the time, preservation by Israel or the church, a claim to be absolute, persistence through time, a God-like motivation, validity for all men in all times?

liberal is not sure whether his faith is rooted in historical facts or personal speculation. When he tries to give credence to the conclusions of biblical scholars, he wakes up one day to read they have changed their minds. Since he is not sure what to believe, he finds it safer to believe in nothing. If there is any single reason why Christian commitment is weakened in liberalism, it is precisely because there is neither a historical core nor a theological essence which substantially survives change and the vacillating conclusions of theologians.

Recently the liberal has sought to bring the Christian who has been set adrift by historical studies back to some kind of dock. One proposed solution to bridge this gap, we have already seen, is to say that commitment is possible because we possess a continuity within the historical traditions of Christian beliefs. But is historical continuity alone an adequate theological standard? It could preserve error as well as truth. And who is to say how much or how little is to be included as authentic in this continuum of Christian thought? We would not expect the liberal and evangelical to agree. There is also the practical difficulty that the typical Christian does not have enough theological background to know what lies within the Christian tradition and what is simply his own personal opinion. But even more important, this liberal solution does not solve the basic problem of providing Christian truth with some distinctive mark which can command the respect of men.

(3) As we recall, the third criticism of the liberal against the evangelical was that he began with the untested assumption that revelation must be direct and objective. The criticism also works the other way. Evangelicals ask if the liberal does not begin with an assumption about the absoluteness of historical relativity and conclude that revelation must be indirect and nonobjective. Historically, liberals began by trying to solve the problem of relativity and subsequently let that one question determine all other theological questions. As Victor Ferkiss puts it, writing about the technological revolution, "evolution was more than Christianized, it was made the essence of Christianity."[34]

To say the least, the evangelical finds it disturbing that

[34]Victor C. Ferkiss, *Technological Man: The Myth and The Reality* (New York: New American Library, 1969), p. 86.

liberals seem more concerned to construct a theology which meets our experience of reality than to remain faithful to biblical revelation. A concrete example is the controversial report on "Sexuality and the Human Community" prepared by a committee of churchmen and theologians for the Presbyterian Church in the U.S.A.[35] The test of what seems real to us today is allowed to determine what revelation is or is not, which is little more than humanizing theology to the point where man becomes the center instead of God. The evangelical can only cringe when he sees American liberalism returning to an anthropological starting point after such a brief excursion into the transcendency of neo-orthodoxy. We can applaud the attempt by Langdon Gilkey and Peter Berger to uncover those aspects of daily experience which reflect a reality that is ultimate and truly "other" (supernatural), but wonder about a theology that never gets beyond examining our fundamental experiences of being in the world.[36] Evangeli-

[35]Evangelical reaction to this report was unanimous: the document gave greater weight and authority to the research of trained specialists than to the clear teaching of Scripture. In the words of one delegate, "The Sexuality Report was pure situation ethics." As if to save face, the 182nd General Assembly passed an attachment to the report affirming that adultery, prostitution, and homosexuality are sinful. The same controversy was repeated when the question of ordaining homosexuals came before the General Assembly. Here, however, the hermeneutical issue of how best to interpret Scripture was focused more sharply, namely, how to interpret those texts dealing with homosexuality in their wider cultural-historical context.

[36]Gilkey, *Naming the Whirlwind;* Peter L. Berger, *A Rumor of Angels* (Garden City, N.Y.: Doubleday, 1969). Gilkey and Berger might point out that they are not really giving us a theology but a starting point or a prolegomenon. They also argue the necessity to begin with our ordinary experience in a secular age that is marked by the absence of a supernatural God or any inherent order. Other factors have contributed to returning liberalism to an anthropological starting point: the loss of confidence in reason or history to provide faith with certainty, demythologizing, existential theology, and the failure of neoorthodoxy. The end result is the rejection of the premise that theology can begin with objective statements about God.

Both Gilkey and Berger wish to show how the secular mood hides the signals of transcendence that are present in everyday experience. Gilkey finds traces of ultimacy in the negative traits of fanaticism, frantic striving, meaninglessness, boredom, and terror at death and the future;

cals rightly question why liberalism should welcome with open arms the general revival of Friedrich Schleiermacher, champion of an experience-centered faith devoid of the conceptual, when liberalism is already overly subjective and lacking in objectivity. And then Professor Ferkiss wants us to accept a "new immanentism" as one of the basic elements in a new philosophy which must come to dominate human society if man is to survive in a technological world.[37]

Could it be that Karl Barth lives on in the evangelical warning that the study of man is about to replace the study of God, and that what counts is what man says *about* God not what God said *to* man? Is it possible that the liberal has succumbed too readily to the naturalism, temporalism, and autonomy of our age by replacing all absolutes with relatives? Can the liberal entertain the thought that he has spent so much energy in trying to adapt theology to historical relativity that the basic Christian tenets have been undermined and the content of faith buried beneath the shifting sands of historical research? It would be the worst kind of inversion if man is hearing only his own voice when he thinks he is interpreting God's revelation for his own time.

CONCLUSION

Despite what both may say, evangelicals and liberals have both, in opposite ways, been antihistorical in their understanding of revelation and as a result have created an imbalance in their

---

and in the positive traits of joyful wonder, creative meanings, and the resolute character of human life (p. 362). Berger finds signs of the supernatural in the propensity for order, play, hope, and humor (pp. 53–72). Berger states his aim as the inversion of Feuerbach's view that religion is merely the projections of man's own self to the view that man's religious projections are really a reflection of a reality that is truly "other." The question which is not considered, however, by Gilkey or Berger is whether a purely human starting point devoid of revelation can ever assure us that man is not seeing his own reflection. In other words, can a naturalistic theology that excludes special theology ever get beyond the purely human and worldly to the divine and otherworldly?

[37]Ferkiss, *Technological Man*, pp. 207–208.

theologies. When the questions of evolution and historical relativity were raised, evangelicals and liberals sought some way to immunize revelation from the grip of uncertainty which was sure to follow. The evangelical (and fundamentalist) argued that relativity did not really affect biblical revelation, but in reality he reacted by removing revelation to the realm of the superhistorical. Divine truths were posited as timeless and universally valid and therefore safe from relativity. Liberalism acted as if relativity could be included in toto within Christianity, but in reality it reacted by reducing revelation to a formless personal encounter. Faith was transformed into an existential decision, independent of what happened in the past. The evangelical objectified revelation in order to shield it from the taint of human contamination, while the liberal subjectivized revelation in order to prevent it from becoming static and irrelevant. The result is that we find contemporary evangelicalism preoccupied with the conceptual dimension of revelation and struggling to account for its historical-human character, while liberal theology is preoccupied with accommodating revelation to historical relativity and struggling to find a place for authoritative content.

To understand that evangelical and liberal theologies stand in sharp contrast is also to see that each stands as a counterbalance to the other. Existential or liberal theology fills a need which evangelicalism created by failing to allow a significant place for the human contribution to revealed truth. The strength of liberal theology, and the corresponding weakness of evangelical theology, is its insistence that revealed truth be something which can be acted upon and can change one's self-understanding. The evangelical should be willing to subject all of his theologizing to the same kind of questioning Paul van Buren speaks about:

> Let me say this around one example. One of the ways in which the New Testament writers speak about Jesus is in divine and quasi-divine terms—Son of God, and what have you. All right. My interest is in seeing how these terms function, what they accomplish, what difference it makes whether one denies these terms or subscribes to them. . . . What I'm trying to do is . . . to find out how the references to the absolute and the supernatural are used in expressing

> on a human level the understanding and convictions that the New Testament writers had about their world.[38]

This liberal accent should be a reminder to the evangelical that it was not too long ago when his pietistic strain demanded that eternal truths be experienced truths—"Christ may be born in Bethlehem a thousand times, but it does not touch me unless he is finally born in my heart." It is not enough for the evangelical to raise the importance of the conceptual side of revelation and faith; he must demonstrate the ability to weld together objective doctrines about God and the contemporary experience of contingency and autonomy, faith in the scriptural word and confidence in man's rational power to understand God. More than anyone else he should be aware of the inner weaknesses of neo-orthodoxy which brought about its early demise—an uneasy dualism between religious faith and common experience, an unreal biblical positivism, an unhealthy separation between revealed truths and human truths.

In the future evangelicals must also give more attention to the inescapable question of relativity. The books and articles which have dealt with this subject from an evangelical viewpoint have been of little value. There is the understandable fear that to tackle this problem is to open Pandora's box, but nevertheless each year the crack becomes a little bigger. Recognition must be given to the hidden motivation to defend one's position by appealing to absolutes in a time of rapid change and loss of authority. The evangelical has been able to maintain an authoritative concept of revelation and Scripture only by being insensitive to the issue of historical relativity.

Yet the evangelical could benefit from the liberal's mistakes and gains. He would be foolish to fall into the same snare by robbing revelation of its content and transcendence in order to make it existential and pertinent. He must find a place in his theology for the historical self-consciousness of man without excluding every possibility of objectivity and normativeness. On the other side, the liberal has shown that creativity rather than

[38]From an interview with Paul M. van Buren by Ved Mehta, *The New Theologian* (New York: Harper, 1965), p. 63.

defensiveness is a possible response to the secular spirit of temporality. But in order for the evangelical to react positively he must break away from his limiting reliance on supernatural absolutes. And, along with the liberal, he needs to define more precisely what he means by "objective" and "absolute."

By the same ironic swing of the theological pendulum liberal theology now stands to learn something of the transcendent and conceptual aspect of revelation from evangelicalism. One needs to keep in mind that contemporary liberal theology represents an antidote to the sterility and remoteness of neoorthodoxy. It has attempted to take seriously modern secularism and relativity by closing the gap between faith and culture, by translating statements about God into statements about man, and by separating the act of belief from its historical content. In short, liberals have turned theology on its head in order to humanize the gospel and make it serviceable for social action. But it is questionable whether liberals, in spite of all their talk about an I-Thou encounter, were ever led to experience anything of a sustained personal relationship with Christ. Otherwise why would there be a longing to restore a sense of the mysterious and numinous to revelation? If modern, liberal man seems to be closed off from a spiritual sense of the beyond, then part of the blame must be laid at the door of a theology that has been humanized and turned in upon itself.

In addition, the liberal has never solved the thorny question of the interrelation between the content and the experience of faith, between the conceptual and personal dimensions of revelation. Over the centuries liberal theology has been marked by drastic swings rather than by a balance between the two aspects of faith. Surely by now it should be clear that the answer is not the separation of one's commitment to Christ from historical beliefs about him as a person, of one's personal relationship with God from conceptual truths about him. It may be that evangelicals have oversimplified the dynamic and complex relationship between the emotional and intellectual sides of revelation, but this should not prevent the liberal from appreciating an evangelical tradition which has kept both the experience of Christ and the authority of Scripture clearly in mind.

If liberalism is about to swing back to an emphasis on "experienced transcendence" and away from a confining sense of immanence, as some signs indicate,[39] it can of course find resources within its own past. But the chances of repeating old mistakes would be reduced if liberalism would open itself to a tradition which has long been sensitive to the need of a transcendent distance between God and man. In the years ahead liberal theology must be doubly aware of the danger of sinking deeper into a normless relativity as it attempts to relate revelation to the depths of human experience. Yet at the same time it must work toward a conception of revelation which strengthens rather than weakens Christian belief. It cannot afford to continue to preach a faith which has been cut off from the historical content of Christianity.

In the past, classic confrontations over the proper starting point for theology have occurred. Liberals have consistently preferred an anthropological point of departure in order to insure the gospel is not translated into irrelevant terms. Conservatives have argued that special revelation is the only legitimate foundation. In Helmut Thielicke's book, *The Evangelical Faith,* he surveys with sensitivity the complexity of the various positions taken by Descartes, Kant, Schleiermacher, Barth, Bultmann, Herbert Braun, Paul M. van Buren, and Friedrich Gogarten. Thielicke's own position is that natural theology or a Cartesian starting point fails because it concentrates on the addressee rather than the Christian message, the possibility of faith rather than the proclamation of faith. The almost inevitable result of a Cartesian approach is that revelation becomes authenticated by the human situation and by how it is defined in other disciplines. "The question of the self-understanding of secular man," Thielicke writes, "must not become the starting point of theological thinking. It must arise only as the retrospective question of the called concerning that out of which they have been called."[40] Liberals have not exactly been deaf to this criticism. The post-Bultmannian

[39]Besides Berger's *A Rumor of Angels,* a good resource book is Marty and Peerman, ed., *New Theology No. 7: The Recovery of Transcendence*; and the Hartford Appeal (see Appendices).

[40]Helmut Thielicke, *The Evangelical Faith,* vol. I: *The Relation of Theology to Modern Thought-Forms,* trans. Geoffrey W. Bromiley (Grand Rapids: Eerdmans, 1974), p. 223.

reaction is only the tip of the iceberg, and even though liberals have not abandoned an anthropological starting point, they began doing theology with a much greater awareness of "pre-understanding" as the real potential of competing with the Holy Spirit.

If liberals are caught in the web of what Moltmann calls the "anthropological verification schema," evangelicals are trapped in a theological system that depends upon special revelation being self-authenticating. Conservatives only think they have gotten rid of uncertainty, pre-understanding, and philosophical intrusions by positing *a priori* biblical axioms. The history of the close connection between pre-understanding and pre-judgments has its parallel in the close association between proofs of God and sterility. The danger is not simply a reproductive attitude toward the past, but a faith built upon an *a priori* relationship between the Word and reality. The consequence can be not only a message that does not speak to the complexity of our situation but a message in biblical dress that has not penetrated into the deepest meaning of the gospel itself.

One's theological starting point is a good indicator of the kind of imbalance that is likely to appear, but it does not necessarily determine where you end up. The crucial issue is not so much where we begin or where we end, but whether the hermeneutical circle is closed. Revelation is authenticated neither by anthropological anchors (it seems right to the receiving "I" because it touches some universal spring) nor by *a priori* presuppositions (it is right because our theological premises are logical, consistent, etc.). It should be perfectly clear by now that both evangelicalism and liberalism have traditionally had characteristic strengths and weaknesses. Of course we need a theology that is both faithful and continuous, once the biblical message is delivered, and contemporaneous and radical in its search for meaning. Yet, it is not sufficient to freshen up the gospel with new terminology any more than it is satisfactory to probe the depths of our *Zeitgeist*. The biblical test must continually challenge the questions we propose as well as the answers, our pre-understanding as well as our presuppositions. Modernity can exercise hermeneutical authority over Scripture, just as orthodoxy can, because both are incomplete if they do not return full circle and let themselves be tested by the Holy Spirit speaking through the biblical gospel. The final test of a theology is not its starting or ending point, but the fruit it bears in the life of the church.

Finally it must be noted that if the evangelical and the liberal are to learn from each other, they must at least be cognizant that each has his own way of conceptualizing. The evangelical shows a pattern of casting thoughts into *antithetical* categories, because he believes truth is found in the *separation* of opposites. Truth is absolute in nature. There are no gradations: either a statement is true or it is false. Religious authority demands the sharp distinction between the mind of Christ and the mind of man, between the infallible Word of God and the fallible words of man. The evangelical has an inherent love for clearly contrasting ideas and a dislike for fine distinctions and contrapositions. He finds it nearly impossible to speak of "relative truths," because according to his conception of truth these two terms simply do not belong together. Reality consists of two worlds, the natural and the supernatural, the visible and the invisible; and theology is the process by which man's relative thinking may be brought into conformity with the absoluteness of God.

The liberal pattern is essentially *dialectical,* because he believes truth is found in the *synthesis* of opposites. Truth is never a simple matter of black or white but results from the contraposing of assertion and counterassertion so as to produce a higher truth. For example, we can speak of the presence and absence of God, or assert that man is at the same time justified and yet a sinner. In both cases the two statements are true in themselves, but when combined they produce a higher truth. Inherent in this pattern of thinking is a love for paradoxes and diametrical concepts, with a dislike for simple, straightforward assertions. Since reality is thought to be multifaceted, statements can be made about different facets which seem to contradict one another but really do not. From the liberal's perspective the dialectical is the appropriate form of conceptualization in regard to revelation, because man in his finiteness does not have direct knowledge of God.

DISCUSSION QUESTIONS

1. What evidence can you see in today's world and in your own life that God acts directly or indirectly? How does the evi-

dence you give compare with the biblical description of how God revealed himself?

2. A persistent stumbling block between liberals and evangelicals is the word "supernatural." How would you define the word? What, in particular, is the meaning of the prefix "super," e.g. "not," "beyond," "superior to," or something else?

3. What arguments can you give for or against supernatural revelation from your experience of reality? Is your answer determined solely by your personal faith, or is God's action open to verification by an impartial observer?

4. What teachings of the Christian faith do you consider to be absolutes? Why are they absolute? Are absolutes necessary for Christian commitment?

5. What bearing does knowledge gained from historical research have on your commitment to Christ?

6. Keeping in mind that evolution applies both to nature and to the historical development of the human mind, do you believe God is revealing himself in the ongoing processes of evolution?

7. Is it possible for one truth to transcend another truth without invalidating or falsifying the first?

IV. THE INSPIRATION AND AUTHORITY OF SCRIPTURE

Theologically speaking it was proper to deal first with the issue of how God reveals himself, but in the hearts and minds of most Christians this rather abstract question reduces itself to the concrete question of how the Bible is divinely inspired and uniquely authoritative. The evangelical states that without a doubt "the relationship of verbal inspiration to scriptural authority is the crux of all Christian theology and provides a principle which bifurcates all theological systems as resting either in divine inspiration or in human judgments."[1] The authority of Scripture stands squarely upon its inerrancy, and its inerrancy is directly dependent upon the doctrine of verbal and plenary (full) inspiration. The liberal, on the other hand, states that "not everything that is in the Bible is God's Word," and "in the last resort the contemporary controversy is about the truth and falsehood of this proposition."[2] The authority of Scripture cannot be divorced from the critical-historical method, because the very nature of God's written word makes it necessary. All signs indicate that the issue of scriptural inspiration and authority is going to be the one single issue to stir evangelicals and liberals out of their armed neutrality and mutual indifference.

[1]John F. Walvoord, "The Pragmatic Confirmation of Scriptural Authority," in *The Bible—The Living Word of Revelation*, ed. Merrill C. Tenney (Grand Rapids: Zondervan, 1968), p. 182.

[2]Ernst Käsemann, *New Testament Questions of Today*, trans. W. J. Montague (Philadelphia: Fortress, 1969), pp. 272–273.

THE SMOLDERING DIVISIONS

In the previous two chapters it was fairly easy to define the evangelical position over against the liberal position, but when the issue is the origin and nature of the biblical word we find evangelicals and liberals divided among themselves almost as much as they are divided from each other. Behind the facade of asserting an infallible Bible there exists a wide diversity of opinion among evangelicals. During the past several years significant differences have been voiced over standards for responsible publishing, seminary faculties, and entrance into church union. The issue boiled to the surface in June, 1970 (and again in 1979), when the Southern Baptist Convention took the unprecedented action of requesting that the first volume, dealing with Genesis and Exodus, of the Broadman Bible Commentary be recalled and rewritten "with due consideration of the conservative viewpoint." In one of the introductory articles Dr. John I. Durham expressed sympathy for the critical theory that the first five books of the Old Testament are not the product of a single hand, traditionally identified with Moses, but a compilation of several sources. Some explanation must be given, he wrote, for the "anachronisms, repetition, conflicting accounts, a variety of large and small discrepancies, differing conceptions of God, and several markedly different writing styles" within the Pentateuch itself. In trying to open the way for the possible admission of source analysis Dr. Durham went along with the general editor, Dr. Clifton Allen, and the author of the commentary on Genesis, Dr. G. Henton Davis, in showing a preference for a "dynamic view" of inspiration. The delegates obviously had history on their side, for on two occasions, 1925 and 1967, the Convention had declared that the Bible is the Word of God and has for its matter "truth without any mixture of error," even though not a few Baptist professors, religious editors, and laymen found the Convention's action to be offensive and a blow to free thought and expression.

There is a growing consensus that today's watershed for evangelical theology is the doctrine of inerrancy. In 1959 Edward John Carnell prophetically warned that the issue of biblical infallibility is still an issue because it was never resolved. He had in mind the debate that raged in the early twentieth century between Charles Hodge and Benjamin Warfield on the conservative side and James Orr[3] and Henry P. Smith on the liberal side. We are now feeling the effects of this premature termination of a most important question, Carnell wrote:

> The fountain of new ideas has apparently run dry, for what was once a live issue in the church has now ossified into a theological tradition. As a result a heavy pall of fear hangs over the academic community. When a gifted professor tries to interact with the critical difficulties in the text, he is charged with disaffection, if not outright heresy. Orthodoxy forgets one important verdict of history: namely, that when truth is presented in a poor light, tomorrow's leaders may embrace error on the single reason that it is more persuasively defended.[4]

In the past evangelicals stood firmly with fundamentalists in their belief that Scripture is correct about all matters or none at all. Today more than a few evangelicals are reopening the issue by discussing whether plenary and verbal inspiration necessitates inerrancy. To be more precise, the question is whether Scripture includes only that which is revelatory and contains no error, or whether it may also include nonrevelatory matter which contains error. In other words, what matters must be included under the umbrella of infallibility in order to insure the Bible's trustworthiness: (1) matters concerning faith and practice; (2) matters concerning historical and scientific factuality; or (3) matters related only indirectly, such as anthropology, astronomy, physiology, geography, zoology, biology?

When Warfield set out to defend biblical inerrancy against liberal modernism, he rested his case on the single foundation that Scripture witnesses to its own inspiration. The Bible, he argued, testifies to its own verbal inspiration in two ways. First, a number of doctrinal verses assert full inspiration, including II Timothy 3:16: "All Scripture is inspired by God. . . . " (Other

[3]It would be misleading to label James Orr a liberal, but in this controversy he took a relatively liberal position.

[4]Edward J. Carnell, *The Case for Orthodox Theology* (Philadelphia: Westminster, 1959), p. 110.

commonly cited texts are Matthew 5:18; John 10:35; and II Peter 1:20–21.) Secondly, Scripture bears certain patent marks which provide inescapable evidence to its divine origin. Warfield has in mind those marks outlined by Calvin and put forth in the Westminster Confession (Ch. I, section 5):

> We may be moved and induced by the testimony of the Church to an high and reverent esteem of the Holy Scripture; and the heavenliness of the matter, the efficacy of the doctrine, the majesty of the style, the consent of all the parts, the scope of the whole (which is to give all glory to God), the full discovery it makes of the only way of man's salvation, the many other incomparable excellencies, and the entire perfection thereof, are arguments whereby it doth abundantly evidence itself to be the Word of God.

Warfield insisted that the activity of the Holy Spirit did not add anything to Scripture but simply caused men to see the marks of divinity that were already objectively present in the written words. The doctrine of infallibility, he concluded, could be overruled on only two grounds: (1) exegetical evidence that the Bible does not teach verbal inspiration and inerrancy, (2) any internal or external evidence that would undermine our confidence in the trustworthiness of the Bible as a guide to doctrine and a teacher of truth.[5] So Warfield's case, which has become the traditional one, is that Scripture plainly testifies to its own inspiration and inerrancy until that time when the weight of evidence indicates otherwise.

In the tradition of Calvin and the Westminster Confession, Warfield could have appealed to the inner testimony of the Holy Spirit to guarantee the reliability of the written Word of God, but he was willing to allow the "observed characteristics and structure of Scripture" to be heard. He wrote, "The test of the truth of the claims of the Bible to be inspired of God through comparison with its contents, characteristics and phenomena, the Bible cannot expect to escape; and the lovers of the Bible will be the last to deny the validity of it. By all means let the doctrine of the Bible

[5]Benjamin B. Warfield, "The Real Problem of Inspiration," in *The Inspiration and Authority of the Bible*, ed. Samuel G. Craig (Philadelphia: Presbyterian and Reformed, 1948), p. 174.

be tested by the facts. . . ."[6] Warfield also showed his willingness to weigh the evidence of historical criticism when he declared that he did not think the doctrine of plenary inspiration should be made into a prior assumption. "We must indeed prove the authenticity, credibility and general trustworthiness of the New Testament writings before we prove their inspiration."[7]

The door thus left ajar, or at least unlocked,[8] it is not surprising that some evangelicals find it proper and necessary to slip in a foot. Daniel P. Fuller, for example, proposes a corrective to Warfield which would not change the basic outline of Warfield's argument but would limit inerrancy to those statements that are able to make men wise unto salvation. Fuller observes that the doctrinal verses which Warfield relied on so heavily teach or imply infallibility always in connection with revealed knowledge and "not in connection with knowledge which makes a man wise to botany, meteorology, cosmology, or paleontology, i.e., to knowledge which is non-revelational simply because it is readily accessible to men."[9] Fuller is thus arguing that inspiration and

[6]*Ibid.*, p. 217; see also p. 218.

[7]*Ibid.*, p. 212.

[8]Upon careful reading of Warfield, one must question how open he was to evidence that might disprove scriptural inerrancy and verbal inspiration. Warfield admits that there is this "metaphysical possibility" (pp. 217, 218), but it appears to be only a theoretical possibility since the evidence in support of verbal inerrancy is "unassailable" and "compelling." Without a doubt Warfield considered the weight of the doctrinal verses to be so much greater than the secondary evidence of the actual "characteristics and structure of Scripture, especially as determined by some special school of modern research by critical methods certainly not infallible and to the best of our own judgment not even reasonable" (pp. 206, 215, 223). Warfield says he is willing to allow "a study of the facts" occasionally to modify or correct our exegetical processes and conclusions, but he adds that it is quite another matter "to modify, by the facts of the structure of Scripture, the Scriptural teaching itself" (pp. 207, 204). Carnell also points out that Warfield preferred to deal in generalities and with the broad question of doctrine rather than with the historical and exegetical evidence (*The Case for Orthodox Theology*, p. 106). So in the final analysis Warfield tended to cast aside or limit evidence drawn from the actual structure and character of the Bible.

[9]Daniel P. Fuller, "Benjamin B. Warfield's View of Faith and History," *Bulletin of the Evangelical Theological Society*, vol. XII, no. 2 (Spring, 1968), p. 81. Fuller's attempt to initiate a new discussion about

inerrancy are two different matters. Proof texts for the former are not necessarily proof texts for the latter. And Fuller is not alone in thinking the Bible does not, strictly speaking, teach plenary inerrancy.[10]

In comparison to the smoldering divisions among evangelicals, liberals appear to present a united front. But liberals, too, have their internal differences. For over a century biblical research was dominated and nearly determined by the great personalities of the liberal German universities. A leveling-off process has since made the critical-historical method common property, raised Catholic scholarship to an equal footing, and opened the way to an ecumenical approach to scriptural study. The last fifty years have also seen a renaissance of relatively conservative scholarship. We find not only a host of competent conservative

---

inerrancy has resulted in many rejoinders. For example, Richard J. Coleman, "Reconsidering 'Limited Inerrancy,'" *Journal of the Evangelical Theological Society,* vol. XVII, no. 4 (Fall, 1974); Daniel P. Fuller, "The Nature of Biblical Inerrancy," *Journal of the American Scientific Affiliation* (June, 1972); Fuller, "On Revelation and Biblical Authority," *Journal of the Evangelical Theological Society,* vol. XVI, no. 2 (Spring, 1973); and Stephen T. Davis, *The Debate About the Bible* (Philadelphia: Westminster, 1977), pp. 37ff.

[10]See Nash, *The New Evangelicalism,* ch. 5, esp. pp. 75–77. Evangelical qualifications of inerrancy differ somewhat but generally agree with Warfield that the distinction must be drawn between "proved errors" and "difficulties," and that those which do exist are inconsequential. For illustration see Tenney, ed., *The Bible—The Living Word . . . ,* pp. 104–105, 152ff.; René Pache, *The Inspiration and Authority of Scripture,* trans. Helen I. Needham (Chicago: Moody, 1969), pp. 123ff.; and the not atypical ambiguous conclusion of Klaas Runia, "What Do Evangelicals Believe about the Bible?" *Christianity Today,* Dec. 18, 1970, pp. 8–10.

In 1965 *Christianity Today* reported that, judging by the response of 112 members of the Evangelical Theological Society, 2 out of 3 evangelical scholars considered biblical authority to be the crucial theological question. Yet the inner tension between upholding a high view of Scripture and doing justice to the historical-human dimension of the Bible is apparent in the collection of articles in Henry, ed., *Revelation and the Bible;* and Tenney, ed., *The Bible—The Living Word . . . ,* a publication of the Evangelical Theological Society, an organization which subscribes to the doctrine of inerrancy.

exegetes but a general swing of the pendulum among liberal critics. There is no doubt that early proponents of historical criticism overextended themselves by claiming too much for their method and their results. Consequently, liberals are experiencing in their own time a cautious mood among scholars who are more likely to reaffirm traditional conclusions. We see the emergence of vigorous, post-Bultmann alternatives in Germany, a salvation school and a Pannenberg school across Europe, an Uppsala school of Scandinavian scholars, and a growing evangelical influence in America and England. One of the distinctive characteristics of this period, and liberalism in general, is the willingness to utilize research solely on the basis of its merit. Indeed, it is increasingly difficult to separate a conservative liberal, like Joachim Jeremias, from a liberal-minded evangelical, like George Ladd. Yet, as fine as the dividing line becomes, there are still some basic differences.

While Warfield began exegesis believing the preponderance of evidence was in favor of inerrancy and verbal inspiration, the liberal begins exegesis believing the weight of evidence has shifted against Warfield. The one assured effect of a hundred years of biblical criticism has been to call into question the supernatural marks which would lead us to place implicit trust in the biblical words. Historical and literary criticism as well as textual and comparative studies into the language and cultural background of the Bible pointed away from the "heavenliness of the matter." Archeology began to unearth a wealth of discoveries that lessened, not heightened, the uniqueness of Scripture. From the masses of tablets and papyri it became clear that other cultures knew of covenant treaties similar in language and form, codified laws containing exact parallels to biblical texts, a complex ritual pattern resembling the Hebrew celebrations, and even a comparable flood story. In addition, source criticism began to uncover the seams that held together the various strands of traditions. An explanation had to be given, for example, for striking and undistributed alteration of vocabulary (e.g., "Elohim" and "Jahweh"), change of style within what was thought to be the work of one author (e.g., the Pentateuch and Ephesians), change of point of view within a book (e.g., Isaiah I and II), repetitions (e.g., in the

Synoptics), and logical digression (e.g., II Corinthians 6:14–7:1).[11] Not only did it seem impossible for the individual books to be the work of a single author, but questions began to be asked about authenticity, date, and place of writing. Redaction criticism went a step further and sought to find how and why each author (redactor) shaped and colored his material.

The doctrinal verses which conservatives called upon for support were dismissed because they were themselves conditioned by the author's own time. When the prophet wrote, "Thus says the Lord," he was claiming to speak in the name of Yahweh much as a preacher today speaks in the name of Christ, not to transmit the very words of God. His prophecies were not predictions about the future but warnings of the assured consequence if men did not change their ways. The verses in the New Testament thought to assert verbal inspiration were seen as a late development in the early church as it sought to protect its faith from error.

By exposing a diversity of theological perspectives within Scripture itself, historical criticism simultaneously cast a shadow over the organic unity of the Bible and the "system" of doctrine taught by its authors. It appeared that each strand, each tradition, emanated from a different historical and geographical setting and expressed a particular point of view. The creation account in Genesis 1–2:4a is set against a background of watery chaos (water is a threat to creation), portrays a creation in seven majestic days, and emphasizes the creation of the heavens; while the second account in Genesis 2:4bff. is set against a background of dry desert (water is an assisting element), speaks of "the day" that the Lord God made, and lays the primary emphasis on the earth in which man is placed.[12] The style of the unknown Yahwistic writer is full of joyful confidence and concerns itself with God's selection and promises to Abraham; it stands in relief against the style of the writer of Deuteronomy with his formal phrases, cultic

[11] *The Interpreter's Dictionary of the Bible* (New York: Abingdon, 1962), vol. I, p. 412.

[12] For an evangelical interpretation of how the two creation accounts are really the same continuous account, see Pache, *The Inspiration and Authority of Scripture*, pp. 148–149; Tenney, ed., *The Bible—The Living Word...*, pp. 114–115.

flavor, and view of the history of Israel in terms of her obedience and disobedience to the law. Where is the unity between a first Isaiah of Jerusalem in the eighth century and a second Isaiah of the sixth century who knows of an already devastated Jerusalem? Nor can the letter of James in the New Testament be easily harmonized with Paul's letter to the Romans, nor the order of events in Paul's life as reported in Acts with his own account in Galatians.

Thus when the liberal speaks of unity he has in mind the unity of a multitude of witnesses joined together only in their confession to the one God working out his purpose in their midst. Uniformity of ideas and words was never an ideal. On the contrary, Ernst Käsemann says, the diversity of theological positions in the New Testament becomes the basis for the profusion of church denominations. One needs only to be aware that each sect and ecclesiastical body claims scriptural validity.[13] To make each part of Scripture agree with every other part would be to impose a static unity and submerge the variety, change, even disagreements and discrepancies that abound. It is simply not in character with the *nature* of the Bible to expect it to present a system of rational, doctrinal abstractions.

Historical criticism was born and nursed as a reaction to a doctrine of Scripture that externalized the divinity of Scripture, as though its inspiration were immediately evident and demonstrable to every open-minded Christian. Its spotlight brought out the Bible's human character by highlighting every line and blemish and even the slightest stutter in the voices of its authors.[14] While evangelicals work from a heritage that stresses the Bible's uniqueness, the liberal works from a heritage that finds the Bible to be essentially a historical document written by men who were wholly human in all they wrote. At times it has appeared that the choice must be between a human book in which the divine element is minimized and a divine book in which the

[13]Ernst Käsemann, "The Canon of the New Testament and the Unity of the Church," *Essays on New Testament Themes* ("Studies in Biblical Theology, No. 41"; Naperville, Ill.: Allenson, 1964), pp. 95–107 (esp. p. 103); Käsemann, *New Testament Questions of Today*, p. 275.

[14]James D. Smart, *The Interpretation of Scripture* (Philadelphia: Westminster, 1961), p. 164.

human element is reduced to naught. If the logical conclusion of this alternative is carried through, we would have either a mere record of man's nobler thoughts or the deposit of God's revelation inscribed word by word by unknowing men. Liberals and evangelicals are agreed in principle, however, that this would be a false conclusion, because the real paradox is how the words of men can be at the same time the words of God.

LIMITS TO HISTORICAL CRITICISM

Most of us can remember the time when liberals and evangelicals were separated by their acceptance or rejection of a critical-historical approach to the Bible. It is now only a common misconception that liberals accept the method and its conclusions without reservations and that evangelicals do not recognize the validity of critical analysis. Even the hardened skeptic has come to depend upon the dictionaries, atlases, grammars, critical texts of the Old and New Testaments, and general introductions, all of which are products of historical criticism. George Ladd, who urges that a positive approach to biblical criticism be taken by those who acknowledge Scripture to be the Word of God, describes historical criticism in this way:

> To be a critic means merely to ask questions about the authorship, date, place, sources, purpose, and so on, of any ancient literary work. The opposite of a properly "critical" approach to the study of the Bible is, therefore, an unthinking, unquestioning acceptance of tradition. To be non-critical means simply to ignore altogether the historical dimension of the Bible and to view it as a magical book.[15]

The common conclusion is that since the Bible has come to us through historical events, persons, and situations, it is possible by asking critical questions to better understand the historical process by which Scripture came to be written down.

In theory the liberal places no limits on a critical-historical

[15]George E. Ladd, *The New Testament and Criticism* (Grand Rapids: Eerdmans, 1967), p. 38; also Pache, *The Inspiration and Authority of Scripture*, pp. 248–250.

study of the Bible—to do so would be like asking a scientist to reject any evidence which does not agree with his assumptions. Yet one of the significant developments within liberal theology has been the recognition that complete objectivity is impossible. One of the most radical critics, Rudolf Bultmann, has declared that exegesis without presuppositions is impossible.[16] Bultmann insisted that presuppositionless exegesis is not even desirable, because Scripture will only come alive as you ask it specific kinds of questions which arise out of your personal concerns. It is better to understand and be conscious of the presuppositions you are bringing to a text, for you are more likely then to know if they are being rèad into your interpretation. On the other hand, we will never get a fair and unprejudiced interpretation if we go to the text with some rigid, preconceived pattern of thought. Objectivity, the liberal believes, is possible only insofar as we allow our presuppositions to be corrected by the text.

A growing consensus among liberals claims that too much confidence has been placed in the critical-historical method. In the late nineteenth century and the early 1900s, liberals believed the critical-historical method could lay bare the "objective" facts of history and that these facts would be sufficient to insure the future of Christianity. As the century progressed, it became increasingly clear that the exegete could not separate the objective from the subjective because the two were woven into the very events themselves, and what facts or conclusions they were able to excavate were sterile and subject to constant revision. Gerhard Maier proves to be a harsh critic of historical criticism, but liberals are essentially finding themselves in agreement with him when he writes:

> The subtle net woven by the higher-critical method resulted in a new Babylonian captivity of the church. It became more and more isolated from the living stream of biblical proclamation, and more and more uncertain and blind both as to its own course and also in relation to its influence toward the outside.[17]

[16]Rudolf Bultmann, "Is Exegesis without Presuppositions Possible?" *Existence and Faith* (Cleveland: World, 1960), pp. 289–296.

[17]Gerhard Maier, *The End of the Historical-Critical Method,* trans. Edwin W. Leveranz and Rudolf F. Norden (St. Louis: Concordia, 1977), p. 48.

While Maier wants to substitute a "historical-biblical" method for the historical-critical method, a substitution that involves limiting the critical role of exegesis, liberal scholars feel the answer is not a simple elimination. Walter Wink, James Smart, and Peter Stuhlmacher concur that the critical process is of more value than the results it produces; and its value lies in the fact that it serves to "distance" the interpreter from the text. They would remind Maier that one must first be made aware how foreign the biblical witness is before we recognize that our own identity is tied up in those stories of old. The critical method not only keeps us honest, it probes every question to its depths. According to Smart, the critical-historical method serves to expose "both conscious and unconscious dishonesties in the church's interpretation of Scripture that rob the church's voice of its integrity, and it sets a standard of honesty that is bound to affect every aspect of the church's life."[18] What these three liberal thinkers are driving at is the necessity of maintaining a critical stance in the interpretation of Scripture in order to hear its original voice, but at the same time recognizing that its conclusions are only tentative because this method is a fallible tool in the hands of humans. A "historical-biblical" method sounds just great, but the liberal wonders if the conservative is not finding another way to smuggle in dogmatic prejudices that might prevent the text from being understood on its own terms.

The evangelical would not deny that he also approaches Scripture with a set of presuppositions. The difference, however, is that he states frankly that these presuppositions limit the role and the results of the critical-historical method. The evangelical is careful to make his position clear so as not to give the impression that he is hostile towards science or nonscientific in his study of the Bible. Yet there are several reasons why he believes there is a proper and an improper critical-historical method. First, we can misuse the critical-historical method by regarding science as

[18]James Smart, *The Cultural Subversion of the Biblical Faith* (Philadelphia: Westminster, 1977), p. 87. Similarly, Peter Stuhlmacher, *Historical Criticism and Theological Interpretation of Scripture*, trans. Roy A. Harrisville (Philadelphia: Fortress, 1975), pp. 62ff.; and Walter Wink, *The Bible in Human Transformation* (Philadelphia: Fortress, 1973), pp. 26ff. and 53ff.

inflexible. Certainly the scientific method is not applied in the same way in psychology and sociology as in astrophysics and computer programming. Nowhere is this general principle clearer than in our study of Scripture. If the Bible were a purely historical book then a purely historical method would be appropriate, but since faith and history, supernatural and natural, are intertwined the historical method must be adapted. H. N. Ridderbos amplifies in terms of the New Testament:

> The New Testament can be correctly approached by science only when the latter recognizes that the witness of Scripture . . . is the witness of the Holy Spirit and that any infringement upon this aspect of this witness, on the part of science, results in a faulty appraisal of the object under study, and the truly scientific approach is thereby lost.[19]

For example, science would not only be overstepping its bounds but seriously misunderstanding the witness of Scripture if it tried to pass final judgment on the mighty acts of God in the Old Testament or the resurrection of Jesus Christ. When George Ladd suggests the term "historical-theological criticism," he indicates clearly the evangelical position that historical conclusions cannot be completely divorced from theological propositions.[20]

Second, revealed knowledge, not scientific knowledge, provides the overarching world view in which the smaller details of history and science will find their place. Historical criticism must play a subsidiary, or helping role; otherwise the historical and doctrinal foundations of Christianity could be swallowed up by the onslaught of an unbelieving biblical criticism. In other words, the authority of science is not all-inclusive, for there are many matters of faith which it can neither prove nor disprove.

Third, the past has taught us to be more careful to distinguish between fact and theory. The tendency has been to accept as fact what later turns out to be only a theory, and still later proves to be a false theory. Too often premise is translated into proposition to be translated into certainty. The evangelical feels

[19]Herman N. Ridderbos, *The Authority of the New Testament Scriptures*, trans. H. De Jongste (Grand Rapids: Baker, 1963), p. 66.

[20]Ladd, *The New Testament and Criticism*, p. 40.

he need only point to the recent swing back to an early date for the book of John, renewed confidence in a discernible Jesus of Nazareth behind the gospel accounts, acceptance of the basic historicity of the Abraham narratives, and the trustworthiness of the Old and New Testament texts which was demonstrated by the Dead Sea Scrolls. Critical conclusions are as fallible as the men who posit them.

Fourth, as we saw in Chapter III, evangelicals are committed to a doctrine of revelation that demands a word-event complex. God acts and God speaks, and the two testify to each other. One problem with historical criticism is its disposition toward isolating God's word from his deed, so that we have either a purely historical event separated from its divine interpretation or a purely spiritual, existential interpretation separated from its objective happening. The inadequacy of this method is that it does not respect the inextricable pattern of history and faith, event and interpretation, that constitutes the uniqueness of the biblical word.

The liberal sincerely believed the critical-historical method would free exegesis from the rigid dogmaticism of orthodoxy. It did achieve this limited goal, but in the process biblical interpretation became subjugated to a new set of liberal presuppositions. Critical analysis and form criticism became so alloyed with principles of a philosophical or theological nature that history was closed off to divine intervention, miracles and prophecies were inadmissible, faith was so defined as to be indifferent or even incompatible with historical truth, and the creative faith of the community was given priority over the faithful witness of the apostles.[21] Liberals have shown an increasing awareness of how the critical-historical method acted to establish certain boundaries over which the text dare not climb.

On the other hand, conservatives sincerely believed a starting point of verbal inspiration and inerrancy would guarantee the authenticity of the biblical testimony. The interpreter begins his exegesis with an admirable attitude of reverence and respect for the written word, but that is not enough. James Barr has ex-

[21]A similar movement and recognition has occurred within the Roman Catholic Church. A position paper of the Pontifical Biblical Commission states these dangers.

posed a sensitive nerve when he coins the phrase "maximal conservatism."[22] In the past, the conservative interpreter approached the text dogmatically, that is, the first five books of the Old Testament were written by Moses, the psalms by David, all of Isaiah by Isaiah, the Gospels by the apostles, etc. More recently, Barr explains, dogmatic arguments are being replaced by a maximal-conservative one. The approach here is akin to a linear scale ranging from radical to maximal-conservative. The commentator begins by considering evidence or data revealed by the critical-historical method and then chooses or weights the evidence in favor of the most conservative position.

As Barr points out, the dogmatic approach to biblical interpretation has to work exactly, or it does not work at all. Evangelicals are increasingly trying to make their voices heard through scholarship rather than through purely dogmatic assertions. Thus we have evangelicals in the ambivalent situation of widely accepting the four-source theory of the Gospels but rejecting the documentary hypothesis for the Pentateuch, or accepting a late date for some of the psalms but standing firm on the Pauline authorship of all the epistles attributed to him. Once the dogmatic approach is given up in favor of a maximal-conservative one, there are bound to be inconsistencies. Yet, it must be recognized that even a hermeneutic formed entirely by a doctrine of infallibility must allow for certain qualifications.[23] The issue, therefore, becomes not whether certain qualifications to dogmatic norms will be allowed, but how far and what kind of qualifications will be permitted.

Barr's major criticism is that evangelicals are not consistent. Either they should acknowledge source criticism as a legitimate solution to some of the conflicts posed by the text or reject all such proposals. If the interpreter only "pretends" to exegete the

[22]James Barr, *Fundamentalism* (Philadelphia: Fortress, 1977), p. 85.

[23]I have in mind not only the usual qualifications concerning the requirement to have the reading of the "original" autographs or literal interpretations where they would be absurd, but a wide range of qualifications permitted by all evangelical scholars except the most fundamentalist. See Richard J. Coleman, "Another View: The Battle for the Bible," *Journal of the American Scientific Affiliation* (June, 1979).

passage historically and critically while concealing his or her maximal-conservative bias, this leads us to question the honesty of the interpreter. Clearly the inductive method is being given lip service only. But even more important and fundamental: is biblical interpretation being *guided* by dogmatic presuppositions or *ruled* by them? Conservative scholarship wants us to believe that theological norms do not affect the interpreter's reading of Scripture because the presuppositions are inherent in the text itself. What we have is not only a circular argument, but a hermeneutical circle that does not allow the text to speak its own word. The critical-historical method is not given a fair chance to assist the interpreter to penetrate behind and beyond the literal meaning of the text. The method itself simply becomes another pawn in the hands of dogmatic presuppositions.

THE NATURE AND ORIGIN OF THE BIBLE

When you probe beneath the commentaries and general introductions written by evangelicals and liberals, there come to light a number of contrasting positions concerning the nature and origin of Scripture. By no means are the contrasts absolute, but they do reflect significant differences in emphasis.

(1) *Oral vs. Written*. The most obvious contrasts appear when we inquire into the origin of the Pentateuch and the Gospels. The more conservative evangelical accepts the traditional view that Moses wrote the first five books of the Old Testament and the disciples and other eyewitnesses wrote the Gospels. There is, however, a growing acceptance of the critical view that behind the written accounts stands an oral stage of transmission. The liberal gives a greater significance to the oral period. Not only does he assume that a longer time span was involved in which traditions were passed on by word of mouth, but he sees this period as having been dynamic and formative.

In the case of the Old Testament separate oral traditions were in existence for centuries. Different traditions grew up and coalesced around certain heroic figures like Moses, Joshua, and David and around certain cultic centers like Bethel, Shiloh, and Hebron. According to the specific "life situation," each tradition received a particular stamp—the enthronement festival giving rise to the royal psalms, the conquest of Canaan giving birth to the battle songs (e.g., I Samuel 18:7). Definite forms developed which gave shape to previously independent and formless traditions, such as popular stories (David and Goliath), myths (the serpent in the Garden of Paradise), and historical narrative (I Samuel 13–14). In time, basic motifs emerged—the election of Israel, Exodus, law-giving—around which freely circulating traditions clustered. Almost simultaneously, external destruction from the foreign nations precipitated the collection and writing down of oral traditions. The final step was that of a redactor or author who put the written document or documents into the final form we find in the Bible. Throughout, a continual process of selection was at work, for no community preserves a tradition that it no longer finds useful for its own self-understanding.

In the New Testament the same basic process was operative but was telescoped into a shorter period. The life of Jesus was neither written down immediately nor passed along orally as a connected whole (with the possible exception of the Passion narrative). Rather, traditions about Jesus were preserved in smaller individual units such as sayings, short stories, parables, teachings, legends, and liturgical pieces. As in the Old Testament a final author collected and shaped the various traditions into a coherent whole.

Basic, then, to the liberal's understanding of the origin of the Bible is the conclusion that the different writers did not see themselves as reporters anxious to record in writing what they heard and saw. The idea of the importance of the written word over the oral or spoken word was foreign to them and appeared only later. The biblical writers were first and last theologians and preachers concerned with transmitting an oral tradition that preserved their identity as God's chosen people.

In evangelical theology the written word has primacy over the oral. The evangelical cites archeological evidence that writing was known in the time of Moses. He disputes the argument that the biblical writers were not concerned to preserve an accurate account of what took place. The early church, for instance, preserved the record of Jesus' life not only because it was useful but also because of an interest in Jesus himself. The oral period was not as long as the liberal thinks. We know of many examples from the Near East of cultures that wrote down their traditions while they were still flourishing in oral form. And insofar as an oral stage existed, the evangelical emphasizes the reliability of ancient people to preserve unchanged material passed on by word of mouth. There were numerous methods employed to insure accuracy, such as a monotonous style, recurrent expressions, and a certain rhythm and euphony. The rabbinic way of life was also committed to transmitting the exact wording as well as the exact thought: "Everyone who forgets a word of Scripture accounts to him as if he has forfeited his life." To safeguard the whole process only properly trained rabbis and pupils were permitted to pass down tradition.[24]

Clark H. Pinnock remarks that "Christianity was born a book-religion."[25] Although parts were transmitted orally, the natural disposition was to trust the written word, for only then could the sacred words be preserved from error and copied without limitation. The very fact that the sacred books were copied by hand over a period of three thousand years with such accuracy, as no book of man has ever been or ever will be, were subjected to all the catastrophes and captivities of Israel, and have survived so much persecution and destruction since the time of Christ is itself a testimony to God's concern for his word to be written.[26]

(2) *Freedom vs. Faithfulness.* The question of origin goes deeper than whether the Bible basically reflects an oral or a writ-

[24]For a conservative approach to the issues of memory, tradition, and transmission see Birger Gerhardsson, *Memory and Manuscript* (Uppsala, 1961); Harald Riesenfeld, *The Gospel Tradition and its Beginnings* (London: Mowbray, 1957); Eduard Nielsen, *Oral Tradition* ("Studies in Biblical Theology, No. 11"; London: SCM, 1954). For a liberal treatment of the same issues see Brevard S. Childs, *Memory and Tradition* ("Studies in Biblical Theology, No. 37"; Naperville, Ill.: Allenson, 1962); W. D. Davies, *The Setting of the Sermon on the Mount* (Cambridge: Cambridge Univ., 1964), pp. 464–480. Also see *Jesus and Scribal Authority* (Lund, Sweden: C. W. K. Gleerup, 1978), an interesting treatment by Stephen Westerholm, an evangelical scholar who studied under Birger Gerhardsson.

[25]Clark H. Pinnock, "The Inspiration of the New Testament," in Tenney, ed., *The Bible—The Living Word . . .* , p. 147.

[26]See Pache, *The Inspiration and Authority of Scripture*, p. 196, who quotes a fine passage from Louis Gaussen.

ten tradition. The deeper issue is the manner in which traditions were passed on and committed to writing. As the liberal studies the Bible he finds one characteristic to stand out, namely, a remarkable freedom to adapt and interpret tradition to changing circumstances and requirements. Gerhard von Rad explains both the reason for and the process of reinterpretation.

> Each generation was faced with the ever-identical yet ever-new task of understanding itself as Israel. Of course, as a rule the sons were able to recognise themselves in the picture handed on to them by the fathers. But still this did not exempt each generation from the task of comprehending itself in faith as the Israel of its own day. However, in this process of actualisation the tradition here and there had to be reshaped. Theological demands altered—thus, for example, the Elohist's idea of the saving history was brought in alongside the earlier one of the Jahwist. No generation produced a perfectly independent and finished historical work—each continued to work upon what had been handed down to it. . . . [27]

Respect for the past always kept the various authors from revising tradition in order to make it conform completely to their own ideas. The problem each generation faced was how to maintain continuity with the past and still freely interpret its new circumstances in God's light.

The authors were more than scissors-and-paste editors who artificially compiled material from diverse sources. They were men with distinctive personalities who employed a number of literary devices to achieve their particular purposes, such as abbreviation, unique emphasis, selective Old Testament passages, expansion, stylization, transportation of scenes, different settings, and catchword linkings.[28]

The freedom of the evangelists is clear in the Gospel of

[27]Gerhard von Rad, *Old Testament Theology*, trans. D. M. G. Stalker (New York: Harper, 1962), vol. I, p. 119.

[28]For specific illustrations of each see Joachim Jeremias, *The Parables of Jesus* (New York: Scribner's, 1963); Günther Bornkamm, Gerhard Barth, and Heinz J. Held, *Tradition and Interpretation in Matthew*, trans. Percy Scott (Philadelphia: Westminster, 1963).

John, for the author obviously did not attempt to relate the exact words of Jesus. Instead he demonstrated a high degree of creativity in reinterpreting the traditions about Jesus in order to bring out what he considered to be the truth of the good news. While it is not so clear on the surface, upon closer inspection Matthew and Luke show a similar freedom and originality in recasting material from Mark and blending it with their own peculiar sources. Matthew, for example, gathers together teaching material in chapters 5–7 so as to present Jesus as the Messiah in word, miracle narratives in chapters 8–9 to present him as the new Messiah in deed.[29] St. Paul, moreover, shows no compulsion to relate the words of Jesus and uses terminology so different that he has been accused of preaching a different gospel.

The liberal concludes from this evidence that the guiding principle was not preservation for the sake of preservation, but reinterpretation for the sake of witness to God. The church, like Israel, was plainly untroubled by differences in detail or emphasis in parallel traditions and certainly did not see them as errors or intolerable contradictions. Quite the opposite seems to be true, because there was a deep awareness that the mere transmission of bare facts does not, as such, establish historical continuity or a vital community. Unless it is freshly appropriated, revelation becomes a dead past unable to resurrect anything.

Most evangelicals go so far as to agree that the Old and New Testaments are the distillation of a larger body of materials after much reflection and present a combination of history and interpretation. But at the same time this admission does not imply that the authors presumed on their own initiative to alter or add to the material they had in order to improve the word of God. E. F. Harrison, for example, writes, "It should be granted that the gift of the Spirit made possible the element of interpretation woven into the fabric of history that constitutes the Gospel tradition, but this interpretive element simply draws out the implications of the history rather than imposing something new upon it."[30] The community of faith may have helped to shape traditions, but it

[29]See Bornkamm in *Tradition and Interpretation in Matthew*, pp. 246–253.

[30]Everett F. Harrison, "*Gemeindetheologie:* The Bane of Gospel Criticism," in Henry, ed., *Jesus of Nazareth . . .* , p. 164.

does not follow that the "life situation" played a decisive role in the actual content.

Although it is often overlooked by liberals, it is highly significant that the biblical authors were conscious of their own illumination and of the inspired nature of the material they were preserving. Their handling of tradition, whether oral or written, was guided by awareness that they spoke not for themselves but for God by the Holy Spirit (see Jeremiah 1:9; Isaiah 6:8; Ezekiel 3:1ff.; II Peter 1:20–21). Paul spoke and wrote with authority only because he was conscious of his apostolic calling "to make the word of God fully known" (Colossians 1:25; Galatians 1:11ff.). The biblical writers were faithful in what they received from God and what they transmitted for God, because they knew it was of God.

(3) *Theological vs. Historical.* According to the liberal, theological considerations were the controlling factor in preserving and interpreting history. The history of Jesus, like the history of Israel, is as much, if not more, the product of faith as the product of eyewitness reports. Ernst Käsemann may have summed up the liberal view when he said, "The Gospels offer us primarily the early Christian preaching about Jesus, and individual words and deeds of Jesus only as they are embedded in that preaching."[31] It was only after the resurrection that the disciples and followers of Jesus knew for certain he was the Messiah, and even then their concern was to proclaim him, not preserve him in the written word. Only as their vivid expectations of his early return began to fade (c. A.D. 60) did the written Gospels begin to take shape. But it was not a historical interest to record the words of Jesus that brought the Gospels into existence, but the theological concern to continue faith in Christ (John 20:31). It was a natural inclination to read their faith back into the original accounts. To heighten, abridge, enlarge, and reinterpret was regarded as not disrespectful but necessary to keep the memory of Christ alive. In this way the proclaimer became the proclaimed, and we today can only see the Jesus of history through the eyes of faith who knew him as Lord.

As a result the Bible reflects a topical order more than a

[31]Käsemann, "The Problem of the Historical Jesus," *Essays on New Testament Themes*, p. 34.

chronological sequence. The biblical critic asks why Matthew so thoroughly rearranged the events in the first part of Mark, and the only suitable answer he finds is that the author was not motivated to write a historical biography. The guiding question was not, "Is this the order of events as they actually happened?" but, "How best can I tell the story of Jesus so my Jewish audience will believe with me that he is the Savior?" As early as 1936 Lohmeyer drew attention to the interesting detail that Galilee is the sphere of redemption in Mark while Jerusalem is the center of the stage in John. Further research has shown that each author wrote from a particular theological viewpoint into which he arranged geographical and chronological information. Since then the growing consensus is that behind every nuance of emphasis, every variation in detail, lies a theological concern.[32]

The evangelical believes the liberal has reversed the priorities. Those who think theological concerns rather than historical interests predominated overlook five important points: the brief period of time which elapsed between the events and the record of the events, the role of eyewitnesses in preserving the tradition, the role of the authoritative apostolic witness, the role of the Holy Spirit, and Jesus' messianic consciousness.[33] If we accept the liberal view, then the creative influence of the authors, the church, and oral tradition has so overwhelmed the historical substratum with its own interpretation that we have no direct access to the historical facts.[34] But such a view seems to

[32]Among the most important books which seek to uncover the framework and theology behind the Gospels are Hans Conzelmann, *The Theology of St. Luke,* trans. Geoffrey Buswell (New York: Harper, 1961); Willi Marxsen, *Mark the Evangelist,* trans. James Boyce *et al.* (Nashville: Abingdon, 1969); James M. Robinson, Helmut Koester, *Trajectories Through Early Christianity* (Philadelphia: Fortress, 1971).

[33]Ladd, *The New Testament and Criticism,* p. 163. The fifth point is my own.

[34]Käsemann virtually says the historical is lost in the kerygmatic. See *Essays* . . . , p. 59: "It is thus quite impossible to extract from our Gospels anything resembling an historical sequence or even a biographical development and all efforts of this kind were, and remained, flights of fancy. Anything which could be used for such a purpose belongs to the later stage of tradition, and for the most part to the Evangelists' technique of composition. But of the individual sayings and stories . . . it was not historical but kerygmatic interest which handed them on." Cf. pp. 15, 20, 46, 61.

assume that all the eyewitnesses were taken out of the church at the time of the ascension of the Lord.[35] The role of the apostles, Jesus' own awareness of the need to provide for historical continuity with future generations, and the work of the Holy Spirit are all practically eliminated. Yet according to Scripture the authoritative witness to Jesus was transmitted through the historical memory of specially commissioned and divinely inspired apostles. W. D. Davies also reminds us that "there was frequent intercourse between figures such as Peter, and other apostolic guardians of the tradition, and Christian communities in various places, so that the transmission and development of the tradition was not unchecked."[36] If the church so readily projected back into the earliest accounts her Easter faith, then it seems odd that she would preserve traditions which were offensive, such as the open division between Jewish and Gentile Christians and between Paul and the apostles (especially Peter), Jesus' own reluctance to proclaim himself as the Messiah, and an apparent denial of the supernatural nature of Christ (the Son of God did not know the time of his return, Mark 13:32).[37] In conclusion the New Testament does not reflect a process by which the church transformed the man Jesus of Nazareth into a divine Savior but rather is a testimony to Jesus' transcendent power that transformed men.

MIRACLE, MYTH, AND DEMYTHOLOGIZING

Another critical issue dividing liberals and evangelicals is the legitimacy of demythologizing. The issue is much broader than it first appears because demythologizing becomes the pivotal point for the whole question of how to reinterpret the Bible for our age.

The liberal begins by defining myth not as a false story but as a way of thinking and speaking which represents a transcendent, unworldly action with immanent, this-worldly objectivity.[38] Mythical thinking acts like a mental projector which en-

[35]Vincent Taylor, *The Formation of the Gospel Tradition* (London: Macmillan, 1933), pp. 41ff.

[36]Davies, *The Setting of the Sermon on the Mount*, p. 417.

[37]Harrison in Henry, ed., *Jesus of Nazareth* . . . , pp. 165–169.

[38]James A. Sanders offers this definition of myth: "Myth, biblically speaking, is not fiction or fable, it is simply a way of telling the

larges a certain inner understanding so it may be seen by everyone. The mythological conception of Satan as a supernatural person projects a visual picture that expresses the universal feeling of a power of evil which is greater than any of us. When myth becomes the language of faith it presents an action of God, whether in history or in the inner life of a person, as an act which intervenes in the natural course of events; it breaks the links of cause and effect, while the divine cause is inserted. The temptation of Christ is mythical in its conceptualization not only because it assumes a prescientific picture of the world, but also because the author has raised what was an inner human struggle to a visible encounter between the power of evil and good.

From a liberal perspective the fact that the biblical writers shared the mythological thinking of their age, much as we share a secular scientific way of thinking, does not necessarily mean the events did not actually happen. It does mean, though, that the biblical authors were not as concerned as we are today with historical factualness or scientific proof. The biblical writers shared a world view that did not make a sharp distinction between natural and supernatural, fact and fancy, scientific and miraculous. Consequently, causality simply was not defined as rigidly as we define it. For ancient man the power of divinity might do what is impossible for men but not what is intrinsically impossible. It aroused astonishment, shock, and horror but did not break any known natural laws. Miracle stories were pressed into use precisely because they served as objective proofs of divine activity. The transformation of the extraordinary into the impossible was therefore a much shorter step for biblical writers, and even a means to give added glory to the God who brought Israel out of Egypt and raised Jesus from the dead.[39]

While myths and miracles once made faith in a divine power easier, the opposite is true today. The very same biblical

---

truth, even that which 'no eye has seen, nor ear heard, nor the heart of man conceived.'" See his excellent article in *Radical Theology: Phase Two,* ed. Christian and Wittig (Philadelphia: J. B. Lippincott, 1967); and the commendable treatment of Brevard S. Childs, *Myth and Reality in the Old Testament* ("Studies in Biblical Theology, No. 27"; London: SCM, 1960).

[39]Käsemann, "Is the Gospel Objective?" *Essays . . .* , pp. 48–54.

myths and miracles make sincere belief more difficult in a scientific age. The language of myths and miracles has the added disadvantage of tending to detract from the real meaning of a revelatory event by focusing attention on the outward appearance. The evangelists themselves saw the danger of a faith that depended upon objective proofs or manifestations (Mark 8:11–12; John 6:26ff.). The liberal thus senses the need and the possibility of peeling off the outer mythical framework and keeping the inner significance for human life. Demythologizing is the method whereby mythical statements are translated into existential statements, i.e., statements directly concerning one's self-understanding. When the method of demythologizing is extended to include all biblical statements which are meaningless because of their language, it is known as existential interpretation.

The interesting aspect of existential interpretation is its avowed lack of concern about the factual content of a story it seeks to translate into a possibility for a new self-understanding. Existential interpretation does not in itself deny the factual content but simply pays little attention to that content. The question of historicity is no longer raised. We are not asking about what happened but about what the story or miracle is saying to our situation now. Whether we deny or affirm the objective reference or suspend judgment about it, the existential significance remains quite unaffected.[40] It is very possible, believes the liberal, to ask the wrong kind of question of the Bible, such as, "Did this really happen?" and thereby distort or sidetrack the real meaning. The kind of question which is appropriate is a question about human existence. No doubt the Bible does contain statements of historical fact, and there may be a proper time to inquire about these facts. But just as surely the general intention of the Bible is not to provide the reader with certain facts but to lead him to accept Jesus as his Lord.

The evangelical has three principal objections to the liberal program of demythologizing and existential interpretation. First, he rejects the liberal assumptions that God never revealed him-

[40]John Macquarrie, *The Scope of Demythologizing* (London: SCM, 1960), pp. 19, 39.

self objectively in the past and that faith today is uninterested in the historical actuality of saving events. To define myth as an outdated mode of representation is to forget that the heart of biblical Christianity is what God did objectively, not subjectively in the hearts of men. Moses did not just sense he was being called to return to Egypt but saw a burning bush and heard the voice of the Lord (Exodus 3:1ff.). The evangelical asks, "How does the liberal know God's supernatural reality did not impinge upon and break through the natural order?" Isn't it to be expected that miraculous signs would attend God's self-revelations?

Secondly, evangelicals reject the idea that the existential (theological) meaning of what happened can be divorced from what actually occurred. Along with John Macquarrie, they ask: "Just how irrelevant can the factual content of the gospel become without its ceasing to be a gospel?"[41] What meaning, for instance, does the statement, "Jesus died for our sins," have apart from the objective suffering of Christ on the cross; or the statement, "Jesus rose that we too might be raised," apart from the objective fact of Jesus' resurrection? Would we be justified in believing God elected Israel to be his special people without trusting the record of the Exodus and their deliverance from the Egyptians at the Red Sea? Unlike some modern theology, the Bible does not separate that which is spiritually true from that which is literally false. Quite the contrary, says John W. Montgomery; "History and theology are painfully intertwined."[42]

Thirdly, the liberal is mistaken in thinking that demythologizing can strip away the pictorial representations without distorting the primary words and basic concepts of the biblical writers. For example, the pictorial description of the Fall of Adam and Eve cannot be stripped away from the doctrine of original sin, because if Adam and Eve are simply fictional characters, then the biblical truth about sin would rest upon a hy-

[41] *Ibid.*, p. 20.

[42] John W. Montgomery, "Remythologizing Christmas," *Christianity Today*, Dec. 20, 1968, p. 4. Helmut Thielicke takes a moderating position between a purely existential interpretation of myth and a purely historical one that does not recognize the transcendent quality of mythological projection. See Thielicke, *The Evangelical Faith*, vol. I, trans. Geoffrey Bromiley (Grand Rapids: Eerdmans, 1974), pp. 66ff.

pothesis, not an actual event. Certainly there are many passages in the Psalms, the Song of Solomon, and the Prophets, as well as in the parables and the book of Revelation, whose language is obviously symbolic. Likewise, there are numerous stories that are cast into a pre-Copernican framework. In these cases the evangelical grants that a limited kind of existential interpretation may be possible. The Genesis view of the heavens holding back the chaos of water, for example, is a descriptive detail, nonessential to the author's purpose of proclaiming the divine nature of creation. The decisive difference, however, is that in this case the means of expression can be reinterpreted without affecting the religious substance.

As the liberal sees it, the real task of theology is to reinterpret and recast the language and thought forms of the Bible, but as the evangelical sees it, the task of theology is to reiterate the biblical message in new terms without changing the fundamental concepts and categories of the authors. One says modern man will not listen to the gospel until its form is radically changed, while the other says the true gospel cannot be preached if the biblical form is radically altered.

INSPIRATION

Running through almost every evangelical and liberal statement is an implied understanding of inspiration, which we will discuss now, and authority, to which we will turn our attention next. In the future, as in the past, the sharpest objections will be raised over these two issues. It will be doubly important, therefore, to express ourselves accurately and clearly on these areas.

By now evangelicals are tired of explaining that they do not believe in, and never have accepted, a theory of mechanical inspiration whereby God dictated every word in the Bible to wholly passive scribes. Such a doctrine would only deny the human character of Scripture and annul the individuality of its authors. What the evangelical does claim to hold fast to is a doctrine of plenary and verbal inspiration. The former signifies that "all the books of Scripture are equally inspired and inspiration extends to all the contents of these several books," in the words of Charles

Hodge. Verbal inspiration asserts that the writer's words as well as his thoughts were "breathed out by God." Verbal inspiration is the necessary corollary to conceptual inspiration, since the right thought cannot be expressed without the right words. What sense would it make to say the thoughts are of God but the words are only those of men? Put succinctly, inspiration is "the determining influence exercised by the Holy Spirit on the writers of the Old and New Testaments in order that they might proclaim and set down in an exact and authentic way the message as received from God."[43]

A few distinctions are necessary to understand fully what the evangelical believes about inspiration. The evangelical says the Bible is the Word of God or contains the Word of God. He does not mean that every word in Scripture came directly from God, because there are words of false prophets and words contrary to God's love; "yet they are inspired as being in the Bible, not in the sense that God uttered them, but in the sense that God caused them to be recorded infallibly, inerrantly, and for our profit."[44] The evangelical also does not say that Scripture contains the full revelation of God, because Jesus Christ was the only complete revelation of God and, secondly, because God's special revelation was prior to and broader in scope than what was written down. The Bible is, however, the fully *adequate* expression of God's will and mind, though it is not a full expression.

The evangelical position is clearly distinguished from the liberal position, which states the Bible is the human witness to divine revelation. If Scripture were only a witness to revelation, then it could not be revelation itself, and therefore could not be the Word of God. The biblical writers were witnesses to revelation, the evangelical agrees, but their writings became more than a mere witness when the Holy Spirit guided their writing. Paul reports that there were more than five hundred witnesses to Jesus' resurrection (I Corinthians 15:6), but not all of them became authors of Scripture, nor did all the apostles write Scripture. Undoubtedly in the history of salvation many men were enlightened and achieved great moral insight. The church also re-

[43]Pache, *The Inspiration and Authority of Scripture*, p. 45.

[44]W. A. Criswell, *Why I Preach That the Bible Is Literally True* (Nashville: Broadman, 1969), p. 66.

cords a long history of such saints. But enlightenment and inspiration cannot be equated here, for the latter is not a human quality. Inspiration is rather a divine activity which involves men as a means to an end but which actually terminates not with them but in what they write.[45] In the words of Warfield, "The Biblical writers are inspired . . . *so that the product of this activity* transcends human powers and becomes Divinely authoritative" (italics mine).

The evangelical understanding of inspiration is outwardly satisfying and filled with confidence, but the liberal believes he detects a host of inner inconsistencies and difficulties. The evangelical's explanation of inspiration is that while the biblical writers were "guided" and "controlled" by the Holy Spirit, they were yet free to choose their own words. For instance, J. I. Packer writes in reference to the inspiration of the prophets: ". . . whereby, having made God's message known to them, the Holy Spirit *so overruled all their subsequent mental activity* in giving the message poetic and literary form that each resultant oracle was as truly a divine utterance as a human, as direct a disclosure of what was in God's mind as of what was in the prophet's" (italics mine).[46] The liberal asks how the biblical writers could be so overruled by the Holy Spirit as to record the very message God intended and yet be permitted the exercise of their own personalities and literary talents. It would seem that either the authors chose their own words to record God's message, or the Holy Spirit chose just the right words for them, but not both. How can words be selected concurrently by both the divine Author and the human authors, as the evangelical argues? The liberal understands perfectly why the evangelical must so often plead ignorance or posit a "psychological mystery" at this point.

The crux of verbal inspiration is that there is a limit to how words can be arranged, substituted, or altered if they are to express the exact message God intended to give to man. Not just any words will do if Scripture is to be the Word of God. To uphold the doctrine of verbal inspiration the evangelical must

[45]J. I. Packer, *"Fundamentalism" and the Word of God* (London: Inter-Varsity Fellowship, 1958), p. 78.

[46]J. I. Packer, *God Speaks to Man* (Philadelphia: Westminster, 1965), p. 67.

therefore insist that the Holy Spirit did indeed limit the freedom of the biblical writers. But that in turn raises the question of why there is such a wide diversity in style, language, and thought form throughout the Bible. At least from where the liberal stands, it appears the biblical writers were freer than most evangelicals are willing to admit and, further, that the writers were not so much "controlled" and "overruled" as they were "filled" and "infused" with the Holy Spirit.

Part of the problem in defining the evangelical's understanding of verbal inspiration is his own imprecision in stating whether the Bible is the adequate, the fully sufficient, or the perfect expression of God's revelation. Whether Warfield began or perpetuated this confusion is hard to say, but it is certain that he promoted it. In his classic definition of the Bible as the Word of God he says the biblical writers were "under such an influence of the Holy Ghost" as to give "the adequate expression of His mind and will." Yet in the next sentence he claims this means the Bible is preserved "from everything inconsistent with a divine authorship—thus securing, among other strange things, that entire truthfulness which is everywhere presupposed in and asserted for Scripture by the Biblical writers."[47] So Scripture is at once the infallible record of God's special revelation and simply the adequate expression of God's mind. It is one matter for the evangelical to claim that inspiration secures "an adequate, authentic, and sufficient vehicle of special revelation,"[48] and another to claim that the Holy Spirit secures a product that is "in every word of the original documents a perfect and errorless recording of the exact message which God desired to give to men."[49] We are thus back to the same question of how inerrant the Bible must be to be the final authority in all matters of faith and doctrine. Can the evangelical allow the possible omission of a letter in the transmission of the original text, occasional differences in incidental details in the Gospels, lack of precision in the chronology of historical events in the books of Kings and Chronicles, a prescientific description of the world, and inconsistency in the

[47] Warfield, *The Inspiration and Authority of the Bible*, p. 173.

[48] Ramm, *Special Revelation . . .* , p. 179.

[49] Frank E. Gaebelein, *The Meaning of Inspiration*, quoted in Pache, *The Inspiration and Authority of Scripture*, p. 71.

narratives relating the baptism of Christ? He might claim that the division comes when we move from minor, understandable errors to gross, intolerable errors; but who is to decide which is which except the individual? One of the demanding questions the liberal places before the evangelical is whether verbal inspiration necessitates *infallibility* on any matter, or whether it is sufficient to believe in a verbal form of revelation that is *trustworthy* for our salvation.

The liberal carries his critique one step further when he questions how the word and thought forms of the biblical writers could be "culturally conditioned" and still be inerrant and verbally inspired.[50] Evangelicals readily admit that inspiration did not bestow on the writers a twentieth-century mind. Nor did inspiration serve to smuggle into the text a timeless world view. Rather, as Bernard Ramm emphasizes, "special revelation comes to a *particular* man, living in some *particular* culture, and speaking some *particular* language," and written in some *particular* literary form.[51] But the liberal questions, "How could the Holy Spirit use their language, their culture, their thoughts, their literary forms, and still produce a verbal record that cannot be transcended in any way?"

The evangelical also points out that God needed to accommodate his revelation so that it could enter our world and be understood.[52] On many occasions John Calvin spoke of the great condescension in which God lowered himself that he might be heard and understood. "Because our weakness cannot reach his height, any description which we receive of him must be lowered to our capacity in order to be intelligible. And the mode of lowering is to represent him not as he really is, but as we conceive of him."[53] Both Calvin and Ramm are saying that only partial, but

[50]Pinnock seems to hold both positions at once. See Tenney, ed., *The Bible—The Living Word*. . . , pp. 152, 159.

[51]Ramm, *Special Revelation*. . . , p. 63.

[52]*Ibid.*, pp. 65–66: "We only wish to assert that *revelation bends itself down, accommodates itself to our natures and worldly conditions, enters into our consciousness in a cosmic-mediated form, and comes to concrete expression in some oratorical or literary form current at the time of its entry into the world.*" Cf. Van Til, *A Christian Theory of Knowledge*, pp. 37–38.

[53]John Calvin, *Institutes of the Christian Religion*, I, xvii, 13. Also I, xiii, 1.

adequate, knowledge of God is given to man because it must always be mediated through human words and historical forms. Dutch theologian Abraham Kuyper also stresses the time-bound nature of revelation when he writes, "The 'spoken words,' however much aglow with the Holy Ghost, remain bound to the limitation of our language, disturbed as it is by anomalies."[54] The liberal again asks whether this does not challenge how revelation can take on historical forms, conditioned by time and culture, and still be given in words and concepts that are without error and wholly adequate (or perfect) in their representation of God and his message. The liberal finds this position to be an outright contradiction. The evangelical cannot escape compromising his position either by reneging on the doctrine of condescension or by claiming the biblical authors were given a reprieve from sin and time while they wrote the words of God. But neither solution accounts for the clear historical nature of the Bible, which the evangelical is willing to grant to an ever-increasing degree.

The liberal thus sees the evangelical reaction against the possibility of an existential interpretation as inconsistent. Does it really make sense to say the biblical writers chose from the vocabulary and ideas available at that particular time, and then to act as if these words and literary forms were not historically conditioned? The very development of more precise conceptualization and language through the ages argues against the proposition that certain words and ideas remain completely adequate. It is also unclear why these very expressions must be the best ones for our modern age. If concepts and pictorial representations are inseparably bound together, as the evangelical argues, then both are conditioned by time. Thus the liberal's criticism comes down to this: *How can Scripture be free from all scientific and historical error and be the fully sufficient expression of God's mind, and still be mediated through the words of men who were themselves conditioned by their own history?*

A final interesting point is that evangelicals and liberals agree that revelation is progressive by its very nature. Over the two thousand years in which Scripture was committed to writing

[54]Abraham Kuyper, *Principles of Sacred Theology*, trans. J. H. De-Vries (Grand Rapids: Eerdmans, 1954), p. 479.

God revealed himself with increasing clarity, culminating in Jesus Christ. This was necessary since God needed to treat humanity like a growing person, teaching him as much truth as he could comprehend at each stage of his growth. But if revelation is indeed a cumulative process,[55] then some expressions and conceptions of God are not as sufficient as others. The inescapable conclusion, the liberal thinks, is the admission that not all parts of Scripture are equally edifying, relevant, or necessary. The large sections of ceremonial law are not immediately useful, yet the evangelical has argued that God caused them to be recorded as he did every word in Scripture, for they, in an indirect way, prepared the way for Christ. The distinction must be made, then, between those texts and parts which directly witness to Christ and those which witness to Christ only indirectly, some very indirectly. It is this very distinction that led Martin Luther to declare that not everything in Scripture is gospel—some of it is obscure, outmoded, historical trappings and folklore. Nevertheless the evangelical has been strongly resistant to recognizing a canon within the canon. And the liberal also wonders why the evangelical is willing to recognize a historical development within the Bible concerning some matters, say from animal sacrifice to prophetic speech to Paul's doctrine of justification by faith, but not concerning matters such as the doctrine of God, say from henotheism to pure monotheism.[56]

Like the evangelical, the liberal appeals to Scripture for the key to the understanding of inspiration. The liberal does not cite any particular texts, but he does argue that the biblical writers give no hint that they saw themselves as adding more infallible words to an already infallible account of God's revelation. The prophets were prime examples of the freedom and independence so characteristic of the biblical authors. They knew full well they stood within a tradition in which a remembrance of God's words and actions was preserved. Yet never do they merely repeat their

[55]Packer prefers the word "cumulative" to "progressive" because it brings out the meaning that revelation was moving toward a particular point while not contradicting itself as each new disclosure presupposed and built upon what had gone before. See Packer, *God Speaks to Man*, p. 60.

[56]Cf. Pache, *The Inspiration and Authority of Scripture*, pp. 103–104.

words as though of themselves they were a completely adequate expression of God's message. It is notable that Jesus renewed this prophetic tradition. In comparison with the rabbis, Jesus seldom quoted the Old Testament in order to validate the truth of what he spoke. When his opponents tried to challenge his authority by quoting Scripture, Jesus countered by showing that he would not be bound by a literalistic interpretation of God's word. Obviously Paul did not see his own inspiration and authority as dependent upon parroting Jesus' words. Instead Paul caught the spirit of Jesus' teaching and felt free to preach the gospel in his own way. Without a doubt one of the main reasons why the Pharisees and scribes wanted to get rid of Jesus was his abrupt break with rabbinic tradition, just as Paul's freedom to interpret the life and teaching of Jesus became an affront to the legalism in the early church.

The liberal feels a close reading of the Bible will show that Scripture is itself an enemy of a static doctrine of inspiration. As James Smart says, "Its many parallel but differing documents are as obstacles thrown in the way by Providence to make literalism as difficult as possible for the Bible reader. A literalistic view can be maintained only by shutting the eyes to many of the plainly visible features of Scripture or by concocting lame apologies to explain away the contradictions."[57] The New Testament as a whole follows the Old Testament attitude toward the written words of God. What has been revealed and recorded was considered to be inspired and authoritative, but inspiration and authority were not equated with inerrancy. Otherwise the church would have never allowed the diversity in details we find in the accounts of Jesus' life and teaching. "A church in the bondage of literalism could never have admitted John's Gospel alongside the three earlier ones that tell their story so differently."[58]

The most striking contrast in the liberal's understanding of inspiration is his refusal to attribute a divine quality to the words of Scripture themselves. Inspiration for the liberal is not centered in the text but in the dynamic relation between the interpreter and the Holy Spirit. Scripture remains a human book, the words of fallible men, until the Holy Spirit enables us to find and see

[57] Smart, *The Interpretation of Scripture*, pp. 167–168.
[58] *Ibid.*, p. 189.

the word of God contained therein. The miracle of inspiration is not the deposit of an inerrant Bible but the freedom of God's Spirit to use this human witness to proclaim his ever-new message of judgment and hope. This does not mean the biblical text is dispensable. On the contrary, the moment of inspiration is available to us only through the text of Scripture, for it is through these words and no others that God intended to speak to us. What the liberal rejects is the existence of some inspired quality residing in the biblical word, objective in character and demonstrable by rational arguments. What he does assert is that God's Spirit did not eliminate the humanity of the writers but used the words of real men, spoken or written in a historical context, to speak his divine word to men of all ages.

The evangelical's criticism of the liberal's doctrine of inspiration is that he has none. Historical criticism either advertently or inadvertently destroyed confidence in the orthodox doctrine of inspiration without offering an alternative doctrine. It raised many more questions than it answered and thereby virtually left liberalism without any assurance of the divine nature of Scripture. Historical criticism had to account for inspiration not only at the written level but also at innumerable levels and stages before the words became fixed. Where is the element of inspiration when tradition is shaped by sociological and historical ("life situation") factors? If inspiration is to have any meaning here, it must be a continual process, not a specific one, extending over many centuries. Where does inspiration begin and where does it end, if one redactor alters what another redactor has already reinterpreted? At what point does the Holy Spirit play a decisive role, if ever? Given the diffuse state of inspiration as defined by the liberal, is there any criterion left to separate the words of men from the words of God? In summary, there is nothing the liberal can claim for the Bible which would confirm its divine origin and authoritative content.

FURTHER CONSIDERATIONS

In recent years, and especially since the publication of Harold Lindsell's book, *The Battle for the Bible* (1976), debate among evangelicals has centered around these three areas.

(1) Questions are being raised concerning the adequacy of the older Princeton apologetic for inerrancy as it was formulated by Alexander Hodge and Benjamin Warfield. Jack Rogers, Associate Professor of Theology and Philosophy of Religion at Fuller Theological Seminary, believes that the Princeton approach became overly dependent upon the reactionary scholasticism of Francis Turretin and Thomas Aquinas.[59] As a consequence of Hodge and Warfield's attempt to ground inerrancy in rational proofs, the Reformers' emphasis on the inner witness of the Holy Spirit was sacrificed. The church's attention was gradually shifted away from the central themes of Scripture and focused on details of history, geography, and science. What mattered most in their defense of biblical authority was the accuracy of the Chronicler instead of applying the words of the prophets to their own situation.

The very nature of the Princeton apologetic was to hold itself up as the only valid option and thus to build into the arguments a kind of domino theory. Warfield felt so confident that inerrancy would not be disproved that he challenged anyone to find just one intentional error in the original autographs. The possibility of placing faith in jeopardy over one error is one of the legacies of the fundamentalist-modernist controversy, and David Hubbard wonders if the strong-handed reasonings of Warfield and his followers not only "saved the faith" of some believers, but may also have "cost the faith" of others.[60]

(2) Similar questions are also being raised about the definition of error. The issue for most evangelicals is not whether the Bible is inerrant, but if inerrancy is the best word to use to describe the Bible's truthfulness and faithfulness. The danger is to define error is such a way that is overly rigid, Aristotelian, and scientific—a definition that may have more to do with the old Princeton theology than the Bible itself. Rogers is concerned that "to confuse 'error' in the sense of technical accuracy with the biblical notion of error as willful deception diverts us from the

[59]Jack B. Rogers, "The Church Doctrine of Biblical Authority," in *Biblical Authority*, ed. Jack B. Rogers (Waco: Word, 1977), pp. 35ff.; and Rogers, *Scripture in the Westminster Confession* (Grand Rapids: Eerdmans, 1967).

[60]David A. Hubbard, "The Current Tensions: Is There a Way Out?" in *Biblical Authority*, p. 158.

serious intent of Scripture."[61]

Harold Lindsell is forced to read the whole history of biblical interpretation through the filter of a twentieth-century concept of inerrancy. He is forced into this straight-jacket reading of history by his initial definition of inerrancy.

> However limited may have been their knowledge, and however much they may have erred when they were not writing sacred Scripture, the authors of Scripture, under the guidance of the Holy Spirit, were preserved from making factual, historical, scientific, or other errors.[62]

Lindsell likewise leads himself into an artificial harmonization of the four accounts of Peter's denial, because he has predetermined the biblical writers must agree on how many times Peter denied his Lord (see pp. 174–176). James Barr again points out the inconsistency when a literalistic interpretation is used in one particular situation and a non-literalistic in another.[63] In order to expound the Bible as inerrant, the conservative must twist and turn back and forth between a literal interpretation and a non-literal reading that disregards the integrity of the text.

(3) The battle over inerrancy, says Bernard Ramm, is a "misplaced battle line."[64] Ramm is one among many evangelicals who are apprehensive about the tendency to make the doctrine of verbal inspiration (or inerrancy) the pivotal doctrine for the Christian faith. When the validity of all other doctrines are

[61]Rogers, *Biblical Authority*, p. 46.

[62]Harold Lindsell, *The Battle for the Bible* (Grand Rapids: Zondervan, 1976), p. 31.

[63]Barr, *Fundamentalism*, pp. 40ff. Barr concludes his critique: "Literality, though it might well be deserving of criticism, would at least be a somewhat consistent interpretative principle, and the carrying out of it would deserve some attention as a significant achievement. What fundamentalists do pursue is a completely unprincipled—in the strict sense unprincipled, because guided by no principle of interpretation—approach, in which the only guiding criterion is that the Bible should . . . be true and not in any sort of error" (p. 49).

[64]Bernard Ramm, "Misplaced Battle Lines," *The Reformed Journal* (July–August, 1976). Besides this review of Lindsell's book, see Ramm, "Is 'Scripture Alone' the Essence of Christianity?" in *Biblical Authority*, pp. 109–123.

made to depend upon the inerrancy of Scripture, then the essence of Christianity has been misplaced. The practical result is that anyone holding a view different from inerrancy is less than truly evangelical or orthodox. Lindsell says as much when he states, "then he who denies the doctrine of infallibility—the only sure guarantee that these other doctrines are true—cannot truly be an evangelical."[65] From a different perspective, Ramm is calling into question a defense of biblical authority that produces a domino effect: If the Bible is not inerrant, then we cannot trust anything it has to say; or, if you do not believe in verbal inspiration, then the Bible automatically falls into the same category as every other book.

Ramm is by no means alone when he argues that inerrancy is a misplaced battle line. The real issue for both evangelicals and liberals is *not* the doctrine of inerrancy. It is rather one's attitude toward the Bible. The evangelical reads the Bible as God's Word. Consequently he tries to listen humbly and obediently. Yet, it is certainly legitimate to ask whether one can accept Scripture as the binding word of God apart from a belief that it is without error of any kind. Inerrancy is undoubtedly a presupposition that encourages the interpreter to listen humbly and obediently, but as a doctrine it can also be detrimental when it does not motivate the exegete to inquire critically about the intention of the author. If one begins with a doctrine of scriptural inspiration, one logical conclusion is inerrancy, but it is not necessarily the best or the most valid conclusion.

In the preface to the third edition of his commentary on Romans, Karl Barth offers an alternative to inerrancy as well as a rejection of historical criticism as it has usually been practiced. For Barth there was no other way to penetrate to the heart of the biblical text except by beginning with an attitude of complete loyalty.

> The commentator is thus presented with a clear "Either—Or." The question is whether or not he is to place himself in a relation to his author of utter loyalty. Is he to read him, determined to follow him to the very last word, wholly aware of what he is doing, and assuming that the

[65]Lindsell, *Battle for the Bible*, p. 210.

> author also knew what he was doing? Loyalty surely cannot end at a particular point, and certainly cannot be exhausted by an exposure of the author's literary affinities. Anything short of utter loyalty means a commentary on Paul's Epistle to the Romans, not a commentary so far as is possible WITH him—even to his last word.[66]

This attitude of "utter loyalty" is not quite a belief in verbal inspiration and it is a long way from reading Scripture as an interesting document with contemporary relevance. The interpreter does not begin his exegesis thinking he may discover the word of God "here and there" and upon proper analysis decide whether to agree or disagree with the writer. Karl Barth confesses, "I cannot, for my part, think it possible for an interpreter honestly to reproduce the meaning of any author unless he dares to accept the condition of utter loyalty" (p. 18).

The issue of biblical authority is very much bound up with one's doctrine of inspiration. It is very doubtful if anyone will ever come to a personal conviction about the truthfulness of Scripture by resolving apparent or real discrepancies. The resolution to the "problem" of Scripture takes place in a personal commitment in faith: a commitment that demands that we expect the biblical text to awaken a "faith that lies beyond the scope of human possibility" (Stuhlmacher).

AUTHORITY

Because the liberal has no doctrine of inspiration he has no doctrine of authority, and what authority Scripture does have is relative and subjective. In essence, then, the evangelical critique on this issue is the same as his criticism of the liberal's understanding of revelation.[67]

According to liberal theology the Bible has no objective authority apart from the work of the Holy Spirit, for it is only the Holy Spirit that makes these human words *become* the word of

[66]Karl Barth, *The Epistle to the Romans,* trans. Edwyn C. Hoskyns (London: Oxford University Press, 1968), p. 17.

[67]See Ch. III, pp. 124ff.

God. Scriptural authority rests not upon how the books were written but on how they continue to communicate the message of salvation.[68] Thus, the evangelical says, the authority of Scripture is transferred from the written word to its interpreter, for biblical authority is made to depend upon some activity of the Spirit upon the reader or hearer. The danger in this approach to scriptural authority is in the reduction of inspiration and the work of the Holy Spirit to a *subjective, present* activity. Ridderbos states the evangelical objection in this way:

> No matter how much truth it may contain, this view [of inspiration] is beset with danger. For by identifying the Word of God with the present operation of the Spirit in the preaching, there is the ever present risk that first the Word of God itself, and then the canon may be completely identified with what the church understands or thinks it understands. The situation may even develop so far that God's word coincides with what the individual person experiences when the Scriptures are preached. In this way the door is thrown wide open to a subjectivistic and existentialistic view of God's word and of the canon.[69]

Whenever subjective and relative standards are allowed to speak for God, the inevitable outcome is confusion and uncertainty about what constitutes the Word of God. If Scripture is not its own authority, and if Scripture does not testify to its own authority and interpret itself, then there is no other choice but to look for other relative authorities which can stand alongside the relative authority of God's written word. And this, says the evangelical, is precisely what we find within liberalism. The authority of Scripture becomes dependent upon other authorities—for example, the results of historical criticism, the interpretive role of the church and oral tradition, human reason and experience. We find a multiplicity of hermeneutical principles jockeying for acceptance as the correct method to interpret Scripture. We find

[68]Edward A. Dowey, Jr., *A Commentary on the Confession of 1967 and An Introduction to "The Book of Confessions"* (Philadelphia: Westminster, 1968), p. 101.

[69]Ridderbos, *The Authority . . .*, p. 8.

the individual free to choose his own method of interpretation, his own philosophical presuppositions, his own rule of thumb to distinguish between historical fact and fable. We find that liberals have lost confidence in the Bible: it is seldom read, generally referred to as a norm among other norms, and conspicuously absent from the church's preaching. And if Scripture is a mixture of law and gospel, a canon within a canon, then who is to decide which passages or books are relevant and authoritative for us today? Do we pick and choose as if the Bible is a fruit basket, or do we preach straight through the Bible believing that all the Scriptures are God-breathed?[70] In the end the evangelical critique comes down to this: *How can one relative and subjective authority take precedence over other relative and subjective authorities?*

The liberal counters by criticizing the evangelical for defending the authority of the words of Scripture more than the authority of the living Spirit to speak its ever-new word of revelation. By making the text an inerrant witness and by binding Christ to every written part, the real authority of Christ is either silenced or imprisoned. The living Lord is no longer free to speak his word, free to call into question the established order of things.

The evangelical conception of biblical authority likewise has its negative consequences. Externalizing and objectifying the authority of Scripture tends to make it a static book unable to speak for itself. The inerrancy of Scripture is easily transferred to our doctrines and presuppositions, which we may come to think are contained within the Bible. By establishing the authority of the Bible in and of itself and apart from the witness of tradition and the responsible church, the evangelical leaves the way open for any group to claim authority for itself. What was once God's confronting word, ever revitalizing and judging, becomes institutionalized and neutralized. And this, the liberal points out, is the danger we see borne out in the history of evangelical and conservative churches. The evangelical has not really solved the problem of authority, because if the Bible can be used to support

[70]Criswell, *Why I Preach . . .* , p. 82. The author tells how he has kept his promise in the past seventeen years to preach through the Bible and gives this comment on his experience: "I have found that even in those sections and passages in the Bible that seem the least profitable are the seedbeds for some of the most profitable and precious sermons."

the most diverse opinions and positions, then it ceases in effect to be serviceable as an authority. The Bible becomes not something to be submitted to but something to be used—the liberal wonders whether the evangelical is standing under the Bible or upon it.[71]

Another inherent danger in the evangelical doctrine of scriptural authority is the tendency to be locked into a literal, inflexible interpretation. A literal, plenary approach to the Bible expects Scripture to speak directly to our present situation as if two thousand years had not gone by. The meaning of the various texts is twisted into a timeless possession, when in truth the meaning of the gospel can never be gained or maintained other than critically.[72] A literal approach also encourages an arbitrary selection of texts as evidence when convenient, while other texts equally germane but inconvenient will be passed over, played down, or artificially harmonized. Any position is tenable if it can appeal directly to Scripture. Perhaps the best example from our nation's past is the defense of slavery on biblical grounds as divinely ordained, or at least permissible.[73] The reverse is also true: no position is tenable unless it has direct scriptural support. So the evangelical feels compelled to find biblical texts which directly attack the institution of slavery. A portion of the Magnificat (Luke 1:51–53) is read as an incentive to social concern; the feeding of the five thousand is cited as a directive to do something about overpopulation and undernourishment; and

[71]Käsemann, *New Testament Questions of Today,* p. 264. It is interesting that W. A. Criswell entitles one of his chapters, "Standing on the Authority of the Word of God" (*Why I Preach* . . . , pp. 132–138).

[72]Käsemann, *New Testament Questions of Today,* p. 264: "To sum up: the Gospel begets the critical faculty and creates the critical community, whereas the absence of criticism is the sign of spiritual impoverishment and deprivation." Also pp. 7–9, 271.

[73]John Bright, *The Authority of the Old Testament* (Nashville: Abingdon, 1967), pp. 46–51. Bright states the liberal approach to the question of slavery in Scripture. No matter how hard one tries, neither the New Testament nor the Old Testament explicitly condemns slavery; rather, from end to end the Bible assumes the existence of the institution (pp. 50–51). The biblical opposition to slavery cannot therefore be based upon specific texts but must be drawn from a much broader base of love, mercy, and dignity.

Luke 12:14 is interpreted as justifying a limited kind of social pronouncement.[74] The true test for biblical authority, as for biblical preaching, is not the number of specific texts which can be found but how broad the base is. To appeal to the Bible in a stilted way, as if it were a rule book or a dictionary, is to misuse and misunderstand the nature of the Bible, according to the liberal understanding.

CONCLUSION

Next to relativity, the critical-historical method has had the greatest impact upon Christian theology. As the divine origin of the Bible became increasingly suspect, liberals reacted by divorcing the authority of Scripture from the words of Scripture. It was much safer to locate the foundation of Christian faith in a present activity of the Spirit than in a fallible historical witness. Liberalism became so enamored with the discovery of the Bible as the words of real men written within a historical context that it allowed the Bible's uniqueness and divine nature to fall aside. The authority which was once attributed to Scripture was even transferred to the critical-historical method itself. Evangelicals reacted to the results of historical criticism, which it considered thoroughly negative and destructive, by welding together biblical authority and the written words. The authority of Scripture was protected by establishing a self-verifying relationship between word and event, verbal and conceptual inspiration, inerrancy and the work of the Spirit. The critical-historical method was controlled and tamed not so much by ignoring it, for this proved to be impossible, but by limiting its "acceptable" results and reducing its role to providing background information. Consequently, contemporary liberal theology demonstrates a peculiar unwillingness to trust the Bible as Christianity's final authority, while evangelical theology suffers from a credibility gap between its claims for Scripture and the evidence it presents.

The time has arrived for liberals to realize the limits and

[74]See for example Sherwood E. Wirt, *The Social Conscience of the Evangelical* (New York: Harper, 1968), pp. 16–18 (slavery), 12–15 (social concern), 60 (feeding the poor), 134 (social pronouncements).

dangers of a completely independent critical-historical method. Liberal theology was correct in assessing the importance of the method but failed to place the method itself under the authority of Scripture. The evangelical insistence on a properly defined critical-historical method has always gone unheeded because the liberal feared that the scientific nature of biblical research would be sacrificed. The evangelical, however, is asking historical criticism not to limit its findings but to limit the authority conferred upon its conclusions. The liberal is slowly realizing the disaster which resulted in the nineteenth century when historical studies were cut loose from theological concerns. For example, history and theology are often inextricably bound in Scripture, and therefore a purely historical approach proved deficient.[75] At this point liberals would benefit from working alongside evangelicals in seeking to define the proper role and limits of the critical-historical method.

The evangelical has by no means welcomed historical criticism—he has instead seen it as a threat to the orthodox doctrine of inspiration. But if one's doctrine of inspiration is not made to conform to the biblical evidence, then the doctrine becomes an authority higher than Scripture. Everett Harrison is very clear about the responsibility facing evangelicals:

> It would seem that the only healthy attitude for conservatives is to welcome criticism and be willing to join in it. No view of Scripture can indefinitely be sustained if it runs counter to the facts. That the Bible claims inspiration is patent. The problem is to define the nature of that inspiration in the light of the phenomena contained therein.[76]

What evangelicals can learn from liberals is to be more open to the critical-historical method as a means of determining the nature and structure of Scripture. To be more open means to be

[75]Compare James Smart, *The Strange Silence of the Bible in the Church* (Philadelphia: Westminster, 1970), Ch. IV and *The Interpretation of Scripture*, pp. 260–307.

[76]Everett F. Harrison, "The Phenomena of Scripture," in Henry, ed., *Revelation and the Bible*, p. 239.

free enough not to set preconceived limits, not to decide, for example, that inerrancy rules out the dual authorship of Isaiah.[77] It also means resisting the temptation to smooth out the rough spots and natural tensions certain to be encountered in approaching Scripture as a historical document.

If the liberal needs to temper his historical conclusions with theological considerations, the evangelical needs to temper his theological conclusions with historical results. By subordinating historical criticism to a prescribed area, evangelicalism has run the danger of removing theology itself from the unending process of radical questioning. Evangelical theology can close its credibility gap most easily by showing the courage and readiness "to think something through to the end come what may."[78] Not only is this a necessary presupposition for the critical-historical method, it is also a most important presupposition for systematic theology.

The evangelical rightly calls attention to the liberal's neglect of the Bible's own testimony to its inspiration. Not only does he lack a doctrine (or even a theory) of inspiration; the liberal frequently attempts to define biblical authority without an adequate account of how Scripture is divinely inspired. Very seldom, if ever, do liberals undertake a study of the doctrinal verses. Are we to conclude from this the liberal finds them valueless? Liberal scholarship has done its work well in bringing to light the numerous similarities between Israel and her neighboring people, between Christianity and the surrounding culture. The same scholarship now needs to highlight with equal clarity the uniqueness of Israel's faith and Jesus' teaching. Likewise, liberal scholarship has created its own dilemma by carefully analyzing the diversity of the biblical message without demonstrating the

[77]For illustration compare Clark Pinnock in Tenney, ed., *The Bible—The Living Word*. . . , p. 154: "No hypothesis which attributes gross historical error and anachronism to the gospel writers, no theory which derides the apostles for inconsistency or fallacy, no pseudepigraphic view of authorship which directly contradicts the inner claim of a New Testament book—none of these critical conclusions can be accepted because they contradict the testimony of God Himself in the Scripture."

[78]Käsemann, *New Testament Questions of Today*, p. 5.

overarching unity within that diversity.[79] Otherwise liberal theology will have no basis for establishing or making credible the authority of Scripture.

It may very well be that evangelicals have placed too much weight on the doctrinal verses. The liberal has the distinct feeling everything is made to rest upon II Timothy 3:16–17 and John 10:35, the only two verses which make a direct statement concerning the inspiration of Scripture.[80] The question being raised is not whether the Bible teaches its own inspiration but whether this slender stem can support the top-heavy claims for inerrancy and verbal inspiration. Just as some evangelicals are willing now to grant that the Bible "says nothing precise about its inerrancy,"[81] a more cautious and studied approach seems to be in order for the other claims. Regardless of how natural a corollary the doctrine of inerrancy may be to full inspiration, it is an assumption, like plenary and verbal inspiration, that must be weighed against the evidence and not used to prejudice the evidence. Oversimplification, like Pache's claim that the Old Testament declares 3,808 times that it conveys the express words of God,[82] is a common pitfall of overenthusiasm. Whether "thus spoke the Lord" means "here are the very words of God," or whether "it is written" means unequivocally "God says it," cannot be assumed but must be exegetically examined. Simply to state the obvious fact that Jesus argued from Scripture is not sufficient, for his use of the Old Testament must be carefully compared with the rabbinic use of Scripture during his time. Can we even impose our standard for accuracy and our conception of inspiration upon an ancient document? The answer must be that each passage is to be considered in its full historical, cultural, and literary context, and then conclusions may be drawn.

It is repeatedly said that evangelicals and liberals are di-

[79]Bright, *The Authority of the Old Testament* (esp. ch. III), and Samuel Terrien, *The Elusive Presence* (New York: Harper & Row, 1978), are but two examples of a corrective to this characteristic liberal deficiency.

[80]Possibly II Peter 1:20–21 should be added.

[81]Harrison in Henry, ed., *Revelation and the Bible*, p. 238. Also p. 250.

[82]Pache, *The Inspiration and Authority of Scripture*, p. 81.

vided over whether the Bible is the Word of God or the normative witness to the Word of God. Evangelicals and liberals generally consider their respective positions to be poles apart. Undoubtedly the difference is real, but is it as irreconcilable as we think? The evangelical has traditionally defined the Bible as "the only infallible rule of faith and practice." In comparison John Bright states, "For my own part, in the sense just defined, I should be prepared to affirm without hesitation, in line with the mainstream of Protestantism, that the Bible is the final authority to be appealed to in all matters of faith and practice."[83] The theoretical difference between "infallible rule" and "final authority" concerning matters of faith and practice is debatable, but for all practical purposes it is inconsequential. The crucial point is that Scripture is the one norm in which the church and individual Christians can place their trust. Whether inerrancy is a necessary requirement seems to be a personal rather than a doctrinal decision. And just how great the theoretical difference is depends upon how the evangelical interprets the phrase, "infallible rule." If he means the Bible is the only adequate and sufficient norm for salvation, then surely there is little substantial difference between most evangelicals and liberals.

On a different level, the issue boils down to how the words of men can be the Word of God. The evangelical has argued the words of men can be the Word of God only if they are infallible, while the liberal has argued that the words of men, by their very human nature, can never be God's direct word. The liberal finds it just as difficult to believe God would inspire an inerrant book as it is for the evangelical to believe God would reveal himself in a fallible witness. Yet evangelicals believe God can speak through the very human words of the preacher, and liberals believe the Holy Spirit can miraculously transform the imperfect expressions of ordinary men into the Word of God.

Why, the liberal asks, must the Bible be inerrant in order to be credible and trustworthy? Has it not been the nature of God's grace to accomplish his purpose through men who were far from faultless? Is it any more logical to assume God could not reveal himself in a fallible record than to assume God had to exempt the

[83]Bright, *The Authority of the Old Testament*, p. 31.

biblical authors from error before their words could bear his revelation?

The final test of biblical authority and inspiration, regardless of the arguments made, is whether evangelicals and liberals will resist the temptation to possess and control God's Word and will instead submit themselves to the Word. Each says he does and accuses the other of not doing so; but the proof will rest in their actions, not their words.

DISCUSSION QUESTIONS

1. On what matters must the Bible be correct in order for it to be considered trustworthy? Can the Bible be authoritative on matters concerning salvation without being authoritative on scientific and historical matters?

2. In what sense are the words of Scripture "inspired" if one assumes they passed first through an oral stage and were then written and rewritten? Does plenary (full) inspiration necessarily mean all parts of Scripture are equally relevant and authoritative?

3. Has your personal faith been strengthened by studying the Bible from a critical-historical viewpoint as well as devotionally? What limits, if any, should be placed upon the critical-historical method?

4. Is the biblical meaning or doctrine of the Fall changed in any substantial way if we do not accept Adam and Eve as literal, historical persons? What about the accounts of Jonah and the whale or the temptation of Jesus?

V. PRAYER, PROVIDENCE, AND THE WORLD

The subjects, "prayer, providence, and the world," are unified in that each directly affects the others. What one believes about the structure of the universe has a direct bearing on one's beliefs about God's purpose and how that purpose is carried out for the course of human life and history. What one prays for is in turn directly influenced by one's conception of what is "possible" according to providence and natural law. And prayer, because it is the resulting human action and therefore a very practical issue, becomes a good place for evangelicals and liberals to further confront each other in open discussion.

THE EVANGELICAL POSITION

The evangelical's belief in God as personal naturally leads him to believe in a personal universe, providential care, and the power of prayer to effect real change. When all of the elaborations are stripped away, the evangelical's beliefs concerning prayer, providence, and the world seem to rest upon three basic assumptions: (1) Because God is a personal God, he does intervene personally in the lives of individuals. (2) Since God is the personal creator of the universe, we are set not in a totally impersonal world but in a world which he directs and controls. (3) Since the universe is subject to God's ordaining, prayer can and does make a difference.

It is inconceivable to the evangelical that God, if he is truly a personal God, would not be moved to act by the petitions of Christians. It is likewise incomprehensible that God, the creator of the universe, would abandon the world to impersonal forces or allow evil designs to triumph. If Yahweh revealed himself to Israel through a series of historical and natural events and intervened in the lives of numerous biblical personalities, would he not be doing the same today? Furthermore God as omnipotent planner does not allow events just to happen but fits each effect to its cause in his grand design. The evangelical does not necessarily claim that everything which happens to us as individuals or as nations is intended, but he does believe that certain happenings have a specific purpose. Israel, for instance, did not record every major event in her history but selected those which had a special or divine meaning for her relationship to Yahweh.[1] Similarly, the evangelical does not expect every incident in his life to be the "hand of God," but he does believe that specific events are expressions of God's will.

Thousands of examples might illustrate the evangelical's conviction concerning prayer and the world, but let us look at two which highlight certain significant patterns. When Catherine Marshall was told she had contracted tuberculosis, she first felt resentment—"Why me? What have I done?"—and then resolution—"If I make myself worthy, God will cure me." The soft spottings on her lungs did not go away in the expected three to four months, however, and the days drew into a year and a half with no improvement. Not until her husband Peter gave her a pamphlet that told the story of a missionary bedridden for eight years did she realize that she had been demanding of God in her prayers. The right way to pray, she suddenly understood, is the way of submission to God and surrender to the situation as it is. That night she prayed, "If You want me to be an invalid for the rest of my life, all right. Here I am. Do anything You like with me and my life." In the early hours of the next morning she was awakened by the sure sense that Christ was there, in person, standing by her bed. In the subsequent months there was steady

[1]See the special attention this is given by G. Ernest Wright, *God Who Acts: Biblical Theology as Recital* ("Studies in Biblical Theology, No. 8"; London: SCM, 1962), esp. ch. III. The selectivity of Israel in recording her history has been a prominent theme in recent Old Testament theologies, e.g., those of Gerhard von Rad and Walther Eichrodt.

improvement, until finally the doctors pronounced Catherine completely well.

The lesson that one cannot coerce God into giving us what we want was not forgotten. Mrs. Marshall experienced anew that God answers prayers when we submit to his will the night her husband lay fatally ill. She prayed then: "Lord, will you overrule all this, so that one of these days both Peter and I will have reason to thank You that *even this* happened?" Time revealed that God heard and answered. Through her own numerous writings, thousands have come to know the faith of Peter Marshall and his wife.[2]

A second example is vividly told by David Wilkerson in his bestseller, *The Cross and the Switchblade.* The story centers around the series of events which led him from a small country church to the city streets of New York City and a continuing ministry with the teenage gangs there. The events themselves were both ordinary and extraordinary, ranging from the chance spotting of a story in *Life* magazine and a broken television set to the miraculous recovery of his grandfather and the raising of the exact amount they needed to make a down payment for the Teen Challenge Center. Individually these events might have been considered coincidental, but taken together they spelled out a clear and direct mandate from God to David Wilkerson. Throughout his experiences prayer played a vital role. Wilkerson made frequent prayer requests known only to himself or a small group of friends. Time and time again those requests were mysteriously fulfilled in such a way that only God could have been the cause.[3]

These two examples give an idea of what the evangelical feels he has experienced over and over again: the personal intervention of God, an event or series of events which came as a directive from God, a seemingly tragic happening turned into a blessing in God's eternal providence. At the same time, the evangelical wishes to avoid making a crass equation between

[2]Catherine Marshall, *A Man Called Peter* (New York: McGraw-Hill, 1951), ch. XIV, XX.

[3]David Wilkerson, *The Cross and the Switchblade* (New York: Pyramid, 1963).

cause and effect, prayer and result. Our prayers of petition cannot alter what God has ordained, but they can open the way for God to do what he wants to do for us. In other words, prayer is not some magical manipulation of God for selfish reasons, but it can release God's power. When Isaiah said, "Here am I; send me," he did not alter God's will but he did release it. God cannot do for the man with a closed heart what he can do for one with an open heart. With Catherine Marshall and David Wilkerson, prayer simply gave God the opportunity to do what his love wanted to do. In a very real sense God does depend upon the cooperation of men's prayers. It is when our prayers are not in accord with his will that we think God has not answered or has not been moved by our pleas. Even though our prayers may be contrary to God's will, he will respond to our lack of faith and ignorance with an answer which in the end will benefit us.

Prayer is also not to be confused with a form of "positive thinking," because God's power is not a modified or intensified mode of human energy. Rather, prayer is an avenue, the chief avenue in fact, to the power of God. Prayer is like a tap into God's transcendent power; but it is a power which belongs to God alone and therefore can accomplish what we cannot do by our own inner strength.

Among evangelicals there is not a complete consensus on how God brings about his will. As we have seen in Chapter III, the evangelical does not see the universe as sealed off to divine intervention. Consequently God in his omnipotence can, in the pattern of Old Testament and New Testament miracles, break the natural order and accomplish what can only be called "an act contrary to nature." The predominant evangelical view, however, is that God does not generally suspend or break natural law but rather uses it to achieve his purpose. Two kinds of arguments are usually put forth to support this idea. (1) If man can redirect and manipulate natural laws for his own good without violating them, surely God is able to do the same for the good of mankind. Every day water is made to run uphill and steel is made to fly because man knows how to utilize the physical laws of the universe. Our limited control of natural law then serves as a counterpart to God's unlimited control.

> The whole analogy of human experience suggests that the world is not governed by law; that it is governed by God according to law. He providentially utilizes, manipulates, and combines his own invariable ways of acting to serve his own eternal purposes.[4]

(2) It is also necessary to take into consideration that man's understanding of natural law is still so elementary and incomplete as to render meaningless the idea of inexorable physical laws.[5] God may at times seem to defy the laws of the universe but how can we be certain he is not working within the created order, since we do not yet fully comprehend the physical laws of our own galaxy? Prescientific men, including the biblical writers, were apt to describe events as miraculous which we, with our superior understanding of natural law, would describe as extraordinary but not opposed to a law-abiding universe. Our future experience may likewise upset our contemporary ideas concerning what is natural and supernatural.

When we pray for God's help, then, we are not asking him to disrupt the ordered universe but asking for his divine power to manifest itself in the operation of natural law. God is the master of all laws, known and unknown to us. When he utilizes his knowledge of his own laws, who can say in advance what is possible? God is free to answer any prayer whatsoever; and if a petition is not granted it is not because the reign of natural law prevents God from acting. The more likely explanation is that

[4]Harry Emerson Fosdick, *The Meaning of Prayer* (New York: Association, 1949), p. 103. It is an indication of just how far we have moved that Fosdick can be quoted as expressing a very typical evangelical position. Between the world wars Fosdick was a leading proponent of the liberal viewpoint, but in this context he sounds very evangelical. We can see how far the liberal position has shifted, at least concerning prayer in a secular age. In contrast to Fosdick, a liberal of yesterday, the liberal of today has serious questions about the power of prayer to change an external situation.

[5]See, for instance, Walter Künneth, *The Theology of the Resurrection*, trans. James W. Leitch (St. Louis: Concordia, 1965), pp. 66–67. For a sympathetic liberal treatment see Richard R. Niebuhr, *Resurrection and Historical Reason* (New York: Scribner's, 1957), pp. 177ff.

there are certain areas where God must not substitute our wish for his plan.[6]

THE LIBERAL POSITION

As much as the liberal wants to believe in this comforting kind of world where certain events are ordained and prayer has the power to change, the liberal's understanding of the purpose of prayer and his conception of the world is considerably different, and it is different principally because of three problems: (1) the question of innocent suffering or radical evil, (2) the question of a religiously ambiguous universe, and (3) the question of projecting meaning where there is none.

The problem of innocent suffering, succinctly stated, is how to reconcile the Christian affirmation in a good and loving Creator with the needless, excessive, and purposeless suffering in the world. The liberal does not deny that some suffering serves a positive end in the maturing process of life. What he does deny is that all evil and all suffering have a necessary place in the totality of God's plan for the world. He is not convinced that "all things work together for good," because he has known both personal tragedies and countless natural disasters that as far as he can see have served no good purpose and never will. Even if the evil we see should prove to have a purpose evident to future ages, the liberal asks what comfort and positive value this can have for the great majority who will never know in their lifetime that their misfortune was part of a divine plan.

Perhaps an illustration will be helpful, as the problem of radical evil is poignantly brought home by a distinguished Jewish theologian, Rabbi Richard L. Rubenstein. Rubenstein points out that according to traditional Jewish belief whatever happens in human history happens because God in his infinite wisdom and justice causes it to happen. On the day that the East Germans closed off West Berlin, Rabbi Rubenstein recalls graphically a discussion he had with a Lutheran pastor, Dean Grüber, who confirmed his belief that everything which happens in history has

[6]Fosdick, *The Meaning of Prayer*, p. 103.

a definite purpose in God's plan. And for that reason Dean Grüber was convinced not only that God was behind the erection of the Berlin Wall, as a punishment for the sins of the German people, but that "it was God's will that Hitler exterminated the Jews." Like many a religious Jew, Dean Grüber did not believe the infinite pain of the death camps was a good thing but nevertheless could not help but believe that God was ultimately responsible for them. As Rabbi Rubenstein listened to the Dean he suddenly realized "that there was no way I could believe in the all-powerful God of traditional Judaism and Christianity without accepting the notion that He was actively involved in the obscene horrors of W.W. II." To accept the traditional belief would be "to affirm that my people got what they deserved at Auschwitz."[7] Likewise the liberal does not see how the traditional belief in the all-powerful God of history can be accepted without affirming that the death of five million Jews was a freely chosen, decisive act of the just God. If the historic conception of God's sovereignty means radical evil is ordained and innocent suffering is a requisite of his plan of salvation, then the liberal finds this God morally intolerable and unacceptably impersonal.

The only answer the liberal can accept to this apparent contradiction between innocent suffering and a loving Father is to acknowledge the freedom of man to sin and to see the world as a self-sustaining, law-abiding, self-enclosed entity which is religiously neutral. That is to say, God purposefully limits his omnipotence by giving man free will in a self-contained world. Radical evil is thus to be traced back to the exercise of this free will and to a religiously ambiguous universe. The floods in Pakistan and the earthquakes in Peru and Alaska are good examples of innocent suffering caused by an impersonal world. The other side of innocent suffering is seen in the starvation in Biafra and the death of so many children and peasants in Vietnam as a result of

[7]Richard L. Rubenstein, "Judaism and the Death of God," *Playboy*, July, 1967, p. 70. For an expansion of Rubenstein's arguments see his *After Auschwitz: Essays in Contemporary Judaism* (Indianapolis: Bobbs-Merrill, 1969). The best-selling novel by Chaim Potok, *The Chosen* (New York: Simon and Schuster, 1967), also presents an interesting illustration of how two different Jewish traditions look at the suffering and death of five million Jews.

human selfishness. The liberal does not deny that human sin leads to much of the world's suffering. He does reject, though, any theodicy which does not account for suffering which has nothing to do with the victim's own sin. Such pain and tragedy, he believes, are not acts of God but are the natural consequences of a law-abiding universe or of the misuse of man's freedom. The liberal formula is as follows: all sin results in someone's suffering, but not all suffering is the result of someone's sin.

A third closely related reason why the liberal feels he cannot accept the evangelical's assumption about a personal world directed by a personal God is the danger of projecting a divine meaning where there is none. If the universe is religiously neutral as he believes, then one cannot say with certainty that some specific incident is "meant" by God while another happening has no particular divine significance. In an inherently self-contained world one cannot legitimately look to a God-hypothesis to explain why something happened. The Christian thus has no right to ask, "Why did God allow this to happen?" or, "Is God punishing me?" or, "What is God trying to tell me?" when something good or bad happens. If in a tragic automobile accident two people are instantly killed while a third person, a personal friend, is miraculously saved, we feel a strong temptation to believe that God has intervened for the sake of that one person. It is this temptation which the liberal feels he must resist, or at least be suspicious of, because of the danger of misconstruing God's will or reading into the incident some meaning which is not there.

The liberal is aware, or at least he should be, that he is in the peculiar situation of affirming belief in a personal God in the midst of an impersonal universe. In a world with its own inherent structure and laws, the liberal cannot logically expect God to intervene for the sake of some good. Neither can the Christian's prayers of intercession take the form of an appeal to God to change our external situation. The legitimate purpose of prayer, as Robert Raines describes it, "is not calculated to move the arm of God but, rather, to make ourselves available to him that our arms may be moved by him; . . . not that our will be done by him but that his will be done in and through and despite us."[8] Prayer

[8]Robert A. Raines, *The Secular Congregation* (New York: Harper, 1968), p. 128.

thus becomes a factor in altering our human situation insofar as it changes our relationship to God's will. We, not the causal structure of the universe, are the ones who are transformed through prayer and who in turn transform the world.

In a world where there are no intentional earthquakes or planned accidents, the "response in faith" is the all-important matter for the liberal. And since no objective purpose is imposed from without on a particular event, it is man who must assume the responsibility for creating meaning in the light of God's revelation in Jesus of Nazareth. From the liberal's perspective, the freedom God gave man assumes its proper place when man uses it to respond to the contingencies of life with love instead of hate, hope instead of despair, and creative aggressiveness instead of resistive passivity.[9] As so aptly said in a prayer by Jo Carr and Imogene Sorley, it is the response and use of freedom, not what happens or does not happen to him, that distinguishes the Christian from the nonbeliever.

> "It is God's will," she said, oozing unctuousness.
> *Thy will,* Lord, that a young mother should die in a senseless car wreck?
> *Thy will* that a house should burn or a tornado strike?
> *Thy will* that an immortal soul should be begotten in such a casual and thoughtless way?
> O Lord, whose other name is Love, *it is incompatible with thy nature* to will such as these. . . .
>
> But you do not sit "up there" dispensing misery, to make me strong—or to try me.
> *That* is incompatible with thy nature.
> Tragedy comes—not "sent" by thee, but it comes.
> So what is thy will in the situation, Lord?
> That I should fold my hands in meek acceptance?

[9]The twin notes of freedom and responsibility are characteristic of a recent movement within liberal theology. See, for example, the articles edited by Martin Marty and Dean Peerman, *New Theology No. 5* (New York: Macmillan, 1968); especially the article by Johannes B. Metz, "Creative Hope," p. 131: "In this approach to the future, man no longer experiences his world as a destiny imposed on him, as inviolable nature surrounding him, but rather as a 'stone quarry' out of which he must build his own 'new world.'"

No!
It must be thy divine will for me to accept what comes *and grow because of it*
and create out of it a new and better situation. . . .
Amen.[10]

It is not true that God sends disease, famine, and war to provide opportunities for self-giving and to test faith; rather, God has set us in such a world with such revelations of himself so that we might meet what befalls us with Christian love and understanding. It is only in this kind of world, the liberal insists, that man can grow in his relation to God and realize his full human potentialities. Conversely, in a world in which rewards and punishments were justly apportioned to our deeds, we could not do the right simply for its own sake, and consequently our moral nature would not have the occasion to develop. A divine arrangement by which suffering could always or sometimes be seen to work for the good of the sufferer would likewise be self-defeating. It is precisely in a world where suffering falls upon mankind unequally and haphazardly that true kindness, compassion, and unselfishness are possible.[11]

While it would seem that the liberal's conception of the world implies that God has forsaken the world and men to their own devices, the liberal nevertheless is confident that God is personally involved in the outcome of his creation. To say the liberal believes in a religiously ambiguous world is not entirely correct. The universe is neutral in its everyday occurrences, perhaps, but not in its final destination. In the first place, the liberal has been deeply influenced by Teilhard de Chardin and others like him in their strong affirmation that history and nature give evidence of converging toward a personal center, namely, God. The universe is not out of God's control but is evolving in the direction of greater consciousness toward a center which is already present and somehow personal. Although science has given this conception of the universe a firmer foundation, it is

[10]Jo Carr and Imogene Sorley, *Bless This Mess & Other Prayers* (Nashville: Abingdon, 1969), p. 90.

[11]John Hick, "God, Evil and Mystery," *Religious Studies*, vol. III, no. 2 (Apr., 1968), pp. 544–546.

really a reaffirmation of the Judeo-Christian belief in history as linear. For the Christian, history is not simply an extension of the past ("man is no better or no worse than before") but is always unfinished, always opening toward a real future of new events.

Contrary to what some think, the liberal does not see this forward movement of evolution as an automatic process. Man, the Christian especially, must bear his responsibility in fulfilling the work of creation. God does not direct us individually any more than he manipulates the laws of the universe. Instead, he has revealed to all of us in the person of Jesus Christ what is expected and how man is to use his freedom in order to insure the movement of evolution. The forward movement of an immanent universe and the upward movement of faith toward a transcendent God are thus intended to work for the common goal of bringing God's creation to its proper end. What *we do*, therefore, is important, because we are cooperating with God's creating; we become, in fact, the living extension of God's creative power.[12]

SUMMARY: TWO VIEWS ON PRAYER

In recent years there has been a lessening of the distance between evangelicals and liberals in these matters. Evangelicals have tended more toward the position that God carries out his will *through* the natural order rather than *against* natural law. At the same time the liberal has tended to be more open to the idea that supernatural or unexplainable occurrences may happen. The crux of their differences centers on the question of whether God reveals his will directly and personally to individuals by regulating the created order, or indirectly and generally without regard to specific individuals and without manipulating the inherent structure of a law-abiding universe.

The evangelical agrees that there are real tragedies in the

[12]Teilhard de Chardin, *The Divine Milieu* (New York: Harper Torchbooks, 1968), p. 62: "We may, perhaps, imagine that the creation was finished long ago. But that would be quite wrong. It continues still more magnificently, and at the highest levels of the world. . . . And we serve to complete it, even by the humblest of our hands. That is, ultimately, the meaning and value of our acts."

midst of a universe governed by law. But to assert a completely neutral world is to forget that natural law is governed by God. In a universe regulated by God according to natural law it is far from naive to believe God uses the natural order to make his will known directly to individuals. What is more, there is reason to believe God initiates his own action (as in the case of Rev. Wilkerson). To speak of "signs" from God is therefore legitimate. The liberal feels we can only go so far as to say that history and science support the biblical message that there is a definite plan toward which we are moving, and that God has revealed himself in Jesus Christ so we can know how life should be lived. Even a universe governed by God does not permit us the inference that he will redirect universal laws for the sake of a single person. The evangelical warns of the agnosticism which discredits direct knowledge of God's will; the liberal warns of playing God by imputing to man divine knowledge of the present and future.

Taking into consideration what we have said thus far in the first two chapters, the difference between evangelical and liberal over the value of prayer is almost self-evident. For the liberal two assumptions have priority: (1) Christ is already present in the world and the other person; (2) the purpose of prayer is to push us deeper into Christian involvement. Recent prayers published by liberals amply bear out these assumptions. The prayers in Malcolm Boyd's book, *Are You Running with Me, Jesus?*, arise not out of a quiet study but whenever and wherever he perceives the presence of Christ. Characteristically, these prayers on location spring from the awareness that Christ lives in my neighbor, the drug addict, the television star, the jazz musician, or the student engaged in premarital sex. The purpose of these prayers is not so much to ask God to enter the lives of troubled people as to demonstrate how *we* can be open to all persons and how *we* can perceive with Christ's eyes the potential goodness of even the worst sinner. Robert Raines exposes the not-so-subtle difference between praying for Christ to intervene and praying for Christ's presence to be fully realized:

> Awareness that Christ lives in my neighbor, though unacknowledged by him, frees me from religious imperialism or proselytism. I am free to regard him as already loved and

> inhabited by Christ, a person from whom I may learn something new of Christ, one whom I am called to serve. . . . Prayer is *awareness* of the potentiality for community which results from Christ's presence in every man and in me (italics mine).[13]

The beautiful collection called *Prayers* by the Roman Catholic priest Michel Quoist is a fine illustration of how God calls us to give of ourselves through the daily events of our existence. The road to total self-giving is through what Quoist calls "the Gospel of daily life." A straightforward example is the prayer entitled "The Telephone":

> I have just hung up; why did he telephone?
> I don't know. . . . Oh! I get it. . . .
>
> I talked a lot and listened very little.
> Forgive me, Lord; it was a monologue and not a dialogue.
> Since I didn't listen, I learned nothing.
> Since I didn't listen, I didn't help,
> Since I didn't listen, we didn't commune.
>
> Forgive me, Lord, for we were connected,
> And now we are cut off.[14]

The nature of prayer, then, is to help us see Christ in our brother and in the common as well as the dramatic events of our lives. Our communion with Christ is with and through our neighbor to the extent to which we give ourselves in love.

When the liberal prays to God he does not intend to move him to intervene or to change his external circumstance. The liberal prays for justice, healing, comfort, peace, thinking that these things will be accomplished if he does them. But it is at this point that prayer becomes indispensable for the Christian, because prayer provides him with both the strength and the vision to bear Christ's suffering in his body. In short, prayer is the activity which brings Christ out of the past and into the present and summons the Christian to total self-giving.

[13]Raines, *The Secular Congregation*, p. 118.

[14]Michel Quoist, *Prayers*, trans. Agnes Forsyth and Anne Marie de Commaille (New York: Sheed and Ward, 1963), p. 19.

The evangelical is also guided by two assumptions in his understanding of prayer: (1) the purpose of prayer is to unite us in fellowship with Jesus Christ; (2) through prayer the power of God can be brought to bear upon another person. Evangelicals and liberals both speak about fellowship with Christ, but the evangelical has in mind the specific, direct relationship the Christian has with God through prayer. "Comfort in hours of sorrow, courage in times of discouragement, spiritual vitality in times of physical sickness, guidance in times of decision, inspiration when surrounded by difficulties and problems"—these are the gifts which flow from daily prayerful communion with God.[15] Prayers of evangelicals naturally tend to be more contemplative than action-oriented, simply because they reflect a stronger sense of fellowship with Christ.

At the same time, evangelical prayers are more truly intercessory because of the firm belief that prayer can release the power of God for the sake of a single life. Liberals and evangelicals agree that "man cannot do it alone," but the evangelical believes in addition that there are times when "only God can do it." In other words, even if God does work through natural means, he takes the initiative to guide those processes, whether mental or physical, toward a definite goal. In the case of a man at the point of death, God can reverse the processes at work and begin others which will put him back on the path of regaining his life and health. In one instance it may be a new will to live, in another the sudden resurgence of some physiological resources, in a third a combination of both, but in each instance God is the initiator. It does not matter whether God acts indirectly or directly, immediately or later, naturally or miraculously; what matters is that God does act on behalf of the petitioner.

The decisive difference, then, is the evangelical conviction that prayer affects events and circumstances as well as the one praying. Harold Lindsell, former editor of *Christianity Today*, comes right to the point when he says:

> No one should succumb to the error of viewing prayers as a means of changing the individual and his at-

[15]Ramm, *Protestant Christian Evidences*, p. 223.

> titudes rather than changing events, circumstances, and history itself. Certainly "prayer changes me"—my outlook, my orientation, and my attitudes. But prayer also changes those situations and circumstances of life which are distinctly divorced from any change which may take place in the individual who prays.[16]

For this reason alone prayers of petition and intercession have a radically different nature and intensity for the evangelical, for as he prays for himself and others he is firmly convinced that God is able to do what he is asked to do. And although evangelicals do not depreciate prayers of adoration, confession, and thanksgiving, prayers of petition and intercession assume the primary place in their daily prayer life.

CONCLUSION

In an article for *Presbyterian Life* John Bodo described the two extreme schools of thought toward prayer as the "nickel-in-the-slot" approach and the "push-up" philosophy. The former holds that a prayer given in good faith automatically assures the desired answer. The latter waves aside the whole question of answer to prayer and claims instead that prayer is like doing push-ups; it builds the muscles of the soul.[17] Caricatures as they are, these pictures do point out something of the dangers the liberal and evangelical tend toward. And perhaps it may be more helpful in the way of a conclusion to emphasize the respective dangers than to attempt a solution satisfactory to all.

Although the liberal would not admit it, his prayer is often little more than the means of renewal for the fight against prejudice and injustice by revitalizing the image of the historical Jesus. When the liberal speaks about responding to God in prayer, he usually means responding to the past revelation of God in the human form of Jesus, "the man for others." Prayer becomes not

[16] Harold Lindsell, *When You Pray* (Wheaton: Tyndale House, 1969), p. 11 (also pp. 21, 106, 160).

[17] John Bodo, "What Should We Pray For?" *Presbyterian Life*, July 1, 1967, pp. 4–5.

so much a dialogue with the divine Christ as a monologue with the human Jesus; not so much a private sharing with the living Savior as a recommitment to the lifestyle of the Suffering Servant. Prayer serves a legitimate purpose when it clarifies our motives, directs our actions, and energizes our intentions. But certainly Jesus intended prayer to be more than this. Can we imagine Christ praying to himself in order to hear his own words? He warned against the man who "stands and prays . . . with himself" (Luke 18:11). His life was so obviously dependent upon another Life that when he prayed he surely met Someone. He felt a Presence that not only disturbed him but comforted him, not only revived him but directed him. What is sadly lacking in the liberal theology of prayer is a sense of true fellowship with another Person.

The liberal practically rules out any specific action of God on behalf of the individual. Consequently God is robbed of initiative to act on his own, and prayers of intercession and petition are rendered pointless. When the neutrality of the world is taken so absolutely, God is necessarily excluded from particular historical events or personal experiences. What one misses in the theology of Teilhard de Chardin, for instance, is a solid basis upon which we can speak about a God who is responsive in love to the individual person. It is as if God's purpose and concern for the individual are lost within his vast cosmic scheme or entombed in his past revelation. What difference is there between the contemporary liberal position and the deistic conception of God who builds his clock-like world in such a way that it continues to keep better and better time? The liberal must ask himself, if God takes the initiative only in the commencing of some general processes, then why ask for God's guidance in our lives?

The liberal has no conceptual reason which says God cannot initiate some direct action through natural law, whether it be a coincidence of events or an unexplained recovery, but he recoils from the idea either because he has not personally experienced it or because he is afraid he may be reading in a meaning which is not there. Granting that men may frequently deceive themselves, the liberal should at least be open to the possibility of God's direct intervention as an expression of his personal love. At a time in liberal theology when the very doctrine of God is being reexamined to allow for a more responsive Deity, it would be unfortunate if more attention were not given to this fundamental question of God's concern for the individual. Liberal theology has worked itself into the awkward position of proclaiming a future open to ever-new acts of God, a style of life centered around involvement, revelation as a word of promise, and a new theism in which God is genuinely affected by all that we say and do, and yet failing to answer how we can meaningfully pray to God as Scripture enjoins us, namely, as the Father who demonstrates his personal love for us.[18] This is one of the important tasks confronting liberal theology.

The evangelical on the other hand does not take seriously enough the reality of innocent suffering resulting from a basically impersonal, law-abiding universe. As a consequence there is a tendency to see a cause and effect relationship between God and event, prayer and result.[19] The evangelical moves onto shaky ground when he attempts to explain away or deny untimely deaths, sudden or prolonged illnesses, unaccountable or irrational accidents, or natural catastrophes by seeking a divine cause. The more significant and personal the event, the more likely the conservative is to assume a divine cause or interpretation. Once it is assumed God is the cause behind some events, the door is then ajar to blame God. And once it is presumed that God is the cause, it is a short logical step to believe prayer can bring about some change in our situation. The way is open to think a happy solution to our misfortune was the result of our prayers or an unhappy outcome the result of our ill-disposed prayers. A vicious cycle is thus established which distorts the purpose of prayer and belittles the freedom given to man by God.

It is one thing to conceive of God as responsive, but the evangelical must ask himself whether his logic sufficiently guards against using prayer to manipulate God. Although the evangelical tries to avoid that danger, it is questionable whether the impres-

[18]Liberal theology is aware of the problem, but barely. See Ogden, *The Reality of God,* p. 67, n. 105.

[19]This criticism might be made in reverse: the tendency to find a causal relationship between prayer and result has led to rejection of the true scope of innocent suffering. But this way of stating the criticism does not seem as accurate.

sion is not left that God will be moved to act only by prayers which employ the right method. The evangelical has attempted to dodge this implication by saying it is not the content or form of a prayer that counts, but the believer's heart. Nevertheless proper formulas are given and conditions are regularly laid down, such as confessed sins, lack of faith or desire, or not praying in the name of Jesus or for the glory of God.[20] But is God moved to respond because we meet certain requirements for prayer or because he has compassion on us? Obviously there are principles which make prayer more effective, but just as obviously these guidelines can in no way restrict the freedom of God to intervene on behalf of the sinner or nonbeliever or to answer unspoken prayer. Isn't there also a real danger that prayer will be narrowed to asking God for what we do not have and importuning him to get us out of tight spots? Prayers intended only to instruct and move God are certainly as bad as prayers which only instruct and move ourselves.

Similarly, are we not in danger of thinking we can manipulate God when we see him as the cause of the incomprehensible, the extraordinary, and the extreme good and misfortune in our lives? By asking God to intervene in our external circumstances, do we not stand in danger of turning God into the great celestial Manipulator who must ever tinker with his creation in order to reach man? If God is the answer or the cause in this sense, then what is to prevent him from being pushed further to the edge of life as we find more reasonable explanations to the once-inexplicable?

If any kind of balance is to be reached between liberal and evangelical, it seems that it must affirm God's freedom to respond to the individual in what is nevertheless an essentially neutral and ambiguous world. We must be careful not to tip the balance, on the one hand, toward a forced cause and effect relation between sin and suffering, prayer and result, because of our anxiousness to believe in a God who loves us personally; nor on the other hand toward reducing God to a powerless, impersonal

[20]Cf. Lindsell, *When You Pray,* who frequently speaks of the spiritual *laws* which govern prayer and the conditions which are necessary for prayers to be answered as well as effective (pp. 24, 47, 56–75, 95–96).

force within history and nature because of our rigid conviction in a law-abiding universe.

Such a balance is required because the evangelical has correctly held fast to Scripture and the church's testimony to a God personally involved with his creation, while the liberal has done justice to man's freedom to respond in the face of a world filled with indiscriminate suffering and death. The liberal cannot write off as a dated world view the undeniable biblical witness to those special moments (*kairoi*) when God freely intervenes more decisively than at other times. Nor can the evangelical deny that it is only within a world where there are real contingencies and tragedies that true kindness, compassion, and unselfishness are possible.

How can one ignore God's personal dealings with Abraham, Moses, Joshua, David, the prophets and apostles, Paul and the saints? The liberal may not want to take the Bible literally when it implies that God spoke to these men directly, but this does not exclude the possibility that God was leading Israel and the church through specific actions with these specific men. Even if we allow for historical timeliness, coincidence of events, extraordinary insight, unwavering commitment, and a divine-human encounter, these episodes still reveal God's interaction with individuals. In his humorous way Archbishop Temple commented that the events which occurred in his wonderful and productive life were merely coincidental, but added that the coincidences came more frequently when he prayed. "When I pray, coincidences happen. When I do not, they don't."

In her biography of her husband, Martin Luther King, Jr., Coretta King provides us with a modern example of divine action which even the liberal could accept. At the junctures in their lives, she writes, there was a sense of a divine plan and purpose. In retrospect Coretta King describes Martin's decision to go to Montgomery to accept his first church in this way.

> Though I had been opposed to going to Montgomery, I realize now that it was an inevitable part of a greater plan for our lives. Even in 1954 I felt that my husband was being prepared—and I too—for a special role about which we would learn more later. Being in Montgomery was like a

drama that was unfolding. Martin and I and the people of that small southern city were like actors in a play, the end of which we had not yet read. Yet we felt a sense of destiny, of being propelled in a certain direction. We had the feeling that we were allowing ourselves to be the instruments of God's creative will.[21]

It is at this point that the liberal's position concerning the world must be considered. The debate between Job and his three "friends" is familiar. Job is convinced that his suffering is unjustified and that his fate is no different from the rest who are victims of chance misfortune (Job 9:21–24; 10:1–3; cf. Ecclesiastes 2:14–15, 17, 20–21; 4:7–8; 5). His companions, however, are positive that Job has done some wrong to deserve this suffering. Job sees a world filled with innocent suffering but his friends argue that a just God does not simply let affliction happen. Certainly it must be granted that the latter idea is present in the Bible. Some Psalms espouse a doctrine that the righteous prosper and the wicked suffer, and the author of Deuteronomy applies the principle to Israel as well as her kings.[22] This view was undoubtedly "orthodox" in some circles but scarcely normative for the Old and New Testaments. The books of Job and Ecclesiastes stand as a strong refutation of this concept of God. Job is declared innocent from the very start (see the prologue, Job 1–2), and the point of the story is to see whether a man's faith in God is dependent upon a favored position or persists *in spite of* what happens. Although the idea of just retribution lasted into New Testament times, it was likewise contested by Jesus when he was asked, "Master, do you think those eighteen who were killed when the tower in Siloam fell on them were more sinful than all the others in Jerusalem?" Jesus answered in effect, "No, you don't understand. You cannot correlate sin and suffering in that way" (Luke 13:1–5; cf. Matthew 5:45; John 9:1–3).

The acceptance of an essentially ambiguous world and the

[21]Coretta Scott King, *My Life with Martin Luther King, Jr.* (New York: Holt, Rinehart and Winston, 1969), p. 97 (also pp. 244–245).

[22]See Psalms 1; 37; 49; 73. The nation and the kings of Israel found success and reaped destruction to the extent that they obeyed the commands of God (see, e.g., Deuteronomy 28).

existence of genuinely innocent suffering which cannot be directly linked with sin or said to be sent by God does not necessarily rule out God's direct involvement in human life. As long as this allowance is made, the evangelical should be more willing to take a second look at the meaning of providence. The Christian must always be open to the possibility that God is not directly behind a certain significant and personal happening. He must be more willing to accept that not everything which happens is initiated by God, even though it would give us added comfort to think so. The acceptance of a basically neutral universe need not have the negative meaning conservatives have always associated with it. One key for a more positive perspective is found in the following understanding of the unexpected delay in Christ's return (*parousia*):

> It is natural that men should wish to see without delay the happy ending of the story in which they are involved. . . . But may it not have been God's intention . . . that life between the incarnation and the *parousia* should be the normal state of mankind? In this way men, caught in the tension of deferred hope but living by the Holy Spirit, might learn the discipline of the life of the children of God, each generation wrestling afresh with fear and defeat, existing under the shadow of death, and discovering what it is to live by faith.[23]

In a real sense, then, providence has meaning only when we hold fast to what the evangelical and liberal have respectively felt to be essential: the freedom of God to respond to his creation and man's freedom to respond in an ambiguous universe. Within this basic framework the question of just *how* God effects his love for the individual is left unanswered. It must be left unanswered, not simply because their separate traditions have led evangelical and liberal in opposite directions, but for the more important reason that both parties by neglecting the role of the Holy Spirit have successfully sealed off a possible solution.

Protestant theology has created its own dilemma by forcing us to choose between a God who acts either from outside (a

[23]C. K. Barrett, *Jesus and the Gospel Tradition* (Philadelphia: Fortress, 1968), p. 107.

transcendent act) or from within (an immanent act). Consequently there is no middle road open between a God who responds directly by intervention or indirectly by evolution. Yet the biblical witness concerning the Holy Spirit is clearly that the *transcendent* God is at work carrying out his purposes *within* this world through the Holy Spirit. The work of the Spirit is not divided between an earthly and a heavenly sphere, but in him the two coincide. The Spirit is one with God the Creator and one with the world; he is distinct from but cannot be separated from what happens in the world. Because the Spirit is to be our Counselor during the period when Christ is physically absent (John 14:26), shouldn't our doctrines about prayer, providence, and the world reflect a corresponding doctrine of the Holy Spirit? If there is to be a way open between evangelicals and liberals, it seems most likely to come about through a joint rethinking of the Christian theology of the Holy Spirit.

DISCUSSION QUESTIONS

1. Since prayer is an individual and highly sensitive matter, it may be helpful for each person to tell something of his belief concerning prayer. What purpose, for example, does prayer have in your life?

2. Relate some incidents in your life when you felt God's will was being carried out. Do you think the term "intervene" is appropriate? Why? If so, explain in what sense God intervened.

3. Is it possible to believe in both the omnipotence of God and a neutral world of chance and tragedies?

4. Examine the following passages in their full context: Matthew 7:7–11; 18:19; 21:22; Romans 8:28–30. On the basis of these texts are we justified in thinking that God responds directly to all sincere prayers and that all things will work for the good in the end?

5. Do you make a distinction between the work of Jesus Christ and that of the Holy Spirit? For example, to whom do you pray and by whom are prayers answered?

VI. THE CHURCH AND SOCIAL INVOLVEMENT

Without malicious intent any congregation, whether Jewish, Roman Catholic, or Protestant, could be split over the single issue of social involvement. "What kind?" "How much?" "Direct or indirect?" "Corporate or individual?" are the dividing questions. In the last decade or more this is precisely what has been happening, either openly or latently, with the result that Christians are hindered from presenting a unified and vital witness. In many respects I believe we are not as far apart as we think. Nevertheless we have been unable to move off dead center. To a large degree the reason is our tendency to isolate the problem of the church and social action from the other issues which divide evangelicals and liberals. As usual we have neglected the underlying motives, the respective historical dispositions, and the broader issues. We have failed ourselves because selfishness and vested interests have let us be content with the same arguments and the same clichés. My purpose then for placing this chapter last should be clear—to place the issue of social involvement in a total context where we can see all the factors at work.

An assessment of our present situation might best begin with how we see one another. The evangelical sees the liberal as compromising the mission of the church by involving it in social and political spheres where it has no special authority or divine imperative. In attempting to transform society by changing its organizational structures, the liberal neglects the priority of reconciling man to God. By substituting a man-centered foundation for a Christ-centered foundation, he deludes himself into thinking that power politics is more powerful than the Word of God. The liberal gives every indication that he is more concerned about man's physical and social well-being than about the basic moral and spiritual poverty of the world; more interested in fanning the fires of social unrest than in reconciliation. Unfortunately he works under the myth that man is an unhappy creature in an unhappy and alienated society. In short, personal regeneration has given way to a Christianized humanism whose goal is to make man fully human—healthy, happy, economically secure, at peace with himself, free in a just society.

From the liberal's vantage point the evangelical must have either a shallow or a limited social conscience which prevents him from envisioning the full scope of the gospel. His exaggerated emphasis on the individual overlooks the degree to which man has become societal and his world political; and his preoccupation with the spiritual overlooks the suffering of the whole man who is both body and soul. Exclusively person-to-person evangelism does not deal with the corporate and institutional sin of our modern, mass society. There is a political and social naiveté behind the evangelical's approach to changing society through "born again" lives. The failure to throw the weight of the corporate church against modern-day social evils leads to a passivity which harms the witness of the church. His great concern for law and order neglects the depth of misery caused by inherently unjust governments, and his support of the status quo disregards the eschatological and radical nature of Christ's good news.

Both the evangelical and liberal would feel these to be unfair assessments of their positions, and in part they are. When we are willing to find out where each assessment is correct and where it is not, and to seek the reasons behind the beliefs of each, we will be in a much better position to engage in fruitful dialogue.

HISTORICAL PERSPECTIVE

By now the reader should be alerted to the underlying theological presuppositions the liberal and evangelical bring to the question of the church and its social involvement. To these must be added presuppositions concerning man and society, economics, and politics. A brief historical perspective will go a long way to illumine the distinctive heritages which condition their respective attitudes toward social involvement.

A. Liberal

Though seldom given due regard, the rise and acceptance of the Social Gospel (approximately 1865–1915) is the most helpful window to view the liberal of today. The Social Gospel was both a positive and a negative response. Positively, it was the attempt of liberal Protestantism to deal with the impact of the industrial age in America. Already in the 1800s and 1890s liberal clergymen were becoming concerned with the dangers of monopolies, the growing conflict between labor and capitalism, the tenement evil, right-to-work laws, and child labor laws. Negatively, it was a reaction to what seemed an exaggerated individualism which did not take account of the extent to which each person is conditioned by society. It reacted likewise to an unrealistic separation between body and soul, between economic and spiritual, religious and political spheres. It sought to minister to the whole man in his total environment. Concretely, the Social Gospel took completely seriously the power of unemployment, for instance, to corrupt man. When a man is robbed of work, he is denied the means of self-fulfilment. He becomes a contented loafer or an embittered self-seeker. The Social Gospel then was an extension of the "old gospel" to a new age.

Three clearly related ideas constituted a logical and unified frame of reference for the Social Gospel. "These were the immanence of God, the organic or solidaristic view of society, and the presence of the kingdom of heaven on earth."[1] As a whole, but especially in its doctrine of the immanence of God, the Social Gospel reflected the newly promulgated theory of evolution and an optimism not yet diminished by two world wars. The belief in a pervasive and ultimately triumphant spiritual reality at work in the universe came naturally. It rode the crest of a feeling that we were on the road to a new social order, a brotherhood of mankind. It saw the theory of evolution not as the descent but the ascent of mankind. The liberal emphasis on the immanence of God was

[1]Charles Howard Hopkins, *The Rise of the Social Gospel in American Protestantism 1865–1915* (New Haven: Yale Univ., 1940), p. 123.

thus the application of the new optimism about man and the world and the theistic expression of the scientific idea of progressive evolution: The vision of God unfolding himself in man and nature at once broke down the rigid distinction between sacred and secular and reinforced the idea of an organic bond uniting the individual and society. The conservation of natural resources and the equal distribution of material benefits became important concerns. The immanence of God meant that a vital and divine indwelling force was already at work in creation and could be brought to perfection with the help of Christians.

A second foundation stone of the Social Gospel was the social solidarity of mankind and the correlative concept of the solidarity of sin. The growing awareness that man is an inextricable part of a larger community caused the Social Gospel to widen its theology of both salvation and judgment.

> The social gospel is the old message of salvation, but enlarged and intensified. The individualistic gospel has taught us to see the sinfulness of every human heart. . . . But it has not given us an adequate understanding of the sinfulness of the social order and its share in the sins of all individuals within it. It has not evoked faith in the will and power of God to redeem the permanent institutions of human society from their inherited guilt of oppression and extortion. Both our sense of sin and our faith in salvation have fallen short of the realities under its teaching. The social gospel seeks to bring men under repentance for their collective sins and to create a more sensitive and more modern conscience.[2]

Walter Rauschenbusch's intention was not to dispense with personal regeneration but to extend it to the larger social groups to which we belong.[3] Typical of the Social Gospel, Rauschenbusch points out that some half-dozen social sins combined to kill Jesus:

[2]Walter Rauschenbusch, *A Theology for the Social Gospel* (New York: Abingdon, 1945), p. 5.

[3]*Ibid.*, ch. x; but esp. p. 96: "Therefore our discussion cannot pass personal salvation by. We might possibly begin where the old gospel leaves off, and ask our readers to take all the familiar experiences and truths of personal evangelism and religious nurture for granted in what follows."

religious bigotry, graft and political power, the corruption of justice, mob spirit and mob action, militarism, and class contempt. Jesus died, then, not only for the private sins of Caiaphas, Pilate, or Judas but bore the weight of the public sins of organized society, "to which all who ever lived have contributed, and under which all who ever lived have suffered."[4]

Flowing forth from this sense of corporateness are a host of other attitudes. A new feeling of solidarity with the poor and minorities prompted a concern for the common laborer. The spiritual and economic realms were seen as interdependent; for without justice in the economic system there could be no realization of the Kingdom of God. There emerged a sensibility that the most important decisions affecting thousands should not be left entirely to unchristian men. There was a willingness to work with humanitarian movements in the hope a common goal or a better society could be achieved sooner. The results and analyses of the expanding social sciences were readily consulted. And not incidentally, the church as the redeemed *community* served as the moral model of the new society.

More than any other concept, the Kingdom of God became the integrating idea for the Social Gospel. In Rauschenbusch's own words, ". . . the essential purpose of Christianity was to transform society into the kingdom of God by regenerating all human relations and reconstituting them in accordance with the will of God."[5] The Kingdom of God as defined by the Social Gospel had certain characteristics. It was first of all the divine *force,* realizing itself *in history*. As a historical force the Kingdom of God would realize itself *on earth* as humanity *organized* according to the will of God. *Collectivity* was also a key principle, since this divinely inspired social order would embrace the whole of mankind. Released by Christ, the power of the Kingdom is *now going on,* a present reality, which continues *progressively* until one day the whole of humanity will live by the rule of God.

In the language of Washington Gladden (c. 1895), "The immanence of Christ, the vital unity of the race, the presence of

[4]*Ibid.*, p. 258.

[5]Walter Rauschenbusch, *Christianity and the Social Crisis,* ed. Robert D. Cross (New York: Harper, 1964), p. xxiii.

the Kingdom—these truths give to life a new sacredness and to duty a new cogency." This, succinctly, was the Social Gospel. Insofar as it is a product of its age, contemporary liberalism has difficulty accepting it in toto. It is obvious that some of the predominant themes remain, but at certain important junctures modifications are necessary.

Two atomic bombs, a Dresden, five million Jews, six Negro children dynamited in Birmingham, three assassinations, a Vietnam, riot-torn ghettos make it impossible for the liberal to face the future with the same optimism and confidence. If at the turn of the century men were struck by the immense opportunity for progress, we today are struck by the persistence of sin and the stubbornness of evil in history. For a host of reasons the liberal no longer looks for a smoothly progressive transformation of society.[6] For some revolution appears to be a better solution to the inherent evil of the structures we have created. Nevertheless there is a persistent hope within liberalism that is linked with God's immanence, evolution, and Christ as the focal point of human destiny. Undiminished and even intensified is the sense of solidarity. The liberal remains just as convinced that an individualistic ethic must be modified with a morality of collectives, whether of class, race, or nation.

Most liberals would agree that Rauschenbusch and the Social Gospel tended toward reductionism when they tried to interpret the life of Jesus almost solely in terms of his social teachings. The Social Gospel advocates did not naively paint Jesus as a political revolutionary or a civil legislator or social philosopher. They recognized that he began by winning souls, not by righting political wrongs. They cast him more as an idealist with a vision

[6]Ever since the severe criticism of the Social Gospel by the Niebuhrs, modern liberalism has fought the danger of returning to a theology naively optimistic, overly romantic, which involves no discontinuities, no crises, no tragedies, and no cross or resurrection. See H. Richard Niebuhr, *The Kingdom of God in America* (New York: Harper, 1959), pp. 189–193. In a conversation with the late Reinhold Niebuhr, Wolfhart Pannenberg elicited this response: "I am almost grateful for the act of mercy that he [Rauschenbusch] died before seeing what the war [World War I] had done to the world. It would have broken his heart." See W. Pannenberg, *Theology and the Kingdom of God* (Philadelphia: Westminster, 1969), p. 32.

than an agitator, more as a revealer than a reformer. Yet volumes were written about his teachings on the family, the state, the industrial order, society, crime, poverty, nonresistance, and democracy. In short, Jesus was seen as the founder of a new society. In retrospect the liberal of today realizes the Social Gospel minimized the futuristic, "not yet" character of Jesus' message in order to make his teaching seem more relevant to an expanding industrial age. Ironically, contemporary New Testament research has moved in a direction opposite to Francis Peabody's statement that "Jesus did not share the eschatological ideas of his age." It is precisely the "not yet" tenor of Jesus' message which biblical scholars tell us cannot be eliminated. The liberal knows better now than to expect any easy transition from the life of Jesus to modern society. What strikes the liberal of the 1960s and '70s is the radical (practically equated with eschatological) way Christ stood "in opposition" to the status quo, instead of becoming identified with it or removing himself from society. Jesus may not have been a political revolutionary in the modern sense, "but he had a habit of reversing the order of things men took for granted (Luke 1:52–53)."[7]

Finally, there is a reaction to the Social Gospel's humanizing and temporalizing the Kingdom of God. The same biblical research has made the liberal aware that the Kingdom of God can never be simply equated with a particular social program or government. The dialectical, the "yet to be realized" nature of the Kingdom seems quite incongruous with Layman Abbott's summary: "The object of Christianity is human welfare; its method is character building; its process is evolution; and the secret of its power is God." Liberalism today is not so quick to say the Kingdom of God is merely a just society, a new social order, or a perfectly organized community. The liberal may not deny the Kingdom is all this; but it is much more than a social Utopia.[8]

[7]John C. Bennett, *Christian Ethics and Social Policy* (New York: Scribner's, 1946), p. 11. In his first chapter Bennett outlines very succinctly the new direction liberalism would take in the next decades concerning Christian social action.

[8]See Martin E. Marty, *The Search for a Usable Future* (New York: Harper, 1969), pp. 31–36, 61–64. Marty marshals a typical contemporary liberal attack on Utopia as a false scenerio. Peter Berger and Richard

The "much more," however, is often ill defined or not defined at all. The transformation of society is still sought, but it alone is not the goal. Evolution is still an integral element, but its course is far from automatic, straight, or unruffled. The method of character building surely is nearly useless in the realm of power politics. The extent to which the concept of the Kingdom of God fell into disrespect is obvious from its gradual disappearance after World War I. It is also interesting to note that initially the Social Gospel's enthusiasm for the Kingdom of God as the coming climactic event came from the evangelical revival,[9] only to be disregarded subsequently by both liberal and conservative. Unfortunately, its neglect coincided with the loss of coherence concerning the final goal the Christian is working toward. At best it can be said the liberal is rethinking what the Kingdom of God stands for in a vastly complex and changing world.[10]

B. Evangelical

Protestantism in early twentieth-century America shows the divergence of two vital movements. Besides the Social Gospel, there was the nascent stirring of a new evangelicalism. The emergence of a distinctive conservatism was due mainly to a new awakening of the Christian's social conscience (see chapter I). There is strong evidence that the evangelical today is just as

---

Neuhaus see the significance of the Hartford Appeal in its call for a recovery of the divine transcendence. Both feel the church has become too identified with the prevailing culture because God, who is always wholly other, is equated with historical movements seeking to overcome injustices in society. Neuhaus writes: "Transcendence relativizes every cause, movement, and thought form—most emphatically including those called Christian." See *Against the World For the World*, ed. Peter L. Berger and Richard J. Neuhaus (New York: Seabury Press, 1976), p. 154.

[9]A fresh examination of the interrelationship between the Social Gospel and the evangelical tradition would undoubtedly show that the two are not irreconcilable. See H. R. Niebuhr, *The Kingdom of God*. . . , pp. 162, 184–198; and Timothy L. Smith, *Revivalism and Social Reform in Mid-Nineteenth-Century America* (New York: Abingdon, 1957), esp. pp. 148–162.

[10]Pannenberg, *Theology and the Kingdom of God*, is a good example of the renewed interest in the Kingdom of God as an integrating symbol.

affected by the mood of social involvement as is the liberal.[11] And as the liberal is both proud and critical of his recent past, so is the evangelical.

The evangelical who understands the imperative to become involved in the world's suffering is acutely aware of a past which handicaps him. During the period when liberals were turning outward armed with a concept of the Kingdom of God on earth, the conservative was turned inward by the battle over evolution, the application of the critical-historical method to the Bible, and the attack on religion by Marx, Freud, and others. The smoke from the theological brushfires too often blinded the evangelical to the vast evils of an industrial-military-bureaucratic age. He knew the significance of a saved soul but barely touched the gigantic questions of segregation and poverty. He found himself confronted with the uncomfortable alternative of going along with the social gospelers, whose theology and methods he could not agree with, or denouncing them and other social reform movements. The result was that

> . . . at the very time when they should have been actively and helpfully involved in working out the huge problems of a society in transition, and speaking up for the rights of man as Jesus did, the evangelical Christians were being driven by the heavy artillery of the critics to consolidate their defenses around the Bible. Valuable spiritual ammunition which could have been put to constructive use was being used up in denunciation and rhetoric. Energy and vitality were drained by argument.[12]

[11]A fine example is Sherwood Eliot Wirt, *The Social Conscience of the Evangelical* (New York: Harper & Row, 1968). The U.S. Congress on Evangelism (Minneapolis, Sept. 1969) was a momentous call to right the social wrongs of our age, but on a personal basis. The speeches given at the Congress are reprinted in George M. Wilson, ed., *Evangelism Now* (New York: World Wide Publications, 1970). In assessing the revived interest in relating gospel and social action, one must also note the prominence of black evangelical leaders such as Tom Skinner, John Perkins, Bill Pannell, Bill Bentley, and Ron Potter.

[12]Wirt, *The Social Conscience* . . . , p. 16. Evangelicals faced a similar dilemma in the 1840s and 1850s over the slave issue. As one observer noted, evangelicals were caught "between the upper and the nether millstones of a *pro-slavery* Christianity and an *anti*-Christian abolitionism." See T. Smith, *Revivalism and Social Reform*, pp. 187–203.

Yet it is misleading to say the evangelical has had no social conscience. This point has been obscured by his single-mindedness about the need for personal regeneration and by the differences in kinds of involvement between him and the liberal. The strong stance taken against racism at the 1966 World Congress on Evangelism was ignored by liberals, for instance, because it was coupled with spiritual dynamism rather than political pressure. Driven by a strong sense of individual morality, a conception of man as free and responsible, a doctrine of distinct spheres of authority for the church and the state, and the requirement of a scriptural warrant, the conservative's social involvement has been characterized by compassionate concern for the *individual's* physical and spiritual well-being. In the twenties and thirties the conservative was in the forefront in the fight against alcoholism, tobacco, gambling, and prostitution, while the liberal fought against the social ills of unemployment, unfair rents, child labor, and poverty. Today the evangelical's concerns include the plight of refugees, hunger, drugs, crime, racial prejudice, political deceit, obscenity in films, violence in television, and pornography. For him the principle remains the same: personal regeneration means personal rectitude and integrity.

The contemporary evangelical sees more clearly that Christian morality applies just as much to the politician who votes out of personal gain as to the adulterer, to the manufacturer of unsafe automobiles as to the mugger, to the policeman who takes money from a prostitute as to the prostitute, to the white grocer who sells bad meat to a Negro customer as to the black rioter. The gap between the evangelical and liberal will continue to exist, of course, to the extent that the former regards the individual sin as worse than the social sin (or vice versa). Nevertheless the evangelical looks to confront the social issues of tomorrow knowing that personal sin is the source of corporate sin, not the reverse, and that Jesus Christ, not social action, is the answer to personal morality. What is required to change the world is to change the individuals in the world, and no way has been more successful than to bring man into a lasting personal relationship with the Lord of life, Christ the Son of God.

In comparing the social action of conservatives with that of liberals before and after World War II, another characteristic stands out. The Social Gospel was critical of capitalism and relatively favorable toward socialism because the latter promised a more equal existence in an unequal society. At the same time conservatives were commending free enterprise and limited government, justifying wealth on the basis of merit while denouncing socialism and welfare states. The conservative maintained his traditional avenues of service—city rescue missions for the outcast; homes for the aged, orphans, widows, and unmarried mothers; emergency relief for disaster victims and homeless; schools for the blind and mentally retarded. The liberal's concern for society, on the other hand, led him to support the labor movement and union strikes, to help the poor in their struggle for civil and economic justice, and to be in constant conflict with industrial managers, landlords, city politicians, government administrators, and so-called capitalists. The social action of the conservative demonstrated the Christian response to individual suffering and the morality of personal worth, while the response of the liberal demonstrated Christian concern for social justice and the ethic of wealth.

Besides the obvious difference in attitude toward politics and economics, the conservative and liberal stood separated by a preference to witness by alleviating personal suffering, independent of government programs, in contrast to a preference to witness by social and political action in cooperation with nonreligious action groups. There are three important reasons the evangelical chooses the former method of social involvement. First, a strong adherence to the separation of church and state urges independent action. The evangelical cherishes and guards the freedom of the church to proclaim the love of God in Christ in conjunction with humanitarian service. The deed alone is not enough. He finds the growing tendency toward government welfare programs distasteful, because they tend to displace the Christian witness of the church. Such programs, though needed, neglect the spiritual and moral poverty of man. Second, the evangelical does not share the liberal hope that man will some day achieve a perfect society. The Kingdom of God is another dimension of being which cannot be established on earth, for "here we have no continuing city." It is not that the evangelical regards social progress as unimportant, but it must be held secondary to the salvation of souls. Third, the conception of man as free and responsible prompts the conservative to help the individual to help himself, rather than change institutional structures in the hope they will regenerate men. Social forces and environmental circumstances are not to be overlooked, but they should not lead us to think man is a helpless victim incapable of directing his destiny. Such notions as rugged individualism, the self-made man, and justification of wealth on the basis of merit spring from this conservative image of man as a free actor, able to determine his future and thus free to choose his own salvation.[13] There is evidence, however, that the evangelical is moving away from the unsophisticated depiction of the rich man as bearing a special mark of God's favor and the poor man as capable of herculean feats to raise himself by his bootstraps ("nothing can keep a good man down"), just as the liberal is realizing the simplification in always suspecting the wealthy and always expecting the ghetto-dweller to be helpless to shape his future. Nevertheless the evangelical holds to the conviction that if the less fortunate are to be helped, ultimately they must be helped directly and personally.

The past and present history of evangelical social action testifies emphatically to a final trait, namely, that Christian social action be distinguishable from secular and humanitarian movements. The evangelical has sought to make his involvement distinguishable principally by providing it with a sound and *explicit* biblical basis. Misinterpreted, this becomes known as "Bible-quoting," but its intended purpose is to preserve the distinctiveness of the Christian message as applied to secular questions. In an age when secularists and atheists are actively engaged in social reform, it is vital for the evangelical to demonstrate a concern which goes beyond the material. When the Christian becomes involved in today's social ills, he must leave no doubt that his motivation is the love of Christ. Where the corporate church must take a stand on sociopolitical questions, it must do so by making perfectly clear the scriptural principles involved and the moral issue which is at stake.

[13]The relationship of belief that the poor and black are responsible for their own plight to certain conservative theological beliefs is an interesting one. See Jeffrey K. Hadden, *The Gathering Storm in the Churches* (New York: Doubleday, 1969), pp. 79–81, 111, 141.

The evangelical faces the concrete problem of where to become involved. The social work once carried on by his forefathers has passed into secular and governmental hands. He finds some other group already raising their voices on nearly ever social or moral issue imaginable. He is also hobbled by the world's suspicion. He does not want to be identified with either the far right or the radical left. He scarcely hopes to become more involved in racial and social justice than the liberal now is. Thus by *choice* and necessity, the evangelical understands his role as insuring the distinctive message of Christianity against humanitarian erosion and preventing the unique person-to-person ministry of Christians from being lost among a host of social do-gooders.[14]

THE GOAL AND THE MEANS

By this time certain general directions of thought within liberalism and evangelicalism are taking form. Further observation reveals the liberal and evangelical do not begin with the same presupposition concerning the goal and the means of the church's mission. There is a *theoretical* agreement that the mission of the church involves the whole man, body and soul, and all areas of human affairs, political, social, economic, and all the rest. The evangelical, for example, acknowledges the intimate relation between the spiritual and the physical and between the individual and society. Modern medicine and psychology have left little doubt about the truth of the former, and sociology has provided

[14]The formation of the organization, Evangelicals for Social Action, as a response to the Chicago Declaration (1973), illustrates how evangelicals see themselves implementing a biblical mandate for social justice. President Ronald J. Sider has been instrumental in putting together an organization that trains and motivates local groups to become involved in the full array of urban social/political problems without losing sight of their Christian perspective to human sin and redemption. The bimonthly magazine, *The Other Side*, has also taken a modest leadership role by the creation of its two ministries—Jubilee Crafts and Jubilee Fund. Only the latter addresses itself to the issue of social change. Not as well known is the Boston (Dorchester) based organization, Christians for Urban Justice, which emulates the style of Evangelicals for Social Action and achieves a good integration of gospel and social justice.

enough evidence about the latter. The liberal joins the evangelical in recognizing the importance of beginning with personal regeneration and the danger of slipping into a social humanism. In practice, however, there is a clear difference in emphasis, balance, and priority.

For the evangelical salvation begins with a commitment to Christ growing out of a radical transformation of life. The primary task of the Christian is to bring other men into this saving relationship with Jesus. The function of the church is not to Christianize social structures but to nourish the members of Christ's body with God's Word and the sacraments. In both cases priority is given to man's spiritual needs, because a man must be changed spiritually before he is changed at all (John 3:1–15). Man's eternal welfare must always take precedence over his temporal needs. Reconciling men to God is the first order of priority before men can be reconciled to men. The evangelical is therefore convinced he is working from the only right foundation.

The liberal begins with the supposition that the spiritual and the physical are so interdependent that it is misleading to exalt one over the other. Similarly, the individual's relationship with his environment is so integral that it is deceiving to talk about salvation for the whole man without including the political and social structures which govern his life. It is not a question of reconciling man to God, as if this happens independently of and prior to reconciling our human relations. Jesus' concern for the quality of human existence was not one-sided but embraced man in his total existence. His concern for others—the leper, the blind and deaf, the disturbed—was directed at their greatest need, whether physical or spiritual. Our additional concern about the way institutions treat people is a modern one, but it is in keeping with Christ's attack on anything which prevents man from realizing his full created self. When human personalities, created in God's own image, live in pathological conditions of squalor, you can be sure they will choose for themselves demonic concepts of life.

The conservative maintains that all mission is ultimately evangelistic, while the liberal claims that not all mission is necessarily evangelism. According to the liberal definition, "Christians often are engaged in the mission of the Church without any explicit or self-conscious verbal reference to their being Christian or to the teachings of Christ. They simply allow their Christ-formed consciences and concerns to cooperate with men, whether Christians, Jews, humanists, or atheists, in working for the welfare of other men."[15] There are times and places which require a silent, pervasive "Christian presence" more than a vocal confession of Christ. For the evangelical there can be no mission which does not let it be known in one way or another—not necessarily a frontal, dogmatic assault—that we are witnessing to God's grace in Jesus Christ. The evangelical feels every opportunity should be used for Christian witness; the liberal does not.

In other words, the social humanist believes a hospital should be built instead of a church. The evangelical believes that both hospitals and churches should be built, but churches have priority. The liberal also believes both hospitals and churches should be built, but according to the greatest need.

In complete fairness it must be pointed out that the difference here is one of emphasis. The evangelical is increasingly recognizing that physical conditions and political decisions can hinder or help people's coming to know Christ. The growth and development of Christian lives is not independent of the soil where the gospel falls. Nevertheless the gospel will be and has been spread without a transformed society. Herein the wedge is made. The evangelical sees the reorientation of social structures as consequential to personal conversion. Where the spiritual is given true priority, the material needs of man will be met also. The liberal does not claim that elimination of unjust laws and ghettos is more important than conversion but argues that socio-political involvement is justified as a form of mission which need not be directly evangelistic. The transformation of structures which hinder love becomes not only a necessary preparation but a legitimate end to be pursued in itself. The Kingdom of God is not identical with just social structures, but it is not independent of them either.

The second basic presupposition concerns the means or

[15]From a position paper by the Division of Evangelism of the United Presbyterian Church in the U.S.A., adopted at the 1967 General Assembly.

catalyst of the church's mission. As previously stated, there is a theoretical agreement that both verbal and nonverbal, direct and indirect, individual and corporate action are involved in changing men and society. Yet differing concepts of salvation dictate a different accent. Theologically and methodologically, the evangelical has reason to value more highly the verbal and personal. From the days of the early church the Word preached has had the unique power to convict the individual of his sin and reveal to him that Christ has acted to overcome sin. Keeping in mind that the goal of evangelism is to bring the individual into a saving *knowledge* of Jesus Christ, it follows that the means must be *conceptual* in nature (e.g., preaching the gospel and teaching Christian principles). The emphasis on revelation as conceptual also adds to the conviction that understanding is to be trusted more than experience. In addition the evangelical displays considerable confidence in the power of the spoken Word to change people. Three thousand souls were saved on the day of Pentecost by the straightforward, uncomplicated preaching of Peter (Acts 2). Who can count the number of lives turned about and given to Christ in small and large tent meetings and crusades? Surely the times require that we use all the advanced communicative techniques at our disposal, but there has been no better way to confront the individual with Christ than the preached Word.

The formulation of the Lausanne Covenant (1974) reflects the evangelical's preoccupation with the spoken Word as the only valid means to evangelize. In a plenary paper John R. W. Stott warns that evangelism must "not be defined in terms of *methods*."[16] Stott proposes announcing the good news by a transformed life, by a Christ-centered home, by works of love, and even by speechless excitement about Jesus. The authors of the Covenant, however, distinguished evangelism from any "presence theology" that might be nonverbal.

> Our Christian presence in the world is indispensable to evangelism, and so is that kind of dialogue whose purpose is to listen sensitively to understand. But evangelism itself is

[16]John R. W. Stott, "The Biblical Basis of Evangelism," in *Let the Earth Hear His Voice,* ed. J. D. Douglas (Minneapolis: World Wide Publications, 1975), p. 69.

> the proclamation of the historical, biblical Christ as Savior and Lord, with a view to persuading people to come to him personally and so be reconciled to God (section 4, Lausanne Covenant).

"Only changed men change society," so the evangelical motto runs. Here the transformed individual is the agent of permanent change in society. Mission history abounds with evidence of how regenerated lives have changed society. Head-hunting cannibals became peaceful citizens; drug addicts were delivered from their addiction; thieves turned to honest labor; wealthy men gave sacrificially for social benefit. While history also teaches us that social action may change the circumstances, will it make the world more just, more human? Was Castro so much better than Batista? the Black Panthers than white bureaucrats? the United States than the French in Vietnam? the Khomeini than the Shah of Iran? Much more effective than general pronouncements aimed at uncommitted masses or parties is the person-to-person outreach of dedicated believers. As Edward Carnell teasingly asks, would Billy Graham be more effective if he shifted from preaching against personal sin to preaching, "Repent of your race prejudice and be saved"? Would he not run the risk of overplaying racial injustice and neglecting the deeper personal pride which is the root of all sins?[17] Realistically, how can society be fundamentally changed unless its individual members are freed from their selfishness and destructive pride?

The liberal is more inclined toward impersonal, nonverbal, corporate, and sociopolitical engagement. Pragmatically, he has serious doubts about the power of spoken words to change men, not to mention ghettos and governments. The social sciences have convinced him that involvement, conflict, and tension are much better catalysts to effect substantial change. As powerful as

[17]Edward John Carnell, "On Reinhold Niebuhr and Billy Graham," in *The Case for Biblical Christianity,* p. 90. Cf. Peter L. Berger and Richard J. Neuhaus, *Movement and Revolution* (Garden City, N.Y.: Doubleday, 1970), chs. II, III, IV, VI. Berger, who is generally known for his liberal theological position, explains why he sides with the conservative approach to sociopolitical problems.

concepts and verbal bombardment can be, the human personality is strangely resistant to words. Many a preacher questions what real change his hundreds of sermons have brought. Since the physical environment and society are to be transformed, the means must be appropriate. Certainly big business, political leaders, and bureaucratic institutions understand the language of action better than words. The latter they can ignore, but direct confrontation they cannot. It is unrealistic to think the entrenched status quo or the military complex of America can be humanized by the diligent work of individual Christians working separately. There are times when the selfish power structures of nations will only heed the united action of many and their corporate political and economic power.

Theologically, the liberal is pushed in the same direction. Since humanitarian goals are highly valued, it is not surprising that the liberal's means are sometimes similar to those employed by non-Christian social activists. His sense of solidarity is more than an expression of the doctrine of the brotherhood of mankind. It is in essence an expression of the theological truth that man finds his true self in relationship with others, that is, in society. Salvation and judgment are corporately conceived insofar as our mutual destinies are dependent upon each other. Even Christ is more deeply revealed in the "depth-experiences" of life than through traditional "religious" experiences. The liberal's reluctance to equate faith with assent to traditional doctrines has led him to stress the nonverbal aspect of faith: experience, self-consciousness, self-understanding, commitment.

Superficially it would be easy to resolve the conflict by admitting the necessity of both verbal and nonverbal methods of communicating the gospel. There is ample evidence that the evangelical is not rigidly opposed to corporate, sociopolitical action. The liberal on the other hand realizes that lasting change in the end must be the product of men who care more about others than themselves because they know Christ. But it is only superficially that the issue can be so easily disposed, because the liberal and evangelical are speaking to each other from quite divergent perspectives. To summarize: The liberal is willing to overlook any final distinction between physical and spiritual, secular and sacred, while the evangelical is not. The liberal perceives God as already present in the world; one has only to discover, develop, and cooperate with the divine spark there. Because Jesus is located in the other person, the liberal finds his faith tied into society—not accidentally but inherently. For the evangelical certain priorities must be kept in order to insure that we do not lose the distinction between natural and supernatural, worldly and divine, body and soul. Redemption is a gift of God won by Jesus Christ, not a human achievement or the evolution of man's goodness. Faith in Jesus is more than faith in an ephemeral presence or an ideal man. It is faith in the living Person who can be known and trusted. Liberal concepts of progress and history, evolution and immanence, secularism and humanism have been translated into an understanding of the Kingdom of God which includes the gradual transformation of society. In contrast, evangelical concepts of fallen man and supernatural redemption, apocalypticism and transcendence, sacredness and regeneration have added up to an understanding of the Kingdom of God as the dramatic intervention of God.[18] The former envisions the end of history as the gradual fulfilment of the present, the latter as the sudden return of the physical person of Jesus.

THE CHURCH'S PRIMARY ROLE

We are now prepared to tackle the issue: Should the corporate church, as distinct from its individual members, become directly

[18]There can be no doubt that as evangelicalism came to adopt a premillennial attitude, notably since the Niagara Prophetic Conference (1868) and peaking around 1925, it became apathetic toward social issues as it awaited an immediate Second Advent. As the fundamentalist-modernist controversy abated, evangelicals felt less alienated from the culture. Contemporary evangelicalism, as a result, exhibits a mixed picture of rejection and acceptance of American cultural values, a reluctance and a willingness to view social change as integral with the Kingdom of God. See George M. Marsden, "From Fundamentalism to Evangelicalism: A Historical Analysis," and Robert D. Linder, "The Resurgence of Evangelical Social Concern (1925–75)," in *The Evangelicals,* ed. David F. Wells & John D. Woodbridge (Nashville: Abingdon, 1975).

[19]Dean Hoge's study brings to the surface the important factor that it is not so much the actor, the church, or the individual, but the type of action that arouses opposition to social mission. Dean R. Hoge, *Division in the Protestant House* (Philadelphia: Westminster, 1976), p. 87. I certainly do not wish to downplay in any way the fact that the issue itself can be as divisive as who chooses to become involved.

involved in the sociopolitical realm?[19] The evangelical has no objection against the individual Christian's working to influence political elections and speaking out on economic questions. He does not object to Christians uniting together for corporate action, whether to form a new political party or a committee on better housing. The Christian, he believes, is called to be involved in every area of human life and to be concerned with the reform of society in accord with Christian principles. It is a different matter, however, for the church as a corporate body to become involved in secular issues, for Christians to become involved in the name of the church, or for groups to speak for the church. The liberal, of course, believes the corporate church has a mandate to commit her authority and power in the secular realm. Both the evangelical and liberal have deeper reasons for their positions, as we have seen and will see further.

To appreciate the perspective of the evangelical one must understand his theological views on the separation of church and state and on the divinely given structures in history and society. The evangelical finds ample scriptural warrant for two distinct spheres of authority, one belonging to the church and the other belonging to the state.[20] The church has been ordained and equipped to govern in the spiritual realm just as the state has been in the secular realm. According to the Protestant Lutheran heritage of the "two kingdoms" of creation and redemption, each receives its authority from God. In the kingdom of creation, the Creator rules all sinful men through Caesar and the laws of civil justice and order. In the kingdom of redemption, the Redeemer rules all regenerate believers through Christ and a personal faith in him. "As both Redeemer and Creator, God is at once the Lord of both kingdoms; as both righteous and sinful, the Christian is at once a subject of both kingdoms."[21]

An evangelical theology of society thus requires the two spheres of authority to be properly distinguished but never separated. The conservative sees the necessity and advantage of sharply differentiating the valid functions of the church and state in

[20]See, for example, Matthew 22:21; Luke 12:14; Romans 13.

[21]William H. Lazareth, "Luther's 'Two Kingdoms' Ethic Reconsidered," in *Christian Social Ethics in a Changing World*, ed. John C. Bennett (New York: Association, 1966), p. 123.

order to preserve the sanctity and freedom of each. He denies, at the same time, a rigorous dualism between the two spheres and assumes the responsibility to permeate all of society with personal love and social justice.

Scripture also warrants certain orders or structures of creation to benefit mankind: marriage, family, divisions of labor, private property, and the like. As social structures they apply to all men and are the direct responsibility of the secular authority, but as God-given orders it is the duty of the church to promote and maintain them. Men should accept these social orders for what they are: the Creator's dikes against sin. Since they belong to the kingdom of creation they will be corrupted by sinful men. Nevertheless they are still the means by which the Creator graciously preserves his fallen order from even greater chaos, injustice, and suffering.

There are definite implications arising from this basic theological stance. The Christian is obliged to respect and be obedient to civil authorities and their laws. The Christian is reminded that those in authority in the secular realm have received their right to rule from God, even if they misuse it or deny its divine origin. The laws they promulgate should be broken only under extraordinary circumstances, even if they are inadequate or unjust, since they are part of God's total plan. The Old Testament supplies many examples of governments (Assyria, Babylonia, Rome) which acknowledged only their own authority but in the end served the will of God nevertheless. Secular kingdoms are manifestly composed of sinful men, but God does not allow them to use him for their own evil purposes. Otherwise St. Paul's injunction to "be subject to the governing authorities" (Romans 13) would be invalidated.

Another basic implication precious to evangelicalism is that while the institutional church has a legitimate obligation to *preserve* what is valuable in society, it does not have a legitimate obligation to *transform* the state into the Kingdom of God. In contrast to liberal theology, the conservative does not look forward to the time when the secular and sacred realms will merge to become one. If he did, he would be scorning the secular orders which have been ordained by God to remain secular and to enjoy a relative autonomy of their own. He would also forget that "in the Kingdom of God persons can be transformed by the gospel, but in the kingdom of men institutions can only be reformed by the law."[22] The evangelical works under the presupposition that the church can Christianize politicians and economists, but not politics and economics. It is men, not society's structures, that can be spiritually transformed, and only changed men can change society. For the church to engage in direct political pressure, endorse legislation, or espouse specific positions on military, economic, and social issues is paramount to Christianizing the functions of the state, denying the "sacred secularity" of God's ordained orders, and confusing the two distinct spheres of authority.

The church's mandate to preach the Word of God constitutes its authority in the spiritual sphere. It is a mandate that we must never forget is grounded in God's direct and absolute revelation of himself. Since this authority is unique to the church and belongs properly to the corporate church and not to its individual members, the church must steadfastly protect it from erosion and use it judiciously. If it tries to apply its authority in secular matters, the church stands in grave danger of wasting and undermining its authority. When the church commits itself directly on the secular scene—to relieve poverty, to influence foreign policy, to enter discussions on political problems—it enters an area of human affairs where it possesses no special authority, where it can only be a poor competitor, where it has much to lose and little to gain. Time and again the church has found that its action was wrong, premature or too late, misinformed, or naive. Inevitably people lose confidence in the church's message and ability to lead in the area of life which ultimately counts.

The role of the church as a corporate body must not be confused with that of its Christian laymen. The individual, because he has only himself to answer for, is free to participate in morally ambiguous political decisions in a way that the church as a whole is not. Man being what he is, government always possesses an element of corruption. Its deliberations are at best imperfect and at worst grievously unjust. Its processes arouse and stimulate human qualities antithetical to Christian integrity: ambition, self-love, greed, envy, love of public attention, desire for

[22] *Ibid.*, p. 124.

power, the appetite for flattery. As Norman Mailer said when considering his new role of candidate for mayor of New York City, "It's very dangerous for your soul to be a politician, because if you get power it can lead you to perdition faster than almost any other form of human activity."

It is for this reason that George F. Kennan, a Christian layman and formerly ambassador to Russia, strongly urges the church to concentrate on its primary duty of arming and strengthening the individual: to maintain him against tremendous forces in his belief, to encourage him in his disappointment, to inspire him in his disillusionment, to extend to him the comfort of the sacraments, and to help him set his Christian principles in perspective against the imperfections and compromises which inevitably belong to man and government.[23]

The liberal seems to overlook or disregard the effect which surely results when the church engages in public pronouncements. Such pronouncements cannot help but give the impression of speaking for the whole church. Since in fact they do not, social pronouncements split the church into opposing groups. What possible witness is gained by involving the authority of the church in such complex problems as the war in Vietnam, the establishment of a defense fund for Angela Davis, labor union disputes involving grape pickers in California and textile workers at J. P. Stevens Co., corporate investments in South Africa, or the boycott of Nestle products? Whatever positive effects such actions may have are lost many times over in the discord and loss of confidence they bring. A divided church is never as potent as a unified church. Certainly the church, which is the corporate body best able to speak to the spirit of man, is visibly reduced in effectiveness when it shows the same disunity and relativity that all other institutions demonstrate.

Public social pronouncements weaken the church in another way. By seeming to accomplish a lot but in actuality changing very little social pronouncements deceive Christians into complacent passivity. Instead of motivating Christians to

[23]George F. Kennan, "The Relation of Religion to Government," *The Princeton Seminary Bulletin*, vol. LXII (Winter, 1969), p. 45. The address had been published previously either in whole or in part in several journals of Princeton University, where it was given.

individual involvement, they allow laymen to sit back, feel good, and do nothing since the church has already spoken for them. As a result the great and lasting changes possible through personal witness tend to be dissipated. In effect, public pronouncements seriously weaken the position of the church for either social or spiritual good. The purity of purpose which should uniquely be the church's is lost in deference to secular involvement.

Consequently "most evangelicals would say it is one thing for Christians to express and act on their convictions on public issues, but it is quite another thing for a corporate church denomination to speak authoritatively on such issues in the name of all its members."[24] It is not that evangelicals would never have the corporate church speak out, but they would limit the church's public pronouncements to the very gravest issues, when "there are spiritual or moral issues which can be supported by clear-cut Biblical authority,"[25] and they prefer that such pronouncements "should be couched in generalities rather than specific terms."[26] The authority of the church is best served when it inspires and equips its members to make choices as Christians between different social and political questions and not when it makes specific recommendations. The church's involvement in social reform is likewise best served when it makes clear the Christian principles at stake and stays clear of partisan disputes.

To understand the liberal's position it is equally important to appreciate some of his general experiences as well as his specific theological doctrines. The liberal has a deep sense that there is something very inadequate about our present social structures. Our national system of priorities which places war and preparing for war far above human life and human values is almost irrational. The liberal has found it impractical and futile to be concerned for the individual as a separate entity cut off from social and political structures. He is acutely aware of how fateful our political decisions are for millions of people, of the inherent pos-

[24]Wirt, *The Social Conscience . . .* , p. 133.

[25]This was the fourth objective of *The Presbyterian Layman*, a monthly publication of the Presbyterian Lay Committee, before it was revised in 1970 due to concern expressed by the 1969 General Assembly over its wording. The change did not affect the meaning or intent of the original objective.

[26]Wirt, *The Social Conscience . . .* , p. 134.

sibilities for tremendous evil or good. Modern society, in both developed and underdeveloped countries, is highly political, and therefore our Christian involvement must be political. The large-scale social changes now in progress, coupled with the view that no existing political structures are sacred, lend a sense of urgency to what we do and how quickly we set about it. The liberal speaks throughout from a history of direct involvement which precludes "Pollyanna" assumptions about how good things are or bland acceptance of the present system as a given.

The liberal's biblical orientation is of course different from that of the evangelical (see Chapter IV). He readily admits that it is vain to search the New Testament for precise social directives, since the biblical message seeks fundamentally to transform individuals within the established order.[27] The transition from the New Testament to modern society, however, must take into account the successive social changes through which we have passed. St. Paul had reason to urge obedience to "the governing authorities" (Romans 13:1), since it was his Roman citizenship which protected him from unjust procedures (Acts 25–26). It was not long, though, before the church saw a different side of the Roman Empire: a blasphemous beast persecuting the Christians (Revelation 13:5–7). Moreover, the early church confidently looked forward to the imminent return of Christ. As soon as this expectation faded, and as soon as the church became powerful enough politically to use its authority, the Christian imperative took on a new aspect. If government in New Testament times had little social function and was limited to maintaining order between individuals, the state today has a major responsibility for social problems and their solutions. It is this vastly complex political world of encrusted prejudices, vested interest, urban crises, surplus wealth, atomic arsenals, sanctioned monopolies, industrial-military complexes which compels the liberal to seek a *new social theology*—a social theology based upon the broadest biblical principles.[28]

Like the evangelical, the liberal feels the principle of sep-

[27]John Howard Yoder's *The Politics of Jesus* (Grand Rapids: Eerdmans, 1972) may be the best available treatment of how Jesus challenged and transformed the social patterns of the established system.

[28]Roger Mehl, "The Basis of Christian Social Ethics," in Bennett, ed., *Christian Social Ethics* . . . , pp. 44–47.

aration in America has served well to preserve the independence of both church and state. At the same time the liberal is very leery of any doctrine which sanctions the authority of the state as ordained by God. To do so is to overlook the important ways the authority of the state is limited and subordinate. The state is limited first of all by the fact that its authority is placed under the higher mandate to "care for justice and peace" (the fifth thesis of the declaration of Barmen). When government neglects this mandate, it is the church's duty to call the state back to its proper role. It is the church, not the state, which has been entrusted with the goals and values which should guide the destiny of mankind. There is a proper course, a right social shape, a more human structure for which the church bears the ultimate responsibility. Man-made laws are always subordinate both to the higher goals of society and to the divine or natural law. Thus Martin Luther King, Jr., found justification for civil disobedience against the state when a civil law conflicted with an eternal law.[29]

The liberal finds the traditional, strict separation of church and state inadequate for another reason. One mark of modern society is that the responsibility of government goes beyond the simple protection of its citizens and the preservation of law and order. The extension of welfare programs, social security and health benefits, a war on poverty, five civil rights acts, and foreign aid are all signs of the government's new role of provider and guarantor of equal opportunity. In general the conservative resists this tendency because it represents an intrusion into a domain formerly dominated by the church, conflicts with the American Protestant concept of private enterprise, and reduces the opportunity for Christian witness. By and large the liberal accepts the tendency as inevitable and welcomes the chance to support the state when it serves the general welfare of humanity. Reversion to a more limited government does not seem the answer in a

[29]Martin Luther King, Jr., *Why We Can't Wait* (New York: American Library, 1964), pp. 82–83: ". . . An unjust law is a human law that is not rooted in eternal law and natural law. Any law that uplifts human personality is just. Any law that degrades human personality is unjust. . . . Thus it is that I can urge men to obey the 1954 decision of the Supreme Court, for it is morally right; and I can urge them to disobey segregation ordinances, for they are morally wrong."

society where human need can no longer be met solely by personal diligence and the resources of immediate families. The staggering increase in the number of people who are starving, ill-housed, sick, elderly, or uneducated makes it both mandatory and expedient for the church to cooperate with secular and governmental agencies.

Coupled with the widened sphere of the state's responsibility is the expansion of the church into an area once dominated by government. Undoubtedly a direct influence is the pronounced trait of liberal theology to tear down any dualism between body and spirit, secular and sacred.

> To the gospel, man is neither spiritual nor secular, nor is he a bifurcated spiritual-secular being. He is man. The restoration of his wholeness as man is one part of that salvation Jesus Christ brings him. When the church treats man as though he were spiritual in one part and secular in another, angel when he kneels in prayer and devil when he dances, morally responsible personally but morally irresponsible collectively . . . when the church thus makes religious schizoids out of men it thwarts the saving power of the Christ who came to make men whole.[30]

The effect is to create a uniquely modern sphere of shared responsibility: the authority of the church and the state overlap where human lives and human values are at stake. The Christian does not play politician nor does the church play legislator, but the Christian's concern does include social structures, and the church's responsibility does penetrate into the lobby halls when the welfare and destiny of human lives hang in the balance.

Because the liberal has felt freer "to intermeddle with civil affairs which concern the commonwealth," as the Westminster Confession puts it (Ch. 31, section 4), he has frequently been criticized both for attempting to Christianize the social orders and for reducing Christianity to an atheistic humanism. The criticisms are understandable but wide of the mark, since they disre-

[30]An editorial, "The Uncomfortable Pew," *The Christian Century*, May 11, 1966, pp. 607–608; which was a response to J. Howard Pew's article, "Should the Church 'Meddle' in Civil Affairs?" *Reader's Digest*, May, 1966, pp. 1–6.

gard the distinction the liberal makes between social action which is nothing more than humanism and Christian social action which *includes* within it humanistic values of justice, equality, and peace. Since most humanistic values stem from and parallel Christian values, the liberal believes the church is obligated to utilize its authority insofar as it benefits the common good.[31] On this basis the liberal has sought to commit the authority of the church on such issues as racism and civil rights, poverty, Vietnam, women's rights, health care, and the elderly. Nonetheless the church must be warned against pressuring the state to enact legislation which depends upon a doctrine or practice unique to the church (e.g., prayer or birth control restrictions).

It is accurate, then, to say the liberal works to humanize the social orders but not specifically to Christianize them. Similarly, the liberal is not reducing faith to a belief in mankind. Instead, he is intentionally filtering out certain particular Christian elements in order to preserve a basic separation between church and state. Even though the church must avoid promoting its own particular biases when it enters direct political action, it must sacrifice none of its Christian motivation. The line being drawn here is admittedly a fine one, but this is a risk the liberal feels is necessary if the church is to be heard at all by the powerful secularists in today's society.

If the evangelical, influenced by a theology of divinely given orders and two spheres of authority, tends as a result to be tolerant of the state, the liberal is influenced by more than one theological consideration which keeps him unreconciled to the present order. One is the acceptance of the Barthian view that God has given the state not as a dike against sin but as an act of his providence. The state, although it does not recognize it, is meant to be an analogue of God's Kingdom. Two important implications are the result. Positively, if we believe the state should

[31]See Thomas Merton, *Faith and Violence* (Notre Dame: University of Notre Dame, 1968), p. 53: "The Church's mission in the world today is a desperate one of helping create conditions in which man can return to himself, recover something of his lost humanity, as a necessary preparation for his ultimate return to God." See also Jürgen Moltmann, *Religion, Revolution and the Future,* trans. M. Douglas Meeks (New York: Scribner's, 1969), pp. 118–128.

reflect the higher moral order, then Christians should have a much greater expectation for the state than has the average citizen. The liberal's optimistic hope for government is therefore the driving motivation behind his effort to reform or revolutionize the social structures of life. Negatively, if we believe the state is to be patterned after God's Kingdom, then every government is revealed to be a far cry from God's Kingdom. Notice that it is stated that the state is only to be an analogue to the Kingdom, not that it is or ever can be equated with the divine order. Barth was emphatic here, because he knew how tempting it is for the nationalist to exalt his nation as ultimate. Rather, it is because God has shown the true nature of his future Kingdom that Christians must oppose all political ideologies. The reason for the liberal's continued dissatisfaction with the status quo is his realization of the constant disparity between the Kingdom of God and the present order.[32]

The prophetic and eschatological have also played a prominent role in the liberal's attitude toward the state. (It can be expected that they will play an increasingly significant role for the evangelical and provide an important common denominator in the future.) The Old Testament prophetic tradition is rich with examples of opposition to the status quo in the name of the Lord. Their message was both verbal and demonstrative, judgmental and hopeful, spiritual and political. Their confrontation was often a direct one which brought them into conflict with the establishment of their age. Jeremiah was beaten, put in jail, and slandered because he stood up against the hypocrisy of his own people and friends (Jeremiah 20); Elijah risked his life when he challenged the prophets of Baal and denounced King Ahab and Ahab's wife and son (I Kings 18:17–19, 21; II Kings 1); Nathan courageously implicated King David of his heinous performance in the Bathsheba affair (II Samuel 12); Micah questioned the right of the aristocracy of Judah to rule and of the prophets to advise when

[32]William Hordern, "Barth as Political Thinker," *The Christian Century*, Mar. 26, 1969, pp. 411–413. When Billy Graham was asked about his unofficial role as chaplain to the White House, he acknowledged a distinction between New Testament evangelists commissioned to save souls and Old Testament prophets who intervened in political matters. It is a distinction that typifies evangelical and liberal stereotypes, but is hardly biblical.

they exploited the poor and profited from war (Micah 3); and Isaiah steadfastly condemned the religious and social economic evils of his time (Isaiah 1–6). It is not surprising, then, that Martin Luther King, Jr., is seen as a modern-day prophet when he is despised and murdered for his direct confrontation of an unjust and racial social system and for his denouncement of the war in Vietnam.

The eschatological is the future dimension of God's Kingdom that prevents us from being entirely at home with any social program or any particular government. "This futurity of the Kingdom opens ever-new possibilities for action while still denying any human institution the glory of perfection that might warrant its making an absolute claim on the obedience of individuals."[33] While the liberal does not have a detailed program for social change, he does resist the institutional cementing of present conditions that can dam up the future. He does not claim to possess any formula for transforming social structures, but he does possess a vision which induces him to work harder for a better society.

Behind the liberal's readiness to involve the authority of the church in specific issues is a different view of authority rooted in a different understanding of revelation from the evangelical's. The church is against *this* war or for *that* economic reform not because it has an absolute Word on these matters. Quite the opposite. The church can and must be specific in its ethical and political teaching because revelation is by nature specific and historical. For the liberal, revelation is not static and unchanging but rather continually evolving as it is applied to every new situation. A church which plays it safe by resorting to generalities or silence is untrue to the gospel because it does not want to be a church under grace. A church under God's grace can afford to be concrete since God did not call it to be infallible. He does call it, however, to be faithful and relevant to its mandate to be a power of redemption in this world.[34]

From the liberal's point of view there are valid reasons why

[33]Pannenberg, *Theology and the Kingdom of God*, p. 115.

[34]Harvey Cox, "Beyond Bonhoeffer? The Future of Religionless Christianity," *The Secular City Debate*, ed. Daniel Callahan (New York: Macmillan, 1966), p. 209.

the church should make social pronouncements from time to time on secular issues. In the first place, the church's pronouncements are meant to speak *to* the individual churches as much as they speak *for* the corporate church. They are meant to instruct, stimulate, and motivate individual Christians in their secular involvement. Secondly, such pronouncements may never change the course of history, and this is not their intention. They are nevertheless a vital means of witness which the church cannot neglect. They let countless thousands outside the church know that the church does care and is willing to risk its authority on their behalf. They fight the growing feeling that the church cares little and is willing to risk even less. Thirdly, the church's ethical pronouncements must be specific, because if they are generic and abstract they will never speak to secular man.

> He does not live "in general." He lives his life in a particular place, doing a certain job, faced with specific issues. Vague moral advice does not interest him. Specific ethical demands may infuriate him, stimulate him, or encourage him. But at least he will hear them. . . . [35]

Finally, the unprecedented merger of secular and sacred in the last few decades makes it impossible to isolate a purely spiritual or moral side of an issue. The legal defense of Angela Davis may seem to be a purely political or social question, but liberals see it also as a moral and racial issue: the Council on Church and Race of the United Presbyterian Church allocated $10,000 to her defense fund. Likewise, the World Council of Churches over the past eight years has given $2,640,000 to various groups opposed to racism. More than half has gone to black organizations in southern Africa who are actively involved in overthrowing white minority regimes. The antiracism grants, admittedly, are given in order to move the council "beyond charity and involve itself in the redistribution of power." If the church attempts to remain securely within the spiritual realm, it is sure to disturb no one and convince no one.

Liberals, it is well known, place a greater emphasis on the church's use of its corporate authority and power. Public pro-

[35] *Ibid.*, p. 214.

nouncements and corporate action to back them up are the two principal ways liberals attempt to effect changes for the commonwealth which are both biblical and humanitarian. The liberal does not blatantly discount the value of personal witness but sees it as ineffective in certain important aspects. Looking at our own country, the liberal asks how potent the diligent work of individual Christians will be against an entrenched status quo, institutional prejudice, ghetto cities, or the excesses of an industrial-military complex. It would be fine to convert all of our congressmen and top business and military executives, but it is unrealistic to expect to do so. Both politically and technologically, the central challenge facing modern man is not whether he will use his newfound power, but how he will use it. The liberal accepts this as our present situation and concludes that the Christian church must not neglect the authority and power it possesses.

Since the church has a moral obligation to utilize its corporate power, it is immoral if it does not. If the church does not use its resources for explicit good, in effect it allows itself to be used by others for implicit evil. If the evangelical reminds us that power corrupts, the liberal does not let us forget that the absence of power also corrupts by allowing evil to take over. Hence the recent decision by some denominations to withdraw their large holdings from banks which directly or indirectly support the apartheid government of South Africa. Whether the church likes it or not, it is big business. "Outside the United States government it is the wealthiest institution in the nation. It is wealthier than General Motors, General Electric, and General Foods all put together—far bigger."[36] (Church holdings in real estate alone are estimated at $100 billion.)

The weight of the corporate church is to be used not preserved, risked not protected, extended not restricted, creative not defensive. The church is truest to its vocation when it spends itself openly, trusting God to use its failures and successes.

A convenient summary is found in the ongoing debate about the validity of civil disobedience and revolution as a means

[36]Charles H. Bayer, "The Minister as Politician," *The Princeton Seminary Bulletin*, vol. LXII (Winter, 1969), pp. 36–37.

of social change. The liberal in his pronouncements on civil disobedience has been careful to point out that such action is a serious responsibility to be practiced as a last resort. Civil disobedience is judiciously defined as "*deliberate, peaceable* violation of a law deemed to be *unjust,* in obedience to conscience or a *higher law,* and with recognition of the State's *legal authority* to punish the violator" (italics mine).[37] It is justified "when a particular government fails to provide justice, peace or freedom," or "where legislation violates an acceptable constitution and no speedy means of legal relief are available."[38] There is no consensus among liberals whether revolution necessarily means violence.[39] There is agreement that revolution must be political and radical and have as its goal a more human quality of life. In America, for instance, revolution means the transformation from a centralized oligarchy to a participatory democracy, a reversal of priority from militarism and destruction to human values and self-dignity, from systematic repression to equal opportunity, from a sense of hollowness and materialism to a sense of community and identity, from an indifferent majority to a sensitive, responsive majority.

The evangelical, however, is very reluctant to justify, much less talk about, civil disobedience because he believes it cannot help but encourage lawlessness, bloodshed, confusion, and dissolution of law and order. Deliberate disobedience of the law is

[37]The official policy statement of the National Council of Churches, "Religious Obedience and Civil Disobedience," adopted by the General Board, June 7, 1968.

[38]*Ibid.;* and the 1966 Geneva Conference on Church and Society.

[39]See the diversity of opinion in Marty and Peerman, ed., *New Theology No. 6* (New York: Macmillan, 1969), subtitled, "On revolution and nonrevolution, violence and non-violence, peace and power." The question of whether it is ever morally justified to liberate oppressed people by resorting to violence has taken on practical significance through the World Council of Churches' recent grant of $85,000 to the radical Patriotic Front. The Front, which hopes to bring down Rhodesia's tottering biracial government, has been involved in ugly killings of unarmed civilians. Even though the anti-racist monies are earmarked for welfare purposes, it does have the effect of freeing funds for military purposes. Paul Lehmann presents a balanced argument both for and against the use of violence—*The Transfiguration of Politics* (New York: Harper & Row, 1975), *passim,* but especially pp. 260–278.

justified only in "cases extraordinary" (Westminster Confession of Faith), that is, instances of unusual urgency where the lines of morality are clearly drawn. The Nazi regime under Hitler is a clear example. Revolution is opposed for the same reasons and simply because the violence and injustice it begets are almost always worse than the violence and injustice it seeks to bring down. It is morally justified and worthy of Christian sympathy "only where it actually protests against an established government's persistent abuse of the norms of government (maintenance of law and order, protection of the innocent, repression of bad works). . . . "[40] Civil disobedience and revolution remain very poor alternatives to inner renewal, because they aim to change and overthrow without regard to the spiritual and moral transformation necessary for lasting change.

If we review what we have exposed, there are obvious reasons for this difference of opinion. The liberal's faith is more likely to draw him into conflict with the state. He finds it difficult to accept the authority of the state as inviolable because it is God's agent to preserve order.[41] The evangelical is more willing to accept as given whatever society he finds himself in so long as he is able to proclaim the gospel and practice the Christian ethic. He is better prepared to consent to the authority of the state as sovereign in its own sphere. While the liberal seeks a positive, aggressive role from government, the evangelical prefers a more limited, conservative role.[42] To the evangelical way of thinking a

[40]Carl F. H. Henry, *Aspects of Christian Social Ethics* (Grand Rapids: Eerdmans, 1964), p. 179.

[41]According to John Bennett this is one of the major theological changes from the 1937 Oxford World Conference to the 1966 Geneva Conference on Church and Society. See John C. Bennett, "The Church in a Revolutionary Age," *Social Action and Social Progress*, Jan.–Feb., 1966, p. 18.

[42]Cf. Carnell, *The Case for Biblical Christianity*, p. 132: "There is one, and only one, indubitable justification for government, and that is to bear the sword as an agent of God in the forceful restraining of wrongdoers." The consequence of Carnell's statement is obvious in his conclusion about when a Christian should go to war. There appears to be this point of inconsistency in Carnell's argument: he is quite willing to recognize the sinful nature of man but reluctant to recognize the sinful nature of governments.

stable order is almost always better than the risk of no order at all, but the liberal is not always certain whether the established hierarchy is worth preserving. If the liberal seeks to transform society by revolutionizing its social structures, the conservative seeks societal change by the spiritual regeneration of its citizens. When the evangelical speaks of revolution he means the violent substitution of one government, probably equally unjust, for another. For the liberal revolution means a basic change for the common good or a new consciousness. The conservative associates revolution with communism and socialism and tends to reject it outright. If the liberal makes the same association, he concludes that socialism has its Christian elements and that communism is not always the worst fate that can come to a nation. The liberal wonders about the logic which justifies violence in Vietnam but roundly denounces the violence of embittered black people in America. The evangelical wonders about the logic which condemns violence from the right wing but encourages it from the left. The evangelical talks about salvation for the whole man and has in mind his *soul* and also his body, when the liberal has in mind his *body* and also his soul. As the liberal looks to Revelation 13 for theological justification, the evangelical looks to Romans 13.

CONCLUSION

At this point both the liberal and the evangelical must be chided for their bickering over the proper method of witness and their subsequent neglect to enact the gospel however they see fit. Much too much energy has been diverted to verbal diatribes and internal jockeying for power within the community of Christ. If the evangelical feels a person-to-person ministry directed at changing the inner life is the primary goal, then let him demonstrate its power to change men *and the world*. And if the liberal feels compelled to be involved at the level of changing the structures which shape our lives, then let him demonstrate the gospel's power to change the world *and men*. We should know by this time the world has need for both kinds of Christians, and the church will always have room for both kinds of Christian witness.

A. Goals and Methods

In the long run what is required is a balance in the church's mission. To a considerable extent the division between evangelicals and liberals is the result of different goals. The evangelical accepts organized social change only as a consequence of personal salvation. The liberal agrees that the *primary* mission of the church is to save men, but his definition of salvation includes direct social change. *Both undoubtedly have been guilty of an unbiblical separation between witness and service, between evangelism and secular involvement, between the preached gospel and the social gospel.* The evangelical has too frequently been more enthusiastic about preaching Christ than about embodying his lifestyle in a modern world. The liberal too often has been socially active but silent about the object of his faith, Jesus Christ. We will make no progress as long as one side believes the church's mission is simply preaching Christ while the other side believes mission is simply acting for social justice. Telling the good news about Jesus requires both word and deed—not simply because it takes both to get the message across but, more importantly, because the gospel is both *demonstrating* the love revealed in the cross and *making known* the source of this love.

The fatal danger the evangelical Christian faces is leaving the social consequences of the gospel to take care of themselves, when there are too many changed men who are not changing society. It would be unrealistic for the evangelical to think sound doctrinal preaching will so motivate, stir, direct, support, and train laymen that they will automatically bear the cross of Christ in the marketplace. The evangelical minister cannot assume his parishioners will apply the principles of the gospel to secular conditions at the urging of their individual consciences. Experience and sociological studies show that individuals are unable or unwilling to relate theology or their religious commitment to *specific* issues.[43] The morning sermon is not the place for advice on sociopolitical questions, but isn't it the time to reflect upon the specific implications of the gospel for the entirety of human living—which includes in no small way the political and social? I can think of nothing more deceiving for a church than to hear

[43]Hadden, *The Gathering Storm* . . . , pp. 90–99, 126–131.

constantly how the gospel requires us to serve our brother but to do nothing about structuring the church so that the task can be done.

The evangelical must still resolve in a practical way whether "evangelism first" means "social involvement second" and whether the salvation of the individual as the primary goal means the redress of political evils must be a subsequent goal. If the evangelical of the future is going to have a true social conscience, he must provide a stronger theological foundation which more completely integrates personal salvation and social structures. Have we not learned that social structures can shape men as much as they are shaped by men? Have we not learned, in a political world, how unjust structures may direct men to act unjustly? Personal relations based on love are the most powerful means to transform a sick society, but ghettos, immoral laws, depersonalizing programs, and robot bureaucrats can go a long way to nullify the most dedicated work, the strongest will, and the best intentions.[44] By no means are all forms of social and political life alike; for some deceive and corrupt while others nurture and instill integrity and sound values. Does the evangelical see where he has been misled by the logic that since the Good Samaritan did not confront the Roman Empire in the first century to make the Jericho road safe for all travelers, the corporate church in the twentieth century does not have to concern itself directly with political decisions and social legislation? Does he see from his history that because antislavery reform was made an appendage to converting souls, there are still black people today who are captives of a white establishment? And does the evangelical see the fallacy in the statement that social problems are merely the conglomerate of personal problems, and therefore social ethics is no more than the extension of personal morality? Let us pray the answer is yes.

The ensuing debate between Arthur Johnston and John R. W. Stott, who both have been actively involved in the Lausanne Congress and other national and international conferences on evangelism, illustrates the vital relationship between goals and

[44]This point is beautifully illustrated in the book by Jenny Moore, *The People on Second Street* (New York: Morrow, William, and Co., 1968).

means. Stott's position is that social action is a partner of evangelism.

> As partners the two belong to each other. Each stands on its own feet in its own right alongside the other. Neither is a means to the other, or even a manifestation of the other. For each is an end in itself. Both are expressions of unfeigned love.[45]

Johnston, on the other hand, argues that evangelism is more important than social action, and that social action is only a result of evangelism. To make his point Johnston quotes Harold Lindsell.

> The rule of service is twofold. First, it is a means to an end. By service it is possible to confront men with the Gospel of Christ. . . . As long as service makes it possible to confront men with the Gospel, it is useful. The second role of service is as fruit that grows on the gospel tree and leads the people of God to fulfill the law of God.[46]

Thus, according to Johnston, the mission of the church is evangelism, and he is unwilling to integrate evangelism and social action. "To say that mission is a comprehensive word 'embracing everything that God sends his people into the world to do' may be too great a concession to ecumenical theology and without biblical foundations."[47]

Johnston's defense of evangelism, it seems to me, fails to recognize the consequences that history repeatedly demonstrates. First, the mission of the church becomes truncated. The individual is forced to make unbiblical distinctions between what is personal and what is social, between what is evangelism and what is mission. Richard Mouw, for example, asks what criterion we use to decide that racism is a "social" issue and pornography

[45]John R. W. Stott, *The Lausanne Covenant* (Minneapolis: World Wide Publications, 1974), p. 26.

[46]Arthur P. Johnston, *The Battle for World Evangelism* (Wheaton: Tyndale House, 1978), p. 312.

[47]*Ibid.*, p. 303.

is a "personal" one. Protestant orthodoxy, he continues, has applied its concerns to a very narrow range of issues and this kind of doctrinal myopia "has resulted in a situation in which evangelicalism has perpetuated a very limited understanding of the scope of redemption."[48]

Secondly, unless sociopolitical action is integrated with personal evangelism, we enter the world *only* to convert others. Those outside church walls hear a truncated gospel and they in turn embody a truncated gospel, and in this manner Christians begin to believe in the gospel as a dead-end call to repentance. In the mission of the church, the ends and the means cannot be separated, and it is terribly misleading to understand social justice *only* as a means to another end. When "servanthood" is reduced to merely a "means" or a form of pre-evangelism (preparing the soil), then it will not be long before we entirely neglect Jesus' commission to be sent into the world to serve.[49]

Thirdly, Johnston's definition of mission as evangelism does nothing to reverse the individualization that has made the evangelical witness less than what it should be. The ideology of individualism is an important reason why Christians cannot translate, for example, their concern for a Vietnamese mother whose family may be exterminated by American bombs into a political concern of war in general. The ideology of individualism makes it impossible for Christians to integrate specific, individual cases, such as the black family on welfare, with the general concern of the American economic system.

Even though this issue of individualization has been raised again and again, Jim Wallis warns of yet another danger.

> An individualistic understanding of the gospel carries the danger of making salvation into just another commodity that can be consumed for personal fulfillment and self-interest, for a guarantee of happiness, success, moral justifi-

[48]Richard J. Mouw, "Evangelicals in Search of Maturity," *Theology Today*, vol. XXXV, no. 1 (April, 1978), p. 47.

[49]Stott places the mission of the church in a broader context when he utilizes Jesus' twofold commission: "to love your neighbor as yourself" and "to go and make disciples" (The Great Commandment and The Great Commission). See Stott, "The Biblical Basis of Evangelism," in *Let the Earth Hear His Voice*, pp. 66ff.

> cation, or whatever else a consumer audience feels it needs .... Reducing the gospel to only personal and existential terms, the Christian message is easily co-opted by larger social and political forces which seek to make religion an appendage of the established order.... [50]

Wallis' critique rings especially true in light of the way the gospel is being packaged for "non-commercial" broadcasting and mass distribution. Would evangelism be so vulnerable to being co-opted by big business if it had a social and corporate dimension? Would we be as likely to forget that personal sufferings are often the result of sociopolitical systems if we understood how sin and death manifest themselves politically, institutionally, and economically as well as personally?

The fatal danger facing liberals is sacrificing the offensive nature of the gospel in order to be accepted by the humanist as inoffensive. Considering the secular nature of society, one cannot doubt the need to work along with the humanist toward a common good. But one can wonder whether the corporate church serves society best by underplaying and softening its distinctive proclamation. Does not the church bear the unique responsibility to reconcile the antagonisms which sap our strength and fracture the good intentions we have? Instead of being jealous of the state's power, the church should stimulate political leaders to exercise their authority more impartially and more responsibly. If the church does not, who will make clear the general and specific *Christian* principles and values to be applied to secular problems?[51] And what other corporate body is singularly concerned with confronting men with the ultimate meaning of life, with the eternal God and his purposes in history? Has the church done all it can to encourage its individual members to exert their influ-

[50]Jim Wallis, *Agenda for Biblical People* (New York: Harper & Row, 1976), p. 31.

[51]After a detailed study, James Adams warns about "generals" (religious lobbyists) without "armies" (laymen who back their positions). He summarizes, "If the reader has detected a certain amount of cynicism throughout this book, he has not been misled. I believe that the church lobbyist... has an important role to play. He should add a moral dimension to issues, however, rather than resorting to power politics" (p. 287). See James L. Adams, *The Growing Church Lobby in Washington* (Grand Rapids: Eerdmans, 1970).

ence on particular questions in their own name as citizens? Has the church actually armed its parishioners spiritually and morally to stand above the corruption and self-deceit they face when they assume political authority? And has the church been a witness to the transcendent power we have in the Holy Spirit, or has it fostered a self-sufficient attitude?

The liberal's passion for relevance has often led him to speak out when he did not know the inside story. His anxiousness to be "with it" and "where the action is" has led to some dubious involvements. Of course we cannot expect to know all the evidence before we can engage in a morally responsible or politically effective act; yet some liberals have been guilty of acting without taking the time to become well informed. If liberals are going to assume an active role in sociopolitical issues, they have the obligation of playing the role well. They must learn that their competence does not reach into all areas of secular life. If only for practical reasons, the precarious authority of the clergy urges them to be right at least most of the time when they take a stand. If silence due to apathy is one form of sin, overzealous pronouncement is the other side of the same coin. The liberal must also ask himself to what extent his reliance on structures outside the parish, such as antipoverty agencies,[52] reveals a failure to motivate and engage the local church in his kind of social action. Does he see that an unresponsive congregation may be the result of his own unwillingness or inability to incorporate different ways of thinking and doing Christian social involvement? In the future let us pray the liberal will be more sensitive to the division he causes by his insistence on corporate action and social resolutions. Let us also hope for less dogmatic stands on fewer specific issues in order to create a broader basis of acceptance for the Christian principles involved.[53]

If evangelicals and liberals could agree that the mission of

[52]Also denominational, interdenominational, and unaffiliated groups which are answerable to a liberal board rather than a local church. The same trend is apparent in the Roman Catholic hierarchy, e.g., the former Benedictine monastery and now Center for Intercultural Documentation at Cuernavaca, the National Association of Laymen, the Chicago priests' senate, the "underground Church," and the exodus of priests from the parish ministry.

[53]I am indebted in this paragraph to the conclusions of Hadden, *The Gathering Storm . . .* , pp. 232–235.

the church embodies both "loving our neighbor" and "making disciples of all nations," then evangelism would be the essential core of the church's mission whereby we proclaim the gospel in the power of the Holy Spirit. If liberals would be willing to concede that evangelism has a particular historical priority, then evangelicals should be willing to broaden their definition of evangelism to include "liberation of individuals from sin and all its consequences" (Bangkok). Salvation does not, therefore, become identified with humanization or psycho-physical wholeness but neither does it exclude social and political justice.

One can only be encouraged by the way various ecumenical councils, both conservative and liberal, have moved toward a dynamic integrating definition of mission and evangelism, and the gospel of justice and the gospel of proclamation. Progress has indeed been made, but we have not yet arrived. We can continue to make progress, I am convinced, as long as we keep the biblical witness before us. The Gospels are our best teacher because they are full of stories about Jesus' feeding the hungry *and* his teachings about the spiritual food of God, his healing the sick *and* his offer of personal salvation, his comforting the heavy laden *and* his invitation to carry his Cross, his releasing the imprisoned (and guilty) *and* his command to go and sin no more, his restoring sight to the blind *and* his teaching that he is the light that shines in the darkness, his resurrection of the dead *and* his claim that he is the way, the truth, and the life.

B. *Theological Issues*

Behind the clamor over proper goals and methods, one wonders if the real source of division does not lie elsewhere. For example, it must be asked whether the evangelical is opposed to corporate social pronouncements in principle or to the content of those largely liberal statements. The latter seems the case, since the National Association of Evangelicals has in fact passed resolutions dealing with the new morality, federal aid to education, religion in the public schools, race, and other issues.[54]

[54]The resolutions are considered merely expressions of the opinion of those present and are not binding upon members or related agencies. The pronouncements of the major denominations, the World Council of Churches, and the National Council of Churches are similarly not binding on members or lower judicatories but carry, for several reasons, a greater obligation to become policy guidelines.

The liberal stands for a less rigid separation of church and state yet supports the Supreme Court's decision on prayer and Bible reading in public schools. The evangelical stands for a more rigid separation, yet he does not generally support the Court's decision. The only conclusion possible is that separation of church and state is a one-way street for the liberal. He justifies a loose interpretation of the law when the church moves into the political sphere but reverts to a strict interpretation when the state encroaches into the ecclesiastical sphere. On the other hand, the doctrine of separation is a two-way road for the evangelical. He favors a strict separation when it means cooperation with Roman Catholics or humanists, but is willing to cross political boundaries when it is a question of religious freedom or personal morality (e.g., pornography or gambling). The liberal and evangelical say they cannot get together because they disagree about tactics for social change. But in reality we find evangelicals and liberals acting on different issues but employing similar methods. History shows the evangelical is willing to use direct political action, lobbying, or corporate pressure when it is a matter of defending the Protestant ethic or a precious moral principle.[55] In spite of what the liberal says, he frequently finds it more effective to work on a person-to-person basis outside of the corporate structure, especially when general humanitarian ends are at stake (e.g., in air pollution and gun control). Neither evangelical nor liberal will admit the obvious fact that vested interests and personal biases sometimes take priority over theological principles.

It is doubtful if any substantial progress toward a unified witness is possible until the many theological issues raised here are openly discussed. If no other purpose is served by this book, it should at least make us aware of how deep-seated and varied are the theological roots and general attitudes which contribute to our division.

Certain questions need to be addressed to the liberal. To

[55]Recent examples include the movement to return the Bible to public schools, the drive to halt the spread of pornography, the defeat of legislation which would legalize gambling, and opposition to federal aid to parochial schools. The National Association of Evangelicals presently maintains an Office of Public Affairs and staff in Washington in order to protect the religious interests of evangelicals.

what extent have the emphasis on God as immanent in the world, interpretation of the Kingdom of God as this-worldly, uncritical acceptance of evolution, corporate morality, location of Jesus in the other person, overlapping concerns of church and state, loss of distinction between physical and spiritual, and coolness toward conversion contributed to a social involvement which lacks a vital witness to Jesus Christ and neglects the power of God? To what degree has the emphasis on revelation as experiential led to precipitant secular action, or the emphasis on faith as a commitment without specific content to apathy about discerning the biblical perspective in what the church does and says?

Can the liberal admit that it is very difficult for the church to assume its *unique* role in society when the distinction between sacred and secular, divine and human, is lost? While the liberal tradition of prophetic criticism has prevented the hardening of present social structures and political policies, has it been so overwhelming as to render inaudible the prophetic role of positive encouragement and faithfulness to God's providence? The dangers inherent in a doctrine of the state as an analogue of the Kingdom of God are well known, but less obvious is the danger of failing to define the Kingdom of God and leaving it an ambiguous symbol. Finally, isn't it incumbent upon a theology of relatives to make a double effort to demonstrate how the Christian faith goes beyond the goals of humanism?

These questions can almost be inverted and addressed to the evangelical. To what extent have the emphasis on God as transcendent and distinct from the world, interpretation of the Kingdom of God as otherworldly, antagonism toward evolution, individualistic morality, location of Jesus in a personal experience, two separate spheres of authority, a disjunction between body and soul, and apprehension toward corporate power hindered broad and deep involvement in the world's suffering? To what degree has the present emphasis on revelation as conceptual led to a secular involvement characterized by indirectness and lack of initiative; or an emphasis on faith as assent to creeds and doctrines led to the priority of moral principle over human life (legalism over law)?

Before any attempt to recover a "holistic" view of salvation can succeed, evangelicals must develop an incarnational theology.[56] The criticism of an inherent dualism throughout conservative thought patterns is valid enough, but the antidote to date has been simply a confession that their understanding of salvation has been too individualistic and otherworldly. The direction that must be taken is a total reworking of such traditional concepts as creation, redemption, reconciliation, incarnation, and eschatology that reaffirms the proper co-inherence of the objective-subjective, spiritual-material nature of the universe. This persistent tendency toward separate spheres and distinct orders is reflected in a host of issues evangelicals are ill prepared to handle. In his review of the Chicago Call, Fr. Benedict T. Viviano (O.P.) strikes a sensitive nerve: "Billy Graham is very good. But when it comes to resolving the tensions between science and faith, he is not so successful or satisfying."[57] The reason, of course, is that evangelicals do not possess a long tradition, such as the Dominican Thomistic one of Fr. Viviano, of serious effort to relate the data of revelation to philosophy and science.

What can be done to correct the false individualism within evangelicalism, which tends to limit the Christian's ethical concern to his own immediate environment and personal contacts? Does not a theological doctrine which accepts the authority of the state as providentially ordained require an equally strong accent on the prophetic tradition of judgment and criticism of the status quo? One would like to see a counterdoctrine that prevents the passive toleration of a government that maintains law and order, religious freedom, and middle-class values. Is there a source of theological hope and positive expectation for the state which the evangelical could tap to overcome a basically pessimistic view of man and a negative understanding of government? Finally, is it possible the evangelical might be giving theological justification to those structures which meet his standard of democracy, capitalism, voluntary charity, and limited wars against the communists?

Not least among the theological problems we must rethink together is the meaning of the Kingdom of God, which has a long

[56]I am indebted to Lane Dennis for his suggestive thoughts along these lines. See Robert Webber and Donald Bloesch (eds.), *The Orthodox Evangelicals* (Nashville: Thomas Nelson Inc., 1978), pp. 94–111.

[57]*Ibid.*, p. 226.

history in both evangelicalism and liberalism. What does it mean in Jesus' teaching, as the goal of history, and in its relationship to the church? In what sense is the Kingdom of God societal or realized in history? What role does man play in cooperation with God in bringing in the Kingdom? Will the Kingdom be realized without regard to social conditions, human freedom, or peace? Recognizing that the church is not to be equated with God's future Kingdom, how is the church necessary for the sake of the Kingdom? In Jesus' teaching about the Kingdom the present and future are inextricably interwoven. We must therefore avoid the two extreme interpretations which deny either the Kingdom's "not-yet" character or its temporal character. God's rule is not dependent upon human effort, and yet he does not leave men to do nothing but wait quietly for the Kingdom's arrival. A perfect society is not equal to the Kingdom, yet society is more than a mere antechamber to eternity in which all men's works are incidental. The fulfilment of man's social relationships must wait until the millennium, but our Christian faith calls us to prepare ourselves and the world for that day. Perhaps within these boundaries the liberal and evangelical can begin to confront each other on the substantive issues which divide them. Let us pray that our efforts may hasten the time when God will fulfill his promise.

DISCUSSION QUESTIONS

1. What do you feel is the proper role of a church's Christian social action committee? Is it to make specific recommendations on particular issues? To speak out on crucial issues in the name of the church? To ask the ruling body to pass a resolution? To alert the congregation to an important social issue, gather facts, and clarify the issue? To urge church members to become involved in an issue of their particular competence? Do we need to distinguish between those actions which tend to divide a church and those which provide individuals with the opportunity to exercise their own Christian consciences?

2. Why is it that in most churches the Christian social ac-

tion committee is divorced from the committee on evangelism and outreach? What can be done in your church to reunite social action and evangelism?

3. Did Jesus' ministry to the poor, outcast, and oppressed indicate that poverty, bigotry, and tyranny are unworthy of the Kingdom of God? Must they be done away with before his return?

4. As an evangelical or liberal, do you find the following formula acceptable: "Mission, Christian involvement for the common good, is a *necessary* preparation to evangelism"? Can mission ever have a limited goal, e.g., passage of the Civil Rights Act? Is evangelism possible in spite of unjust social structures and corrupt government?

5. How do the liberal doctrine of the state as an analogue of the Kingdom of God and the evangelical doctrine of the state as ordained differ? What are the strong and weak points of each doctrine?

POSTSCRIPT

Our times require more than a reluctant tolerance of different opinions and viewpoints. They demand an open and honest exchange of ideas. I hope I sense a heightened feeling that the church is a unique community precisely because it can *accept* in Christian love, and not simply tolerate, people who strongly hold different convictions and perspectives. We must believe that the church can be a shining example to the world of how a higher obedience to God can transcend the human temperaments which divide men. If we in the church cannot be concerned about each other in spite of our differences, then how can we possibly be God's agents of reconciliation outside the church? For too long we have tried without success to squeeze Christians into a single mold. Undoubtedly what is needed is a new humility which comes through a sense of common guilt about the past, acknowledgment of a higher truth which none of us possesses, and sincere appreciation of the contribution each person and tradition can make to discerning God's revelation of himself.

What I am calling for is no less than an open debate of the issues which divide us. Editors of periodicals and denominational magazines have the obligation to elicit articles and news from both evangelicals and liberals and publish them side by side. Editors of theological journals and books need to encourage, not discourage, scholars from both camps to submit articles and manuscripts on specific issues. Conveners and planners of conferences should invite theologians and spokesmen from both liberal and evangelical persuasions to share the same platform. Judicatories and other authoritative bodies need to set aside time to talk through their internal differences. Councils of churches should sponsor forums and panels which deal with particular divisive questions. Above all, local churches should be forming dialogue groups to deal openly and prayerfully with their hostilities. We must all stop telling ourselves that it is better to leave well enough alone and begin acting like Christian brothers who love each other and our common Lord.

There is no reason why compromise should be a dirty word, why truth must always lie to the right or the left and never somewhere in between. Truth does not fear itself. Instead, Jesus has promised that the truth will set us free. What a beginning we will have toward speaking the truth in love if we all pray to God to remove the pride which blinds us to our own faults and the smugness which causes us to dwell on the shortcomings of others!

APPENDICES

THE CHICAGO DECLARATION

This 473-word Declaration was hammered out by a diverse group of evangelicals at a Thanksgiving Workshop on Social Concern in 1973. It came at a time when there was a growing need to commit the evangelical movement more deeply to the pressing social issues of the day.

As evangelical Christians committed to the Lord Jesus Christ and the full authority of the Word of God, we affirm that God lays total claim upon the lives of his people. We cannot, therefore, separate our lives in Christ from the situation in which God has placed us in the United States and the world.

We confess that we have not acknowledged the complete claims of God on our lives.

We acknowledge that God requires love. But we have not demonstrated the love of God to those suffering social abuses.

We acknowledge that God requires justice. But we have not proclaimed or demonstrated his justice to an unjust American society. Although the Lord calls us to defend the social and economic rights of the poor and the oppressed, we have mostly remained silent. We deplore the historic involvement of the church in America with racism and the conspicuous responsibility of the evangelical community for perpetuating the personal attitudes and institutional structures that have divided the body of Christ along color lines. Further, we have failed to condemn the exploitation of racism at home and abroad by our economic system.

We affirm that God abounds in mercy and that he forgives all who repent and turn from their sins. So we call our fellow evangelical Christians to demonstrate repentance in a Christian discipleship that confronts the social and political injustice of our nation.

We must attack the materialism of our culture and the maldistribution of the nation's wealth and services. We recognize that as a nation we play a crucial role in the imbalance and injustice of international trade and development. Before God and a billion hungry neighbors, we must rethink our values regarding our present standard of living and promote more just acquisition and distribution of the world's resources.

We acknowledge our Christian responsibilities of citizenship. Therefore, we must challenge the misplaced trust of the nation in economic and military might—a proud trust that promotes a national pathology of war and violence which victimizes our neighbors at home and abroad. We must resist the temptation to make the nation and its institutions objects of near-religious loyalty.

We acknowledge that we have encouraged men to prideful domination and women to irresponsible passivity. So we call both men and women to mutual submission and active discipleship.

We proclaim no new gospel, but the gospel of our Lord Jesus Christ, who, through the power of the Holy Spirit, frees people from sin so that they might praise God through works of righteousness.

By this declaration, we endorse no political ideology or party, but call our nation's leaders and people to that righteousness which exalts a nation.

We make this declaration in the biblical hope that Christ is coming to consummate the Kingdom and we accept his claim on our total discipleship till he comes.

THE HARTFORD APPEAL: *An Appeal for Theological Affirmation*

The signers, who were drawn from a broad theological spectrum, met in Hartford in late January of 1975 to draw up a final draft. Their aim was not to develop a new ecumenical creed but delineate the "pervasive, false and debilitating" themes which were undermining contemporary Christianity and its influence in society.

The renewal of Christian witness and mission requires constant examination of the assumptions shaping the Church's life. Today an apparent loss of a sense of the transcendent is undermining the Church's ability to address with clarity and courage the urgent tasks to which God calls it in the world. This loss is manifest in a number of pervasive themes. Many are superficially attractive, but upon closer examination we find these themes false and debilitating to the Church's life and work. Among such themes are:

Theme 1: *Modern thought is superior to all past forms of understanding reality, and is therefore normative for Christian faith and life.*

In repudiating this theme we are protesting the captivity to the prevailing thought structures not only of the twentieth century but of any historical period. We favor using any helpful means of understanding, ancient or modern, and insist that the Christian proclamation must be related to the idiom of the culture. At the same time, we affirm the need for Christian thought to confront and be confronted by other world views, all of which are necessarily provisional.

Theme 2: *Religious statements are totally independent of reasonable discourse.*

The capitulation to the alleged primacy of modern thought takes two forms: one is the subordination of religious statements to the canons of scientific rationality; the other, equating reason with scientific rationality, would remove religious statements from the realm of reasonable discourse altogether. A religion of pure subjectivity and nonrationality results in treating faith statements as being, at best, statements about the believer. We repudiate both forms of capitulation.

Theme 3: *Religious language refers to human experience and nothing else, God being humanity's noblest creation.*

Religion is also a set of symbols and even of human projections. We repudiate the assumption that it is nothing but that. What is here at stake is nothing less than the reality of God: *We did not invent God; God invented us.*

Theme 4: *Jesus can only be understood in terms of contemporary models of humanity.*

This theme suggests a reversal of "the imitation of Christ"; that is, the image of Jesus is made to reflect cultural and countercultural notions of human excellence. We do not deny that all aspects of humanity are illumined by Jesus. Indeed, it is necessary to the universality of the Christ that he be perceived in relation to the particularities of the believers' world. We do repudiate the captivity to such metaphors, which are necessarily inadequate, relative, transitory, and frequently idolatrous. Jesus, together with the Scriptures and the whole of the Christian tradition, cannot be arbitrarily interpreted without reference to the history of which they are part. The danger is in the attempt to exploit the tradition without taking the tradition seriously.

Theme 5: *All religions are equally valid; the choice among them is not a matter of conviction about truth but only of personal preference or life style.*

We affirm our common humanity. We affirm the importance of exploring and confronting all manifestations of the religious quest and of learning from the riches of other religions. But we repudiate this theme because it flattens diversities and ignores contradictions. In doing so, it not only obscures the meaning of Christian faith, but also fails to respect the integrity of other faiths. Truth matters; therefore differences among religions are deeply significant.

Theme 6: *To realize one's potential and to be true to oneself is the whole meaning of salvation.*

Salvation contains a promise of human fulfillment, but to identify salvation with human fulfillment can trivialize the promise. We affirm that salvation cannot be found apart from God.

Theme 7: *Since what is human is good, evil can adequately be understood as failure to realize potential.*

This theme invites false understanding of the ambivalence of human existence and underestimates the pervasiveness of sin. Paradoxically, by minimizing the enormity of evil, it undermines serious and sustained attacks on particular social or individual evils.

Theme 8: *The sole purpose of worship is to promote individual self-realization and human community.*

Worship promotes individual and communal values, but it is above all a response to the reality of God and arises out of the fundamental need and desire to know, love and adore God. We worship God because God is to be worshiped.

Theme 9: *Institutions and historical traditions are oppressive and inimical to our being truly human; liberation from them is required for authentic existence and authentic religion.*

Institutions and traditions are often oppressive. For this reason they must be subjected to relentless criticism. But human community inescapably requires institutions and traditions. Without them life would degenerate into chaos and new forms of bondage. The modern pursuit of liberation from all social and historical restraints is finally dehumanizing.

Theme 10: *The world must set the agenda for the Church. Social, political, and economic programs to improve the quality of life are ultimately normative for the Church's mission in the world.*
This theme cuts across the political and ideological spectrum. Its form remains the same, no matter whether the content is defined as upholding the values of the American way of life, promoting socialism, or raising human consciousness. The Church must denounce oppressors, help liberate the oppressed, and seek to heal human misery. Sometimes the Church's mission coincides with the world's programs. But the norms for the Church's activity derive from its own perception of God's will for the world.

Theme 11: *An emphasis on God's transcendence is at least a hindrance to, and perhaps incompatible with, Christian social concern and action.*
This supposition leads some to denigrate God's transcendence. Others, holding to a false transcendence, withdraw into religious privatism or individualism and neglect the personal and communal responsibility of Christians for the earthly city. From a biblical perspective, it is precisely because of confidence in God's reign over all aspects of life that Christians must participate fully in the struggle against oppressive and dehumanizing structures and their manifestations in racism, war, and economic exploitation.

Theme 12: *The struggle for a better humanity will bring about the Kingdom of God.*
The struggle for a better humanity is essential to Christian faith and can be informed and inspired by the biblical promise of the Kingdom of God. But imperfect human beings cannot create a perfect society. The Kingdom of God surpasses any conceivable utopia. God has his own designs which confront ours, surprising us with judgment and redemption.

Theme 13: *The question of hope beyond death is irrelevant or at best marginal to the Christian understanding of human fulfillment.*
This is the final capitulation to modern thought. If death is the last word, then Christianity has nothing to say to the final questions of life. We believe that God raised Jesus from the dead and

are ". . . convinced that there is nothing in death or life, in the realm of spirits or superhuman powers, in the world as it is or in the world as it shall be, in the forces of the universe, in heights or depths—nothing in all creation that can separate us from the love of God in Christ Jesus our Lord" (Romans 8:38 f.)

THE CHICAGO CALL:
An Appeal to Evangelicals

In May, 1977, a group of evangelical leaders and scholars from different backgrounds gathered together to issue a call for modern evangelicalism to reappropriate the balance of historic Christianity. The Appeal itself outlines the areas the drafters believed must be addressed before evangelicalism can reach maturity.

Prologue

In every age the Holy Spirit calls the church to examine its faithfulness to God's revelation in Scripture. We recognize with gratitude God's blessing through the evangelical resurgence in the church. Yet at such a time of growth we need to be especially sensitive to our weaknesses. We believe that today evangelicals are hindered from achieving full maturity by a reduction of the historic faith. There is, therefore, a pressing need to reflect upon the substance of the biblical and historic faith and to recover the fullness of this heritage. Without presuming to address all our needs, we have identified eight of the themes to which we as evangelical Christians must give careful theological consideration.

A Call to Historic Roots and Continuity

We confess that we have often lost the fullness of our Christian heritage, too readily assuming that the Scriptures and the Spirit make us independent of the past. In so doing, we have become theologically shallow, spiritually weak, blind to the work of God in others and married to our cultures.

Therefore we call for a recovery of our full Christian heritage. Throughout the church's history there has existed an evangelical impulse to proclaim the saving, unmerited grace of Christ, and to reform the church according to the Scriptures. This impulse appears in the doctrines of the ecumenical councils, the piety of the early fathers, the Augustinian theology of grace, the zeal of the monastic reformers, the devotion of the practical mystics and the scholarly integrity of the Christian humanists. It flowers in the biblical fidelity of the Protestant Reformers and the ethical earnestness of the Radical Reformation. It continues in the efforts of the Puritans and Pietists to complete and perfect the Reformation. It is reaffirmed in the awakening movements of the 18th and 19th centuries which joined Lutheran, Reformed, Wesleyan and other evangelicals in an ecumenical effort to renew the church and to extend its mission in the proclamation and social demonstration of the Gospel. It is present at every point in the history of Christianity where the Gospel has come to expression through the operation of the Holy Spirit: in some of the strivings toward renewal in Eastern Orthodoxy and Roman Catholicism and in biblical insights in forms of Protestantism differing from our own. We dare not move beyond the biblical limits of the Gospel; but we cannot be fully evangelical without recognizing our need to learn from other times and movements concerning the whole meaning of that Gospel.

A Call to Biblical Fidelity
We deplore our tendency toward individualistic interpretation of Scripture. This undercuts the objective character of biblical truth, and denies the guidance of the Holy Spirit among his people through the ages.

Therefore we affirm that the Bible is to be interpreted in keeping with the best insights of historical and literary study, under the guidance of the Holy Spirit, with respect for the historic understanding of the church.

We affirm that the Scriptures, as the infallible Word of God, are the basis of authority in the church. We acknowledge that God uses the Scriptures to judge and to purify his Body. The church, illumined and guided by the Holy Spirit, must in every age interpret, proclaim and live out the Scriptures.

A Call to Creedal Identity
We deplore two opposite excesses: a creedal church that merely recites a

faith inherited from the past, and a creedless church that languishes in a doctrinal vacuum. We confess that as evangelicals we are not immune from these defects.

Therefore we affirm the need in our time for a confessing church that will boldly witness to its faith before the world, even under threat of persecution. In every age the church must state its faith over against heresy and paganism. What is needed is a vibrant confession that excludes as well as includes, and thereby aims to purify faith and practice. Confessional authority is limited by and derived from the authority of Scripture, which alone remains ultimately and permanently normative. Nevertheless, as the common insight of those who have been illumined by the Holy Spirit and seek to be the voice of the "holy catholic church," a confession should serve as a guide for the interpretation of Scripture.

We affirm the abiding value of the great ecumenical creeds and the Reformation confessions. Since such statements are historically and culturally conditioned, however, the church today needs to express its faith afresh, without defecting from the truths apprehended in the past. We need to articulate our witness against the idolatries and false ideologies of our day.

A Call to Holistic Salvation

We deplore the tendency of evangelicals to understand salvation solely as an individual, spiritual and otherworldly matter to the neglect of the corporate, physical and this-worldly implication of God's saving activity.

Therefore we urge evangelicals to recapture a holistic view of salvation. The witness of Scripture is that because of sin our relationships with God, ourselves, others and creation are broken. Through the atoning work of Christ on the cross, healing is possible for these broken relationships.

Wherever the church has been faithful to its calling, it has proclaimed personal salvation; it has been a channel of God's healing to those in physical and emotional need; it has sought justice for the oppressed and disinherited; and it has been a good steward of the natural world.

As evangelicals we acknowledge our frequent failure to reflect this holistic view of salvation. We therefore call the church to participate fully in God's saving activity through work and prayer, and to strive for justice and liberation for the oppressed, looking forward to the culmination of salvation in the new heaven and new earth to come.

A Call to Sacramental Integrity
We decry the poverty of sacramental understanding among evangelicals. This is largely due to the loss of our continuity with the teaching of many of the Fathers and Reformers and results in the deterioration of sacramental life in our churches. Also, the failure to appreciate the sacramental nature of God's activity in the world often leads us to disregard the sacredness of daily living.

Therefore we call evangelicals to awaken to the sacramental implications of creation and incarnation. For in these doctrines the historic church has affirmed that God's activity is manifested in a material way. We need to recognize that the grace of God is mediated through faith by the operation of the Holy Spirit in a notable way in the sacraments of baptism and the Lord's Supper. Here the church proclaims, celebrates and participates in the death and resurrection of Christ in such a way as to nourish her members throughout their lives in anticipation of the consummation of the kingdom. Also, we should remember our biblical designation as "living epistles," for here the sacramental character of the Christian's daily life is expressed.

A Call to Spirituality
We suffer from a neglect of authentic spirituality on the one hand, and an excess of undisciplined spirituality on the other hand. We have too often pursued a superhuman religiosity rather than the biblical model of a true humanity released from bondage to sin and renewed by the Holy Spirit.

Therefore we call for a spirituality which grasps by faith the full content of Christ's redemptive work: freedom from the guilt and power of sin, and newness of life through the indwelling and outpouring of his Spirit. We affirm the centrality of the preaching of the Word of God as a primary means by which his Spirit works to renew the church in its corporate life as well as in the individual lives of believers. A true spirituality will call for identification with the suffering of the world as well as the cultivation of personal piety.

We need to rediscover the devotional resources of the whole church, including the evangelical traditions of Pietism and Puritanism. We call for an exploration of devotional practice in all traditions within the church in order to deepen our relationship both with Christ and with other Christians. Among these resources are such spiritual disciplines as prayer, meditation, silence, fasting, Bible study and spiritual diaries.

A Call to Church Authority

We deplore our disobedience to the Lordship of Christ as expressed through authority in his church. This has promoted a spirit of autonomy in persons and groups resulting in isolationism and competitiveness, even anarchy, within the body of Christ. We regret that in the absence of godly authority, there have arisen legalistic, domineering leaders on the one hand and indifference to church discipline on the other.

Therefore we affirm that all Christians are to be in practical submission to one another and to designated leaders in a church under the Lordship of Christ. The church, as the people of God, is called to be the visible presence of Christ in the world. Every Christian is called to active priesthood in worship and service through exercising spiritual gifts and ministries. In the church we are in vital union both with Christ and with one another. This calls for community with deep involvement and mutual commitment of time, energy and possessions. Further, church discipline, biblically based and under the direction of the Holy Spirit, is essential to the well-being and ministry of God's people. Moreover, we encourage all Christian organizations to conduct their activities with genuine accountability to the whole church.

A Call to Church Unity

We deplore the scandalous isolation and separation of Christians from one another. We believe such division is contrary to Christ's explicit desire for unity among his people and impedes the witness of the church in the world. Evangelicalism is too frequently characterized by an ahistori-

cal, sectarian mentality. We fail to appropriate the catholicity of historic Christianity, as well as the breadth of the biblical revelation.

Therefore we call evangelicals to return to the ecumenical concern of the Reformers and the later movements of evangelical renewal. We must humbly and critically scrutinize our respective traditions, renounce sacred shibboleths, and recognize that God works within diverse historical streams. We must resist efforts promoting church union-at-any-cost, but we must also avoid mere spiritualized concepts of church unity. We are convinced that unity in Christ requires visible and concrete expressions. In this belief, we welcome the development of encounter and cooperation within Christ's church. While we seek to avoid doctrinal indifferentism and a false irenicism, we encourage evangelicals to cultivate increased discussion and cooperation, both within and without their respective traditions, earnestly seeking common areas of agreement and understanding.

ORIGINAL SIGNERS OF THE CHICAGO CALL*

Marvin W. Anderson, *Bethel Theological Seminary*
John S. Baird, *University of Dubuque Theological Seminary*
Donald G. Bloesch, *University of Dubuque Theological Seminary*
Jon E. Braun, *New Covenant Apostolic Order*
Virgil Cruz, *University of Dubuque Theological Seminary*
James Daane, *Fuller Theological Seminary*
Donald W. Dayton, *North Park Theological Seminary*
Jan P. Dennis, *Good News Publishers*
Lane T. Dennis, *Good News Publishers*
Gerald D. Erickson, *Trinity College, Deerfield, IL*
Isabel A. Erickson, *Tyndale House Publishers*
Donald C. Frisk, *North Park Theological Seminary*
Pete Gillquist, *Thomas Nelson Publishers*
Alfred A. Glenn, *Bethel College*
Nathan Goff, *Pastor, College Church, Wheaton, IL*
Jim Hedstrom, *Student, Vanderbilt University*
Richard Holt, *D.D.S., Wheaton, IL*
Thomas Howard, *Gordon College*
Morris A. Inch, *Wheaton College*
Herbert Jacobsen, *Wheaton College*
Kenneth Jensen, *New Covenant Apostolic Order*

Kathryn Lindskoog, *Author*
Theodore Laesch, *Pastor, St. John Lutheran Church, Wheaton, IL*
Howard Loewen, *Mennonite Brethren Bible College*
Richard Lovelace, *Gordon-Conwell Theological Seminary*
F. Burton Nelson, *North Park Theological Seminary*
Ray Nethery, *Grace Haven Farm, Mansfield, OH*
Roger Nicole, *Gordon-Conwell Theological Seminary*
Victor R. Oliver, *Vice President, Haggai Institute, Atlanta, GA*
M. Eugene Osterhaven, *Western Theological Seminary*
Lois M. Ottaway, *Wheaton College news service*
Gordon W. Saunders, *Trinity College, Deerfield, IL*
Rudolf Schade, *Elmhurst College*
Luci N. Shaw, *Harold Shaw Publishers*
Kevin N. Springer, *Graduate Student, University of Michigan*
Jeffrey N. Steenson, *Student, Harvard University Divinity School*
Donald Tinder, *Christianity Today*
Benedict Viviano, *O.P., Aquinas Institute of Theology*
Gordon Walker, *Pastor, Grace Fellowship Church, Nashville, TN*
Robert E. Webber, *Wheaton College*

*The signers' employing institutions are included for descriptive purposes only; the inclusion of these institutions does not indicate either their explicit or implied approval of the call.

A POLICY STATEMENT
Evangelism Today

This statement was developed by the Working Group on Evangelism of the Division of Church and Society, and expresses a common ground where representatives of a wide range of churches outside the National Council of Churches could meet with those who are members of the NCC. It was not intended as a comprehensive theological treatise on evangelism, but as a corrective to the recent dichotomy between "personal" evangelism and "social action." It was adopted by the Governing Board of the N.C.C., March, 1976.

One way of setting forth what evangelism means in the ecumenical experience today is to review the journey of the past twenty-five years of that experience—a period in which evangelism has been a central issue in American church life. During this period of changing concepts of evangelism, its fullness has never been totally disclosed at any one time or place, and this statement does not attempt a final or definitive description of it.

In the 1950's two major methods were utilized in evangelism: mass meeting campaigns and lay visitation programs, both inviting persons to make decisions for Jesus Christ. Although other factors probably contributed, these modes of sharing the Gospel coincided in the 1950's with a season of growth in church membership unparalleled in American church history.

However, growth in church membership and calling people to Christian discipleship were not necessarily the same. In the early 1960's it became apparent that for many people joining the church had not produced a significant change of attitude or behavior.

This failure of new church members to be enlisted in a pilgrimage toward fuller Christian discipleship called into question the effectiveness of the methods then being used. There followed an intense theological re-examination of what the demands of Christian discipleship should mean both for individuals and for society.

In the process of that re-examination, the practice of evangelism as a congregational function in which people are confronted with the Gospel and called to Christian discipleship was minimized in those denominations which were working together in the National Council of Churches. Denominational attention was focused on social injustices, and efforts were made to mobilize church members to help rectify them. A false division resulted. Instead of social awareness and action being seen as natural expressions of Christian discipleship to which people are called by evangelism, social action was thought to be a contrast and corrective to evangelism. In this mistaken polarization between them, both—and the whole life of the church—were weakened.

Today we can see the futility of that polarization, but the churches still seem strangely bound by a reluctance to name the Name of Jesus as Lord and Savior. Christians seem to lack the facility today to exclaim with excitement, "Jesus loves me; therefore, I love you!" At this moment in history, there is great need for the churches to recover the ability to name the Name of Jesus Christ as Lord and Savior and bear witness to that Name in word and deed.

But naming the Name and bearing witness to it must be better understood: the commitment to Jesus Christ is a profound event. It is a *personal* event; by the power of the Holy Spirit sinners experience the divine forgiveness and commit themselves to live obediently to Christ the living Lord. It is a *social* event; relationships with friends, neighbors and family are radically altered by the revolutionary demands and allowances of divine love. It is a *community* event; it engrafts one into the community of believers, the church. It is a *public* event; new confrontations with the institutions of society occur, for the "principalities and powers" which impoverish and enslave humanity cannot go unchallenged by Christians!

Commitment to Jesus Christ must be made in the context of the issues posed for us by the moment of history in which we find ourselves—history in which God is at work, through us and sometimes in spite of us. That commitment to Jesus Christ must have an impact on the issues of social and economic justice through the stewardship, integrity and interdependence of Christian disciples. Thereby commitment to Jesus Christ is inescapably a personal, social, community, and public historical event which affects the world and the human beings in it for whom Christ died.

Commitment to Jesus Christ is not a once-for-all event. It is the beginning of one's spiritual pilgrimage of discipleship. Those who are disciples of Christ face continual turning-points which offer new experiences rooted in being "born anew to a living hope" (I Pet. 1:3). We never move beyond the need to hear the renewing call to "repent and believe in the gospel" (Mk. 1:15), in order to live more obediently to the word of the Lord in every area of life, turning from the dead values of self-centered living, acquisitive consumption and upward social striving.

Commitment to Jesus Christ means to embrace more completely in our *personal* lives the new way of life which God's grace initiates, manifesting the Spirit's fruit of love, joy, peace, goodness, meekness, gentleness and self-control. Commitment to Jesus Christ means in our *social* life to love others more deeply, even as Christ loves us and gave himself for us, a love which is giving, accepting, forgiving, seeking and helping. Commitment to Jesus Christ in *community* life means to be called out from the isolation of individualism, from conformity to the ways of the world into the fellowship of disciples which is the church, where by obedience we discover freedom, by humble service we are fulfilled, by sharing the suffering of others we are made whole. Commitment to Jesus Christ in our *public* lives means to be engaged more earnestly in the work not only of relieving the poor and hungry but removing the causes of poverty and hunger in the struggle to remedy both inequities and iniquities, in the liberation of the oppressed and the vindication of the deprived, in the establishment of God's rule in the affairs of humanity. Commitment to Jesus Christ brings confidence that, however dark the present hour, the ultimate victory is assured through Him who is the Lord.

The task of evangelism today is calling people to repentance, to faith in Jesus Christ, to study God's word, to continue steadfast in prayer, and to bearing witness to Him. This is a primary function of the church in its congregational, denominational and ecumenical manifestations. It challenges the most creative capabilities in the churches while at the same time depending upon the Holy Spirit to be the real evangelist.

Now, after the journey of the past twenty-five years, we can call upon people to confess the Name of Jesus Christ and to bear witness to that Name in their lives with a fuller understanding of Christian discipleship and a deeper commitment to share the Good News we have found.

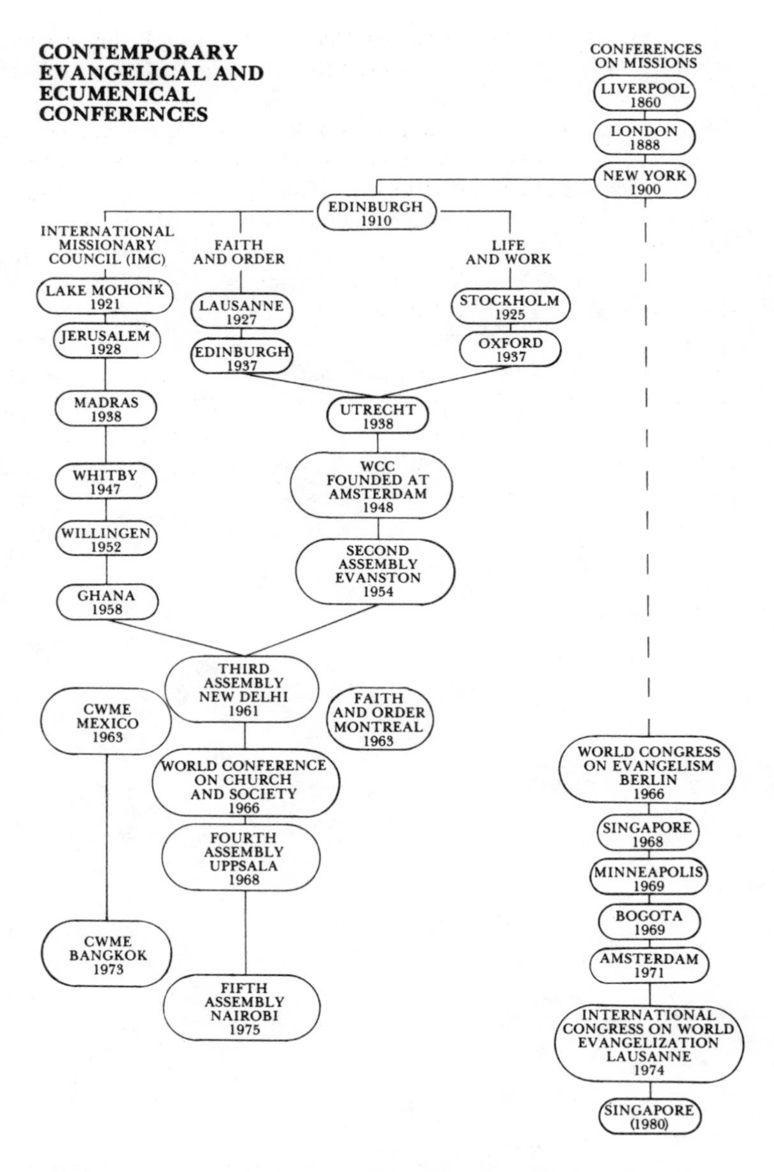

This chart is from Arthur P. Johnston, The Battle for World Evangelism (Tyndale House, 1978).

SELECTED BIBLIOGRAPHY

This is not a complete bibliography but a selection of books which represent evangelical and liberal scholarship.

UNDERSTANDING EVANGELICALISM AND LIBERALISM

A. Theologically

Barr, James. *Fundamentalism*. Philadelphia: Westminster Press, 1977. A rabid critique of British fundamentalism. The reader must be careful about making direct parallels with American evangelicalism, but some of Barr's iconoclastic barbs must be taken seriously.

Carnell, E. J. *The Case for Biblical Christianity*. Grand Rapids: Eerdmans, 1969. A collection of articles by the late forerunning evangelical theologian. Seen in their historical situation, Carnell's insights are provocative.

Henry, Carl F. H. *Evangelicals in Search of Identity*. Waco: Word Books, 1976. A rather short book describing the author's continued effort to push evangelical Christianity toward a new maturity. Henry in his position as a leading evangelical spokesman becomes a window through which we can view how neoevangelicalism has changed; namely, *The Uneasy Conscience of Modern Fundamentalism* (Eerdmans, 1947) and *Evangelicals at the Brink of Crisis* (Word Books, 1967).

Kelley, Dean M. *Why Conservative Churches Are Growing*. New York: Harper & Row, 1977 (rev. ed.). Kelley's book has had a significant impact upon liberals and did much to initiate their own self-evaluation.

Nash, Ronald H. *The New Evangelicalism*. Grand Rapids: Zondervan, 1963. The author skillfully presents and defends the new evangelicalism against liberalism and fundamentalism.

Quebedeaux, Richard. *The Worldly Evangelicals*. New York: Harper & Row, 1978. A helpful compendium to the who, what, and where of the contemporary evangelical movement. The nature of the book excludes historical analysis and has been criticized for being overly optimistic about the rise of a younger, more radical leadership among evangelicals.

Smart, James D. *The Cultural Subversion of the Biblical Faith*. Philadelphia: Westminster, 1977. The author recognizes the secularization of liberalism and how it has affected witness to the biblical faith.

Webber, Robert and Bloesch, Donald (eds.). *The Orthodox Evangelicals*. Nashville: Thomas Nelson Inc., 1978. This volume contains papers and background to "The Chicago Call" issued in 1977 to evangelicals interested in recovering a broader Christian heritage.

Webber, Robert E. *Common Roots*. Grand Rapids: Zondervan, 1978. In this book Webber begins to extend the implications of "The Chicago Call." Historic Christianity, especially the second-century church, is used as a measuring rod to urge evangelicals toward a fuller understanding of Christianity and the worshiping community.

Wells, David F. and Woodbridge, John D. (eds.). *The Evangelicals*. Nashville: Abingdon Press, 1975 (rev. ed., 1977). This is a collection of essays covering a wide range of topics. Because it draws upon critics and adherents, the book is most valuable.

B. Historically

Averill, Lloyd J. *American Theology in the Liberal Tradition*. Philadelphia: Westminster, 1967. An examination of the American liberal tradition in light of its origins.

Erickson, Millard. *The New Evangelical Theology*. Westwood, N.J.: Revell, 1968. The book begins with a historical sketch and then proceeds to outline the theology of neoevangelicalism in language the layman can understand.

Marty, Martin E. *Righteous Empire: The Protestant Experience in America*. New York: Dial Press, 1970. A very insightful analysis of the American religious experience from the point of view of Protestants who came as pilgrims to establish a new righteous empire.

Pauck, Wilhelm. *The Heritage of the Reformation*. Boston: Beacon Press, 1950 (rev. ed., 1961). A historical interpretation of the Reformation as it informed the Protestant faith—both conservative and liberal.

Ramm, Bernard. *The Evangelical Heritage.* Waco: Word Books, 1973. The roots of the evangelical movement are explained in terms of the Reformation.

Sandeen, Ernest R. *The Roots of Fundamentalism: British and American Millenarianism 1800–1930.* Chicago: The University of Chicago Press, 1970. A scholarly treatment of the origins of fundamentalism which Sandeen traces back to British and American millenarian thought.

C. Sociologically

Bellah, Robert N. *The Broken Covenant.* New York: Seabury Press, 1976. Everyone today is critical of civil religion but Bellah wants to give it a fair hearing. Bellah, of course, first raised the subject in his ground-breaking article, "Civil Religion in America," in *Daedalus* (Winter, 1967).

Hadden, Jeffrey K. *The Gathering Storm in the Churches.* Garden City, N.Y.: Doubleday, 1969. While the conflict between clergy and laymen has passed its peak, Hadden's conclusions are still valid. The author has continued his sociological dissection of the church in *Religion in Radical Transformation* (Transaction Books, 1973) and *Gideon's Gang: A Case Study of the Church in Social Action* (United Church Press, 1974).

Hoge, Dean R. *Division in the Protestant House.* Philadelphia: Westminster Press, 1976. In probing the reasons behind the Protestant division, Hoge provides an analysis of Christian commitment that cuts across denominational lines, even though he was primarily concerned with the United Presbyterian Church.

Marty, Martin E. *A Nation of Behavers.* Chicago: The University of Chicago Press, 1976. Marty maps the contemporary religious scene according to six categories: mainline, evangelicalism and fundamentalism, Pentecostal-charismatic, new religions (cults), ethnic, and civil.

D. Other

Howe, Reuel L. *The Miracle of Dialogue.* New York: Seabury Press, 1965. Although there are hundreds of books on communication and dialogue, this one is still basic.

I would be remiss if I did not at least mention such authors as William Barclay, Jacques Ellul, C. S. Lewis, Elton Trueblood, and Michel Quoist.

THEOLOGY

Berkouwer, G. C. *A Half Century of Theology*. Grand Rapids: Eerdmans, 1977. For those who do not have time to read Berkouwer's fourteen volume *Studies in Dogmatics*, this book serves as an introduction to liberal evangelicalism (my terminology) on a wide range of subjects.

Bloesch, Donald G. *Essentials of Evangelical Theology*, 2 vols. New York: Harper & Row, 1978. The title aptly describes the author's purpose. His previous book, *Jesus Is Victor!: Karl Barth's Doctrine of Salvation* (Abingdon Press, 1976), is a vital contribution to the issue of whether neoorthodoxy has anything to say to our religious situation.

Gilkey, Langdon. *Naming the Whirlwind: The Renewal of God Language*. Indianapolis: Bobbs-Merrill, 1969. This book is a thorough analysis of the cultural and theological background to contemporary liberal theology. Unfortunately, the author's recent book, *Reaping the Whirlwind* (Seabury Press, 1976), is not quite an update as it focuses on the specific question of a theology of history.

Henry, Carl F. H. *God, Revelation and Authority*, 2 vols. Waco: Word Books, 1976. Henry tries to ask the really important questions (vol. I) but never quite does, and therefore he falls short of answering them (vol. II).

Thielicke, Helmut. *The Evangelical Faith*, 2 vols. Grand Rapids: Eerdmans, 1974, 1977. Thielicke's scholarship cannot be ignored when he argues against a natural theology. Anyone attempting to do theology in an ecumenical sense must reckon with these volumes.

SCRIPTURE, INSPIRATION AND AUTHORITY

Barth, Karl. *The Epistle to the Romans*. London: Oxford University Press, 1933. A commentary of enduring quality. The prefaces to the six editions make for interesting reading as Barth develops his own principles of hermeneutics.

Beegle, Dewey M. *Scripture, Tradition, and Infallibility*. Grand Rapids: Eerdmans, 1973 (rev. ed. of *The Inspiration of Scripture*, 1963). One of the better books that deals specifically with the issue of infallibility and the difficulties encountered when this doctrine of the Bible must be defended.

Berkouwer, G. C. *Studies in Dogmatics: Holy Scripture.* Grand Rapids: Eerdmans, 1975. Berkouwer takes a mediating position on all the central issues. His treatments are fair, open, and carefully presented.

Childs, Brevard S. *Biblical Theology in Crisis.* Philadelphia: Westminster, 1970. Biblical theology is not dead, but Childs plots the course it has already run so we do not repeat the errors of the past.

Coleman, Richard J. "Biblical Inerrancy: Are We Going Anywhere?" *Theology Today,* XXXI (January, 1975), pp. 295–303; and "Another View: The Battle for the Bible," *Journal of the American Scientific Affiliation* (June, 1979). In both articles the purpose is to set the inerrancy issue into its proper context and demonstrate that nearly everyone practices some form of limited inerrancy.

Davis, Stephen T. *The Debate about the Bible.* Philadelphia: Westminster, 1977. After arguing against a doctrine of inerrancy, Davis develops the claim that the Bible is "the only infallible rule of *faith and practice.*"

Hasel, Gerhard. *New Testament Theology: Basic Issues in the Current Debate.* Grand Rapids: Eerdmans, 1978. A good review, with a good bibliography, of current issues and Hasel's case for not separating biblical theology from biblical history. This book is a companion to his *Old Testament Theology: Basic Issues in the Current Debate* (Eerdmans, 1975).

Krentz, Edgar. *The Historical-Critical Method.* Philadelphia: Fortress Press, 1975. One of several books in the "Guide to Biblical Scholarship" series. It brings the reader up to date on contemporary liberal thinking on the use of the critical-historical method, but the usual presuppositions are not taken for granted.

Lindsell, Harold. *The Battle for the Bible.* Grand Rapids: Zondervan, 1976. The author marshals the classic arguments in favor of biblical inerrancy. In many ways, though, a superficial treatment of a complex problem—but Lindsell's honesty is refreshing.

Pinnock, Clark H. *Biblical Revelation—The Foundation of Christian Theology.* Chicago: Moody Press, 1971. Alongside Bernard Ramm's *Special Revelation and the Word of God* (Eerdmans, 1961), this book is the best explanation of why evangelicals believe inerrancy is the proper attitude toward biblical interpretation.

Ramm, Bernard. "Misplaced Battle Lines," *Reformed Journal* (July–August, 1976). Here, as elsewhere, Ramm wants us to see the dangers in making inerrancy a central doctrine of the Christian faith, and yet Ramm is one who sees validity in a doctrine of verbal inspiration.

Rogers, Jack (ed.). *Biblical Authority*. Waco: Word Books, 1977. This volume represents a new breed of biblical scholarship among evangelicals. Each contributor is critical of the usual "formula" defenses for biblical inerrancy but moves toward a positive approach concerning biblical authority.

Robinson, John A. T. *Redating the New Testament*. Philadelphia: Westminster, 1976. This book is not just a demonstration that a liberal can change his mind. Its content is solid and the liberal understanding of the critical-historical method is not sacrificed.

Smart, James D. *The Strange Silence of the Bible in the Church*. Philadelphia: Westminster, 1970. Smart was one of the first to know why the Bible has become a silent book in the liberal church. Not to be forgotten is his treatment of biblical inspiration, authority, and unity in *The Interpretation of Scripture* (Westminster, 1961).

Stuhlmacher, Peter. *Historical Criticism and Theological Interpretation of Scripture*. Philadelphia: Fortress Press, 1977. Coming from the German liberal tradition, Stuhlmacher exposes the limits of the critical-historical method as it has developed within that tradition; he then joins with many others who refuse to separate historical criticism and theological thinking.

Wink, Walter. *The Bible in Human Transformation*. Philadelphia: Fortress Press, 1973. Wink is likewise aware of the bankruptcy of historical biblical criticism as an end-to-itself, but this only pushes the author to develop a new paradigm that combines objectivity and subjectivity.

EVANGELISM AND MISSION

Berger, Peter L. and Neuhaus, Richard John. *Against the World For the World*. New York: Seabury Press, 1976. Eight participants in the Hartford Appeal offer their reflections and commentary on the significance of this document.

Douglas, J. D. (ed.). *Let the Earth Hear His Voice*. Minneapolis: World Wide Publications, 1975. This volume contains position papers and background material of the Lausanne Covenant and the International Congress on World Evangelism.

Johnston, Arthur P. *The Battle for World Evangelism.* Wheaton: Tyndale House, 1978. Beginning with the assumption that evangelism is the only legitimate aim of mission, Johnston evaluates the major ecumenical and evangelical conferences on mission.

Krass, Alfred C. *Five Lanterns at Sundown: Evangelism in a Chastened Mood.* Grand Rapids: Eerdmans, 1978. As one who has participated in and acted as a consultant on evangelism for both liberal and conservative mission conferences, Krass has an integrated understanding of the Kingdom of God.

Moberg, David O. *The Great Reversal: Evangelism and Social Concern.* Philadelphia: J. B. Lippincott, 1977 (rev. ed.). Something of a historical review of how and why the conservative movement lost its social conscience during the early twentieth century. This book needs to be read alongside Donald Dayton's *Discovering an Evangelical Heritage* (Harper & Row, 1976).

O'Connor, Elizabeth. *Call to Commitment.* New York: Harper & Row, 1963. This book started many of us believing a church could be both evangelical and socially involved. I have enjoyed all of her subsequent books but especially *Journey Inward, Journey Outward* (Harper & Row, 1968) and *The New Community* (Harper & Row, 1976) as they continue the story of the Church of the Saviour in Washington, D.C.

Padilla, René C. (ed.). *The New Face of Evangelism.* Downers Grove, Ill.: Inter-Varsity Press, 1976. In this book of fifteen essays we see the wide spectrum of theologies hidden beneath the Lausanne Covenant.

Paton, David M. (ed.). *Breaking Barriers: The Report of the Fifth Assembly of the World Council of Churches, Nairobi, 1975.* Grand Rapids: Eerdmans, 1976. A very insightful look into the Fifth Assembly for anyone who thinks it was just another conference.

Sider, Ronald J. (ed.). *The Chicago Declaration.* Carol Stream, Ill.: Creation House, 1974. A deeper look by those who gathered in 1973 to express an evangelical concern for the social message of the church.

Sojourners. Published monthly at 1309 L St. NW, Washington, D.C. 20005. As one of the ministries of the Sojourners Fellowship, this magazine has made many Christians realize that a concern for individuals and social justice are not antithetical. Similar in nature is *The Other Side* (300 W. Apsley, Box 12236, Philadelphia, Pa. 19144), though a little less doctrinal and more popular in style.

Stott, John R. W. *The Lausanne Covenant.* Minneapolis: World Wide Publications, 1974. Stott strives for a more inclusive definition of mission—one that sees evangelism and social justice in partnership.

Stringfellow, William. *An Ethic for Christians and Other Aliens in a Strange Land.* Waco: Word Books, 1976. His remarks are so insightful and true to life that everyone feels their sting.

Wallis, Jim. *Agenda for Biblical People.* New York: Harper & Row, 1976. A forthright exposé that cuts across traditional labels concerning the church's captivity to the prevailing culture.

Yoder, John H. *The Politics of Jesus.* Grand Rapids: Eerdmans, 1972. One of the few really good books that returns us to the teachings and ministry of Jesus as a foundation for the church's mission in the world.